Wordsworth
and the Question
of "Romantic Religion"

Wordsworth and the Question of "Romantic Religion"

Nancy Easterlin

Lewisburg
Bucknell University Press
London: Associated University Presses

Associated University Presses
440 Forsgate Drive
Cranbury, NJ 08512

Associated University Presses
16 Barter Street
London WC1A 2AH, England

Associated University Presses
P.O. Box 338, Port Credit
Mississauga, Ontario
Canada L5G 4L8

The paper used in this publication meets the requirements of the American National Standard for Permanence of Paper for Printed Library Materials Z39.48-1984.

Library of Congress Cataloging-in-Publication Data

Easterlin, Nancy.
  Wordsworth and the question of "romantic religion" / Nancy Easterlin.
    p.   cm.
  Includes bibliographical references and index.
  ISBN 0-8387-5309-4 (alk. paper)
  1. Wordsworth, William, 1770–1850—Religion.   2. Religion and literature—England—History—19th century.   3. Religious poetry, English—History and criticism.   4. Romanticism—England.
I. Title.
PR5892.R4E27   1996
821'.7—dc20   95-42863
                                                                          CIP

PRINTED IN THE UNITED STATES OF AMERICA

To my mother's memory

Blake, like the poets of sensibility, lingered in that theatre of the mind, that *kenoma* or sensible emptiness, which lay between Enlightenment truth and High Romantic meaning. He could not ruin the sacred truths, either to fable and old song, or to a story that might emerge clearly from the abyss of his own strong ego, as it emerged from Wordsworth, even as Blake wrote his own brief epics. Blake is one of the last of an old race of poets; Wordsworth was the very first of the race of poets that we have with us still. Blake is archaic, as perhaps he wanted to be. Wordsworth is more modern than Freud, more postmodern than Samuel Beckett or Thomas Pynchon, because Wordsworth alone found the new way, our way alas, to ruin sacred truths.

—Harold Bloom, *Ruin the Sacred Truths*

Contents

Preface

THIS STUDY DRAWS ON RESEARCH IN THE PSYCHOLOGY AND SOCIOL-
ogy of religion to offer an interpretation of transcendent experiences,
metaphysical concerns, and conflicting beliefs—those elements that
make up the religious dimension—of some of Wordsworth's major
poetry. My thesis, based on correspondences between the poetical
texts and social scientific analyses of religion, is that Wordsworth's
work demonstrates an identifiably consistent, though by no means
ubiquitous, tendency to resolve conflicting beliefs and experiences
through the formal and semantic unities of poetry. That is, Wordsworth on occasion seeks to structure belief, traditionally structured
in the social sphere by dogma and participation in group ritual,
through the private act of poetic composition. Ultimately, I suggest
that Wordsworth's problematic struggle with the ambiguously related
spheres of the imaginary and the religious is in part accountable for
his poetic decline; in effect, he loses faith in poetry and the naturalistic
knowledge toward which it leads because it cannot provide the certi-
tudes of religious orthodoxy. Like all other interpretations that hypothesize a writer's unconscious motivations, then, this one is, by its
nature, speculative.

While my approach is interdisciplinary, like that of many current
critics, my conception of literary interdisciplinarity and my corresponding method departs from poststructuralist practices. The theoretical assumptions that govern this essay have not been adopted from
the presently popular paradigms already imported into literary studies;
rather, the perspective developed here represents my own attempted
synthesis of research in the disciplines relevant to my focus. In addition, my method throughout has been pragmatic, in the Jamesian
sense: acknowledging the impossibility of a purely inductive process,
I have nevertheless endeavored to assess the phenomena (the poems,
the body of relevant literary criticism, the studies of religious experience and religious systems) before theoretical formulation.

One of the chief advantages of this approach is that it yields at the
outset a grounded definition of religion. A meaningful analysis of religion must comprehend its two major dimensions as (1) socially generated and reified beliefs and practices, and (2) private experiences that

tend to reinforce that system *if interpreted in accordance with its beliefs*. Given the historically vague or incomplete use of the word *religion* in literary criticism, it is hardly surprising that scholars have lost interest in this aspect of romanticism. But criticism need not repeat the facing abstractions of mysticism in a sympathetic consideration of such phenomena; the notion that appreciation of and identification with the values of the text *necessarily* subverts judgment and analysis and results in the simple reproduction of those textual values is a fallacy purveyed by recent interventionist criticism. Here, the explanatory structures of the social sciences, by placing discussions of religion in a context of observed human behaviors, especially help to discipline, so to speak, our own disciplinary perspective.

It is ironic that religion, which has arguably served a central function in the evolution and survival of the human species by producing social coherence, has been equated with solipsistic withdrawal in romantic poetry by critics of diverse orientations and beliefs. A primary reason for this view is that critics have concentrated on the transcendent moment to the exclusion of other concerns. Because social psychology focuses on the dynamic nature of belief and on the centrality of the social group in the maintenance of belief, it encourages us to reconsider such assumptions. Stable religious behaviors are emphatically social, as an individual's faith depends on social mechanisms for corroboration and reinforcement. In any assessment of religious phenomena and their meaning, then, more important perhaps than the transcendent moment itself is its perceived goal or function, its meaning *beyond* the brief moment of experience. In this essay specifically, a heightened consciousness of the social nature of religious belief usefully highlights the socially and psychologically *problematic* nature of the religious dimension of Wordsworth's poetry, where the feedback relationship between belief system and private experience no longer functions to stabilize individual religious values.

The redirection of Wordsworth criticism to historical concerns in the past decade has put psychological approaches noticeably out of fashion. But the movement away from psychological interpretation is also a result of the nearly exclusive influence of depth psychology on literary criticism throughout this century. Focusing on intrapsychic processes at the expense of interpreting the relationship between the individual and his social environment, depth psychological approaches foster the erroneous view that the individual can be understood in virtual isolation from his environment. Literary critics have thus felt compelled to follow one of two apparent courses, social and psychological contexts for interpretation. At the very least, it appears intuitively unwise to adopt any model which implies little mutual influence of minds and social worlds. Social and developmental psy-chology, which emphasize dynamic models of the self, bear this intu-ition out: according to current transactional and interactionist conceptions, the self is neither a free, independent entity nor a social construction instantiated in the subject by the governing ideology; instead, it is formed in an interactive process between the individual and the social sphere. In keeping with this, my psychological reading of Wordsworth is concerned with the increased difficulty of that process during a period of rapid social and cultural change, and as-sumes that psychic struggle is more often than not *about* the ongoing relationship of the individual to his world.

In addition to the small insight this study might add to an already overwhelming body of Wordsworth criticism, I have some broader aims here. First, the vexed relationship between literature and religion in Wordsworth's work is paradigmatic of an ambiguity that pervades cultures no longer organized according to primitive unities. I hope readers of this study will be left meditating on what we ask of literary art in light of the possible functions literature might serve in individ-ual and social life in a modern culture. In spite of the fact that recent theory has paradoxically humanized our approach to literature by exploring its function rather than seeking its hidden essence, such questions have not been adequately answered or addressed by post-structuralist theories, which have preferred to offer singular pro-nouncements rather than address complexities. Second, conflicts between individual beliefs, desires, and ways of being on the one hand and the demands of our social world on the other are part of the human condition, and in a modern democratic and industrial (now technological) society, both the level of conflict and our consciousness of it are becoming increasingly pronounced. It is possible to know something about the character of our own struggles through those of Wordsworth, whose natural and cultural similarities to us override, in the final analysis, the differences of historical moments.

As we move out of the poststructuralist era, we need to revise and broaden our notion of interdisciplinary literary studies to achieve a more nuanced consideration of the role of literature in human life and culture than current theoretical models afford. I hope this study suggests how a revised approach to interdisciplinarity, one that pro-motes diverse connections with other fields, can supplement our un-derstanding not just of romanticism but of all literary specializations.

For permission to reprint from various editions of Wordsworth's poetry, I gratefully acknowledge the following sources:

Excerpts from *The Ecclesiastical Sonnets of William Wordsworth:*

A Critical Edition, edited by Abbie Findlay Potts, published 1922 by Yale University Press. Reprinted by permission of Yale University Press.

Excerpts from *The Excursion,* from *The Poetical Works of William Wordsworth,* edited by E. de Selincourt and Helen Darbishire, 2d ed., vol. 5, published 1959 by Clarendon Press. Reprinted by permission of Oxford University Press.

Excerpts from *Lyrical Ballads, and Other Poems, 1797–1800,* edited by James Butler and Karen Green, published 1992 by Cornell University Press. Reprinted by permission of Cornell University Press.

Excerpts from *Memorials of a Tour of the Continent, 1820,* from *The Poetical Works of William Wordsworth,* edited by E. de Selincourt and Helen Darbishire, 2d ed., vol. 3, published 1952 by Clarendon Press. Reprinted by permission of Oxford University Press.

Excerpts from *Poems, in Two Volumes, and Other Poems, 1800–1807,* edited by Jared Curtis, published 1983 by Cornell University Press. Reprinted by permission of Cornell University Press.

Excerpts from *The Thirteen-Book Prelude,* edited by Mark L. Reed, vol. 1, published 1991 by Cornell University Press. Reprinted by permission of Cornell University Press.

Excerpts from *The White Doe of Rylstone; or The Fate of the Nortons,* edited by Kristine Dugas, published 1988 by Cornell University Press. Reprinted by permission of Cornell University Press.

I am grateful to those who have helped this project reach completion through their support and interest. A dissertation fellowship at Temple University in 1989–90 was invaluable to me, providing the funding and time for concentrated effort in the early stages of this project, and summer research funding from the University of New Orleans in 1992 enabled me to revise and complete the manuscript. Timothy Corrigan, Robert Storey, and William Galperin, who worked with me on this project as a dissertation, were unfailingly supportive and helpful. I owe many thanks to those friends, family members, and colleagues who have offered advice and shared in these ideas: Daniel Easterlin, Mary Tiryak, Kevin Moore, Donald Rackin, Barbara Riebling, Elisabeth Magnus, Gary Dyer, David DeLaura, Saul Morson, Paisley Livingston, Peter Schock, Joyce Zonana, and Cynthia Hogue. To Robert Storey (again) and to my father Richard Easterlin, both longstanding examples of intellectual integrity and generosity, I feel a special debt, personal and professional; I hope I may have the privilege of succumbing to their influence. My husband, Peter McNamara, gives me the love and encouragement that sustains my faith in myself and makes my work possible. This book is dedicated to the memory of my mother, Jacqueline Miller Easterlin, because she taught me the love of literature and common things.

Wordsworth
and the Question
of "Romantic Religion"

1

Transcendent Experience, Religious Orthodoxy, and the Mediations of Poetry

Toward a Pragmatic Method in Interdisciplinary Literary Criticism

ALTHOUGH PSYCHOANALYTICAL ASSUMPTIONS HAVE LONG BEEN viewed with skepticism and are currently under attack even from within literary studies, psychological methodologies for literary inter-pretation routinely draw on depth psychology, especially Freudianism and the neo-Freudianisms typified by Lacanian and Kristevian theory.[1] This tradition in literary studies notwithstanding, there is no reason to take the truthfulness or even usefulness of psychoanalysis as an article of faith, particularly because its aim (locating the causes of pathology for clinical purposes) has little in common with literary interpretation. Since, in this study, I am concerned with developing an analysis of religious feeling and belief in Wordsworth's poetry, the problem is compounded, for Freud bore a distinct animus to religious questions. By way of introduction, then, I offer a brief discussion of some of the shortcomings of Freudian theory followed by a prelimi-nary description of my method, in the hope that it will suggest how psychological studies of literary figures and works may be revivified by recourse to the ample research in the subdisciplines of academic psychology.

While the validity of basic psychoanalytic assumptions is far from self-evident, criticism of the institution is easily met with the rejoin-der—surprising as it would have been to Freud himself—that psycho-analysis is not a science but a way of knowing that relies on untestable inner speculation and insight.[2] And indeed, as long as it centers on the validity of the theory as a basis for *clinical* practices, the debate is bound to be an exceptionally long one. Assessing the curative value of specific principles within the relationship of doctor and patient poses all kinds of problems, not the least of which is that a patient's

15

health can improve for reasons utterly outside the clinical purview, and thus, potentially, in spite of an erroneous hermeneutic.

But the issue for literary scholarship is somewhat different, since responsible literary interpretation is not, or should not be, the business of identifying neuroses and effecting their cures. Hence, while scholars need not assert "the wholesale unfoundedness of psychoanalysis as a hermeneutic system,"[3] they should be willing to acknowledge, first, that a paradigm designed from cases of mental illness is of questionable use as a normative explanation of human motivation and behavior, much less of literary artifacts, and, second, that psychoanalytical ideas are *relatively* testable (some more so than others), not in the clinic but through empirical research in those social sciences that take human beings as their object of study.

Important here to understanding the limitations of psychoanalysis is the point made by Daniel Stern, a psychoanalyst and developmental psychologist, that both the original theory and its offshoots are *pathomorphic* and *retrospective*; driven by the clinically urgent need to find the sources of psychological illnesses, Freud and later revisionists placed "pathomorphically chosen clinical issues seen in adults in a crucial developmental role."[4] Stern himself takes a normative and prospective approach to human development, focused on the adaptive tasks faced by the infant and her emerging sense of self. In practice, this approach relies not on the determination of clinical success in cases of mental illness but on an expanding body of empirical research with infants, and is consequently promising for explaining the minds and mental growth of relatively healthy human beings.

And where such research bears results that contradict the Freudian model, it presents a serious challenge to orthodox assumptions. For example, the research of Stern and others overturns a fundamental Freudian assumption that has survived numerous permutations of the theory and become a staple of psychoanalytical literary interpretation. Whereas psychoanalysis posits that the infant exists in a state of narcissistic, pre-Oedipal flow, unaware that it is a distinct being from its mother, Stern maintains that children are never completely without such an unconscious awareness; already at birth, the baby has a sense of emergent self and is busy establishing relationships between divergent experiences.[5]

Thus, the familiar critical practice of discovering regression to states of infantile narcissism in literary works (as Barbara Schapiro, noting the drive toward psychic unity in "Tintern Abbey," criticizes Richard Onorato for doing in his reading of the poem), is probably founded on erroneous assumptions about child development and the mother-child relationship.[6] Though object relations psychology modifies the

interpretive tendentiousness of orthodox Freudianism, it still encourages retrospection, that is, reading back to developmental stages rather
than focusing on present issues. In so doing, it continues to reify and
idealize the concept of reunion with the mother, which seems in this
paradigm like an attractive (albeit fictitious) state of being.[7]

Just as Freud's general theory is open to inspection, his ideas about
religion rest on equally pathomorphic and retrospective assumptions,
and need not—indeed, should not—be taken as the only plausible
explanations of those phenomena. Resting on the a priori assumption
that both religious experience and belief are illusory in nature, Freud's
explanations of the origins of religious belief, religious psychology, and
the function of religion within society are based on atheistic rather
than agnostic premises, and are therefore inherently prejudiced against
the institutions and experiences they seek to elucidate. Inevitably,
then, Freudian explanations of religion are teleological and proscrip-
tive, inhibiting rather than enabling a nuanced understanding of what
I wish to consider in this study, religious consciousness and the emotional and conceptual conflicts therein. (Any study issuing from the
position of orthodox belief, by the way, would be equally restrictive
for explanatory purposes.) Adopting Freud's theories of religion here
would necessarily result in a diagnosis of Wordsworth's neuroses, real
or imagined; by avoiding, at the outset, such overt value judgments,
my purpose is to illustrate the complex relation of religious sentiments
and experience to poetic creation. How religious anxieties and hopes
come to be embodied in literary language, and how the struggle to
communicate those emotions becomes a struggle with language itself—
such speculative directions have, potentially, more far-reaching implications for the relation of imaginative writing to human existence
than a mere judgment regarding the truth or falsehood of the poet's
modes of mediation between self and perceived reality.

Interdisciplinary research on questions of religion need not rest on
either a totalizing atheist model or an equally totalizing model derived
from orthodox commitments, and today, a far wider variety of interpretations of religious behavior and experience is available than classical and revisionary psychoanalysis allow. In a recent introductory text
on the history and theory of the psychology of religion, Joseph F.
Byrnes differentiates theory-bound approaches to religion from the
non-theory-bound, descriptive approach of William James. The first
category includes theorists who hypothesize a fundamental dynamic
in human development and behavior, and Byrnes subdivides these
into conflict theories (Freud and Jung), conditioning theories (Skinner
and behaviorism), and fulfillment theories (Allport and Maslow).[8]
The various theoretical directions emphasize, respectively, the sexual

power struggle with the father as the paradigm for all ensuing human interaction; the paramount influence of social institutions in deter-mining thought and action; and the progressive, goal-oriented aspect of human behavior. As this synopsis in itself suggests, theory-bound approaches court the accusation that their explanations are simplistic and excessively reductive, particularly given the complexity of the phenomena under investigation.

Here, only Freud's hypothesis deserves some specific comment, since his arguments continue to be convincing and influential in literary circles. In *Totem and Taboo,* Freud develops the following argument for the origin of religious institutions: once, in our primitive past, the father and leader of the horde wielded brutal and total power over all its other members, claiming all the females for himself. The sons rose up in rebellion against this totalitarian rule, murdered the father, and consumed him. Totemism, the worship of specific animals within particular tribes, then developed as a sublimated expression of the sons' defiance, guilt, and love subsequent to patricide and cannibalism. At some point later in history, these ambivalent feelings of love and hatred were transferred to the anthropomorphic god of monotheistic religions, and the perpetuation of religion in contemporary society is explained by the racial memory trace of this act. In conclusion, Freud states that

> . . . the beginnings of religion, ethics, society, and art meet in the Oedipus complex. This is in entire accord with the findings of psychoanalysis, namely, that the nucleus of all neuroses as far as our present knowledge of them goes is in the Oedipus complex. It comes as a great surprise to me that these problems of racial psychology can be solved through a single concrete instance, such as the relation to the father.[9]

The Oedipus complex, according to Freud, provides a thoroughgoing and universal explanation of all neuroses (here including religion as a communal neurosis), and is the source of both complex sociohistorical developments as well as the specific, individual psychological conflicts of men in modern culture.

This formulation is not only pathomorphic, but obsessively, even awesomely, so in its globalization of the father-son conflict as the root of *every significant dimension* of human culture. Even while acknowl-edging the widespread anthropological evidence for conflict between younger and older males,[10] the suggestion that "religion, ethics, soci-ety, and art" can be reduced to this conflict seems at the very least improbable, given the enormous variety of adaptive demands early humans faced. (And it appears equally unlikely that such a natively asocial creature would have survived at all.)

The teleology of Freud's aprioritized theory is strengthened by the real dearth of facts or "findings," for the conclusion above is couched scientifically rather than delivered in a truly empirical spirit. The show of surprise over the universality of the Oedipus complex is characteristically disingenuous, suggesting evenhandedness and objectivity, when, in fact, his highly speculative psychological and anthropological theorizing is, in its disdain for evidence, self-supporting. In the words of E. E. Evans-Pritchard, "Freud tells us a just-so story which only a genius could have ventured to compose, for no evidence was, or could be, adduced in support of it, though, I suppose, it could be claimed to be psychologically, or virtually, true in the sense that myth may be said to be true in spite of being literally and historically unacceptable."[11] As Evans-Pritchard here implies, the status of Freud's truth claims coincides with those of other myths, as its validation rests on speculation and intuition rather than an observable relation between hypothesis and an outside set of facts. According to Evans-Pritchard, the idea of filial rebellion is based not in the close study of primitive culture but on intuition guided by the observation of people in modern culture. And as he furthermore points out, modern anthropology shows totemic practices to be of far greater variety than Freud suggests; totems are often not, in fact, the objects of worship, and there is no necessarily causal connection between totemism and monotheism since some primitive cultures develop one without the other. But even if Freud's theory of religion should prove valid on some points in the future, there is still no reason to assume that it constitutes a complete explanation of the motives for religious behaviors.

Freud's analysis of religious feeling, as distinct from that of the origins of religious institutions, takes as its premise the infantile narcissism that, as I indicated above, seems more accurately to represent another manifestation of the Golden Age than a legitimate developmental state. In *Civilization and Its Discontents*, Freud concludes that a friend's purported experience of union with God, the "oceanic feeling," is an illusion based in a regressive impulse which seeks first the mother's breast and second the father's protection, and which "might seek something like the restoration of limitless narcissism."[12] In keeping with this theory, the religious man's perception of wholeness is an illusion based in the experience of an infantile consciousness that has not yet learned to differentiate itself from the objects of external reality.

In addition to the fact that recent developmental research disputes Freud's claim that the human infant exists in a state of egoless flow, there is a second, logical problem with Freud's pathomorphic and retrospective equation of oneness with regression. If wholeness is the metaphor for both psychic health as well as infantilism, what are the criteria for distinguishing between the two? They ought to be behavioral, but here they are ideational. If you exhibit every sign of being a well-adjusted adult—realize that other people are largely in control of their own ideas and actions, realize that the objects of physical reality are not coextensive with your own being, take responsibility for your own welfare and actions—on what psychological evidence are you pronounced mentally regressive? The response Freud himself would have made, that society itself is sick and that the institution of religion is therefore a form of cultural neurosis, evades rather than answers the crucial question of what constitutes the behavioral norm for such a diagnosis. As with the totemism-Oedipus complex equation, the supposition that the oceanic feeling is a symptom of regression eschews factual verification.[13]

In sum, both the anthropological explanation of the origin of religion and the psychological assessment of its perpetuity seek to discredit religion by exposing it as illusory, as do *Moses and Monotheism* and *The Future of an Illusion*, Freud's two other books on religion.[14] Freud shares this purpose with other prominent nineteenth-century theorists of religion, among them Frazer and Durkheim, who also posit the origins and phylogeny of religion based on sparse and unreliable evidence. As Evans-Pritchard points out, "Implicit in their way of thinking were the optimistic convictions of the eighteenth-century rationalist philosophers that people are stupid only because they are ignorant and superstitious, and they are ignorant and superstitious because they have been exploited in the name of religion by cunning and avaricious priests and the unscrupulous classes which have supported them."[15] In their drive to offer all-encompassing explanations for the phenomenon of religion, these theoreticians demonstrate the profundity of their own faith in rationalism and materialism; if the medieval paradigm locates absolute reality in a supernatural realm, Enlightenment rationalists and their followers are equally absolutist in their identification of reality with the material universe and will brook no discussion of potential unknowns. From a contemporary point of view, the absolutism that underwrites such a confident notion of reality and the corresponding urge to deliver global theories and explanations is not only highly problematic but potentially antiscientific, when theory is not subjected to empirical tests. Perhaps most important, the atheistic bias of such a theory dramatically affects the testing process itself, hindering attempts to analyze and interpret objectively the religious experiences and beliefs of specific individuals;

essentially, the built-in bias of Freud's theory is that the analyst always knows better than the subjects whom he studies.

Moreover, while no immovable boundaries can be drawn between kinds of discourse, there are rhetorical tendencies in the analysis and interpretation of religious phenomena that correspond to basic assumptions about the order of the universe and the status of human knowledge regarding it. Aptly, the rationalist view that underlies Freud's thinking finds, generally speaking, its discursive extension in an order-conferring narrative mode, rather than the primarily descriptive mode complementary to a world view based in a modified scientific empiricism. In this respect, the use of Freud's theory of religion in commenting upon romantic poetry would contain an obvious irony, as it entails the application of Enlightenment reasoning to aesthetic objects which emerge from and dramatize the breakdown of Enlightenment ideas and the rationalistic mode of reasoning suited to those ideas.[16]

In recent years, Freud's methodology, along with the theories that either emerge from or constitute this methodology, has been questioned by anthropologists, psychologists, biologists, and literary critics.[17] Yet psychoanalytic concepts continue to exert extraordinary influence in literary studies, partly because important distinctions between hypothesis, fact, and truth are not sufficiently recognized and upheld in our discipline. Although it is to a large extent unintentional, the result has been to treat hypotheses selectively imported from the behavioral sciences as though they represent incontrovertible truths. This not only occludes our perception of the full range of approaches and the levels of debate within various disciplines, but is moreover fundamentally erroneous in its general tendency of superimposing ideas from other fields onto literary study, rather than weighing these ideas against the necessarily more diffuse ideational, emotional, and aesthetic elements of literature. There is no neat equation that determines the extent to which a hypothesis about human behavior applies to an aesthetic artifact. The social sciences frequently offer logical formulations of concepts suggested in literary works, and therefore can serve to corroborate and clarify, but not to prove, a literary critical approach. The nearly exclusive use of Freudian theory in psychologically oriented literary scholarship has served as an effective blockade to the flow of ideas from psychology, sociology, and anthropology into literary study for the better part of a century.

However, this only serves as a partial explanation of why Freud has acted as such a predominant influence in the humanities. Frederick Crews, contemplating the nonrational appeal of what he elsewhere calls psychoanalysis' Wagnerian themes, suggests that, for many critics,

> psychoanalysis has been . . . a means of elevating pride among a corps of privileged knowers who, by subscribing to the Freudian movement, rescue themselves from doubt and insignificance. It is as a cathartic and redemp- tive science that psychoanalysis has claimed our loyalty. "Normal science" is dry and impersonal, narrow in focus, and increasingly incomprehensible to the envious humanist. Psychoanalysis, by contrast, offers each of its believers a total vision that spans the entire history of our species, links biology and psychology, and unveils the innermost scandalous wishes ani- mating heroes and ordinary folk, great works of art, and whole systems of law, philosophy, mythology, and religion. What is so humbling about that? Could Faust have asked Mephistopheles to show him much more?[18]

In possession of the tools of psychoanalysis, then, the modern literary critic is transformed from a being conscious of his marginal function in a scientifically oriented society to a powerful seer, a semidivine figure. Somewhat incongruously, the desire for religious certainties is replaced by psychoanalysis itself, which offers comprehensive synthe- ses in every direction; a mythic unity thus masquerades as science, and literary scholarship retrieves its fixed if somewhat unpleasant notion of truth. Faced in our own field with a bewildering array of artifacts which do not invite a single method or orientation to our domain, we grasp hastily for the seeming authority inherent in theo- ries which claim to explain all.

There is also, though, a simpler explanation for the enduring hold of psychoanalytic concepts in literary studies: literary scholars are always attracted to a good story—and indeed, the recent trend within literary theory, gaining support from some contemporary philosophy, to endorse a nonepistemology in which metaphor and story replace reference to facts, plausible hypotheses, and potential truths has served as a kind of official sanction for this disciplinary tendency.[19] Freudian theory, which combines good writing with a hypothesis whose central metaphor is itself borrowed from myth, seems designed for appeal to literary scholars. The Oedipus complex provides a drama- tized and personalized conception of the struggle for cultural and indi- vidual adaption, which at its most fundamental is mundane, continuous, and extremely impersonal. This is art—the ordering and intensification of conflict that is spread over and through the bewilder- ing, frequently unpredictable ranges of development and experience that comprise human life and history. The conflation of criteria for aesthetic value in literature with those for plausibility in science therefore explains some of the ease with which literary scholars assume the legitimacy of Freudian concepts.

Just as psychoanalytic theory poses many problems for the interpretation of human psychology and behavior, the two remaining categories of theory-bound approaches described by Byrne focus too exclusively on single aspects of human psychology. In light of the current interactionist model governing developmental, social, and evolutionary psychology, strict behaviorism, with its tabula rasa mind, seems completely naive, positing an insupportably passive view of the human agent. On the other hand, fulfillment theories are formulated according to a positivistic, nineteenth-century paradigm that represents an idealized rather than an actual version of human experience, and in the process tend to ignore the social environment so totally determining to the behaviorists. Both ultimately reduce to a single dimension the complex feedback relationship between individual experience and social codes and forms.[20] While each of these theory-bound approaches offers us a useful perspective on the vast and confusing domain of religion, none fully accounts for all the cultural and personal facets of the phenomenon; the interplay between theories is perhaps more productive than any one of the theories in isolation. Most crucially, because analysis of religion rests to a significant degree on interpretation of one of the most subjective phenomena possible— believer experience—the leap to the level of theory is an exceedingly long one. Rather than adopting a theory-bound method, then, my research reflects the tradition stemming from William James's descriptive method, as this avoids the speculative excesses and reductionism of these other approaches.[21]

In a recent article, Jack Hanford describes the methodological problem of the psychology of religion, which is more or less a pronounced version of the problem of the entire discipline of psychology. An exclusively empirical approach, seemingly the most methodologically sound, leads to behaviorism, with its model of the passive mind which reduces ideas to sensory data. Such an approach has little to offer in explanation of religious states, which entail subjective, highly complicated emotions. Conversely, an approach that is solely phenomenological, a case study technique like Freud's, lacks criteria for validation. As a solution to the problem of these two extremes, Hanford cites James, whose method he calls a synoptic approach in which "the empirical and protophenomenological orientations [are combined] within a wide frame of reference."[22]

Far from being revolutionary, the modified empiricism proposed by Hanford for the study of the psychology of religion describes the perspective in which methods are today conceived for most of the social

sciences.[23] Developmental psychologists, for instance, combine observation with interpretation of thoughts and remarks before hypothesizing the mental functioning of a young child; in this field, varied
experiments employing repeated observation have, over the past several decades, refined and modified the belief in discrete developmental
stages theorized by Jean Piaget. Despite the difficulty of simulating
clean experimental conditions for the study of a complex subject like
human beings, developmental and social psychology aspire to a modified empiricism and its contingent demand for objective verification.
Researchers in these fields recognize that preliminary hypotheses and
personal orientations color their results, but they also strive for an
understanding based on observable facts. Valid explanation, in this
view, can only be undertaken after detailed description. Freud, for
example, would have been required to demonstrate his theory of the
Oedipus complex on a much more comprehensive scale: subjects
would have been chosen from a heterogeneous population, and the
attribution of conflict, its specific character and duration, would have
been observed in close detail throughout the human life cycle. Furthermore, such tests would have to be carried out repeatedly over
time by a variety of researchers, for only in this way does observer
subjectivism as well as the mitigating influences of historical moments
come to light. This is the only means for identifying a hypothesis with
a plausible claim to truth.

Of course, James himself would have described this technique as
pragmatic rather than synoptic. In *Pragmatism,* James outlined his
method as a means of testing philosophical discourse, but its mediatory
and comparative technique also serves as a valuable model for combining biology, behavior, and philosophy in the study of religious psychology, as well as for applying ideas from diverse disciplines to the study
of literary works. Indeed, James is an important forerunner of those
who endorse a conceptually integrated, interdisciplinary model of
knowledge in the social sciences; his contribution to modern epistemology has yet to be appreciated by contemporary humanists.[24] Ob-
jecting to the claims on truth issuing both from scientific positivism
and from an increasingly abstruse philosophic practice, James developed pragmatism as a method of reconciling ideas with phenomena.
According to James, pragmatism places value on the practical outcome
of ideas and mediates between rationalism—characterized by theory
and abstraction, and monistic, optimistic, and intellectualistic in approach—and empiricism—skeptical, pluralistic, and fatalistic in approach, and factually oriented. For James, philosophy had become "far
less an account of this actual world than a clean addition built upon
it, a classic sanctuary in which the rationalistic fancy may take refuge

from the intolerably confused and Gothic character which mere facts present." Thus drawing on the instrumental concept of truth favored by the natural sciences, James asserts that "ideas . . . become true just in so far as they help us to get into satisfactory relation with other parts of our experience."[25]

James's premise that ideas are of practical value is consistent with the teleological theory of mind that he later propounded in *The Principles of Psychology*.[26] The central proposition of this theory holds that thought functions toward practical ends. This concept of the mind's workings has had an enormous impact on modern social psychology, manifest in such subdisciplinary areas as consistency theory and attribution theory. In James's words, "Our minds grow in spots; and like grease-spots, the spots spread. But we let them spread as little as possible; we keep unaltered as much of our old knowledge, as many of our old prejudices and beliefs, as we can."[27] Consistency theory, based in Leon Festinger's theory of cognitive dissonance, studies the means by which people reduce conflict and contradiction when their prior assumptions are challenged.[28] Attribution theory studies the way people explain events or establish cause and effect relationships in situations where causality is ambiguous. Consistency theory and attribution theory thus provide the empirical testing of the teleological theory of mind, illustrating how the emotional desire for stability of understanding shapes not only the route to knowledge, but the form and content of what men and women learn.

Clearly, James's view of knowledge is to some extent a relativist one; and the suggestion that our access to truth is limited by the biology of our minds and by our attendant needs, biopsychological and social, was in no small degree discomfiting to his contemporaries. But James is far from denying all knowledge claims, perceiving that even within the limited parameters of our existence the continual testing of hypotheses against the evidence of a world we take to be real leads to their confirmation or disconfirmation over time, and therefore to a circumscribed but nonetheless valid *human* knowledge. Jamesian pragmatism is thus the predecessor of the current bioepistemological perspective within the philosophy of science, which holds that, as a product of natural selection, the mind is predisposed to organize or construct input in specific ways (for example, causally) that were adaptively advantageous during the period of human evolution.[29]

In this sense, James's conception of knowledge and truth differs crucially from the extreme relativism, frequently propounded under the banner of "pragmatism," that currently holds sway in the humanities. In a recent attempt to rescue the humanities from skepticism and relativism, Richard Rorty, a philosopher who currently enjoys great popularity among literary scholars, formulated a theory of liberal ironism which nonetheless founders on its own skeptical assumptions. Borrowing from Nietzsche and Donald Davidson, Rorty asserts that language is nonreferential and that intellectual and moral progress constitute a "history of increasingly useful metaphors rather than an increasing understanding of how things really are."[30] Having eliminated the possibility that our formulations offer some plausible account of a mind-independent reality—itself a broad truth claim that seems inadmissible given the philosopher's premises—Rorty leaves open the question of what mediates in the selection of better "metaphors," and his theory is thus ethically as well as epistemologically troubling. As Erving Goffman, paraphrasing James, pointed out some time ago, what is relevant to our human conditions and decisions (intellectual, moral, or trivially personal) are the circumstances under which we *perceive* thing to be real. And we take things to be real all the time; as Michael Morton reminds us, one never really meets a thoroughgoing skeptic.[31] That we are compelled to evaluate our knowledge and to perform moral acts based on the perception of a mind-independent reality is a fact of human psychology and behavior critically overlooked in Rorty's account.

If Jamesian pragmatism establishes testability as a common ground for validating theories within psychology and philosophy, it can also serve as a paradigm for the use of extraliterary concepts within literary studies. In so doing, it will simultaneously restore and improve communication between disciplines. At the conclusion of *Romanticism and the Modern Ego,* Jacques Barzun writes,

> If . . . I am asked what third choice to the romantic-classic seesaw I personally propose, I should answer that it is the pragmatic pluralism of William James, who clearly foresaw its applicability to the problems of this century. Pluralism means creating unities and uniformities only where and when useful, with no pretense that they are eternal and divinely ordained. Pragmatism implies the giving of straight answers to the question, "What, then, do we want?" and assessing the choices by means of their costs and consequences—not material costs only or physical consequences only, but all conceivable relevant interests.[32]

Although Barzun is here responding to the modernists' rather sensational accusations against the romantics, the seesaw of classic-romantic is still an apt metaphor for the play of intellectual trends in the humanities and social sciences. The pragmatic and bioepistemological view is difficult to embrace, for it acknowledges a priori human limitation in the quest for knowledge and the relative and potentially transient value of any proposition with a claim to that thing called truth. Because pragmatism is the intellectual methodological extension of the awareness of man as an organic entity, adopting it rests in and tends to reinforce our sense of life's precariousness and changeability. But for that reason it represents the only mode of fruitful intercourse between humanistic and scientific disciplines—between, on the one hand, the questions of value and need explored in the humanities and, on the other, insights about our physical and mental universe offered by the natural sciences. Paradoxically, by addressing particulars, pragmatism results in the most complete picture of our world and our way of being.

Furthermore, if British romantic poetry exhibits a striving for new universals, it also exhibits strong misgivings about such possibilities, a mediatory way of knowing that is itself pragmatic and emphatically English. This is particularly the case with Wordsworth, for whom both vision and self-definition are simultaneously enabled and limited by the paramount fact of nature. Robert Langbaum, who does not use the term *pragmatism* in his definition of romanticism, seems nevertheless to suggest exactly what James meant by that word in his careful explanation of the romantic mode of knowing: "Like the scientist's hypothesis, the romanticist's formulation is evolved out of experience and is continually tested against experience. The difference is that the scientist's experiment is a selected and analyzed experience, whereas experience for the romanticist is even more empiric because less rationalized."[33] While the general applicability of this statement to the romantics is debatable (one thinks particularly of the tendency to champion mind or imagination over matter in Blake and Shelley) Langbaum's conception of romanticism as a bridge between knowledge and value which tries to embrace all relevant interests is a fitting description of the blank verse lyric of the period.[34] And it was Wordsworth who developed this proto-pragmatic form most fully in *The Prelude*. If it is not anachronistic, then, to apply Freud's rationalist epistemology to the questions of religion and psychology raised by romantic poetry, it is at least bound to obfuscate rather than illuminate the series of unassimilated facts, as well as the perception of knowledge and belief as process, contained within Wordsworth's poetry.

Romantic Melancholy and the Meanings of "Religion"

Because the association of religion with the cluster of philosophical and aesthetic phenomena known as romanticism dates back to the period itself, it requires no particular retrospective advantage to perceive that some combination of metaphysical questioning, existential need, and borrowings from orthodox language and rhetoric underlies the writings of the later eighteenth and early nineteenth centuries. In Sydney Ahlstrom's words, "So fundamental were the questions the Romantics were posing, and so basic was the overall shift of attitudes toward humanity, nature, and God, that the religious category is probably the most adequate way of dealing with the phenomenon [of romanticism] as a whole."[35]

But while there is general recognition that romanticism, either centrally or in some of its most notable manifestations, is of a religious character, there is decidedly little agreement about the aesthetic, moral, and philosophical value of this aspect of romanticism. Indeed, the arguments of scholars about the effect of romantic thought and art on religion—or vice versa—range across an entire spectrum, from Hoxie Neale Fairchild's summation that "romantic religion" is a belief "in which grace is the echo of man's pride" to M. H. Abrams's assessment that romanticism preserves "traditional concepts, schemes, and values which had been based on the relation of the Creator to his creature and creation, but [reformulates these concepts] within the prevailing two-term system of subject and object, ego and non-ego, the human mind or consciousness and its transactions with nature."[36] If Fairchild's romanticism debases and destroys religion, Abrams's transforms it.[37]

In one sense, the broad differences on the subject of what Fairchild calls "romantic religion" attest to the vitality of critical debate concerning romanticism and whatever that word might mean. But both the sharp judgments against and effusive praise of romantic religious phenomena demonstrate much more than the intellectual fertility of contemporary criticism, as in fact scholarly debate always does. A great number, perhaps even the majority, of romantic poems have about them very little that deserves to be called religious, if we are to insist on any precision at all in the construal of that term. For example, with the obvious exception of "Tintern Abbey," a definition of romanticism as fundamentally a religious phenomenon sits oddly with a reading of *Lyrical Ballads,* ostensibly one of romanticism's seminal texts. Yet in spite of a recent tendency, encouraged by Marxist approaches, to dismiss the metaphysical concerns of romantic poetry as manifestations of a desire for escape, the religious aspect of romanticism has, over the long term, laid constant claim to our attention. Our selective, retrospective engagement with the literary past tells us as much about the preoccupations we bring to reading as it does about the literature itself.

Despite the apparent polar opposition between Fairchild's and Abrams's judgments, the two scholars hold in common the assumption that religion, as it exists within romantic poetry, refers to a coherent entity, some kind of conceptual whole capable of redeeming or destroy-ing universal truth. But it is just as much of a historical misconstruc-tion to presume that the romantic poets aspired to or developed an integrated body of beliefs as it is to define romanticism itself as a common movement or ideology. The entry of the word religion into common parlance in the nineteenth century itself signals the loss in Western culture of the perceived unity such a term logically suggests. The category of religion, from the romantic period forward, encom-passes nothing like this formal certainty, for while it retains connota-tions of higher unity, it no longer necessarily implies an integrated understanding of the personal, social, and supernatural dimensions of experience. Rather, we have inherited from the nineteenth century the habit of using the term *religion* for one or the other of the aspects implied by a total metaphysic and spiritual commitment; our resultingly ambiguous and contradictory sense of the term coupled with our persistent use of it indicates the marked degree to which we share the metaphysical uneasiness of the last century and the hope for some unity that the word *religion* should logically reflect. Is reli-gion best described in terms of individual experience, as a state of feeling or of heightened consciousness? Or as various social practices, established orthodoxies, belief systems affirmed and perpetuated through ritual practices? As we superficially conceive it, religion in some kind of working order must fulfill both of these functions, encom-passing the personal, social, and supernatural dimensions of experience and reality; but it is in fact the paradoxical discrepancy between reli-gion defined, on the one hand, as affective experience—states of heightened consciousness or intuition of the divine, for example—and, on the other, as organized belief systems that describes the characteris-tic and manifestly problematic religiousness of romanticism.

In Wordsworth's poetry there is evidence of both aspects of reli-gion, yet the relationship between the two is decidedly problematic. Most of this study is devoted to elucidating this discrepancy in the poetry between religious form and feeling, and to interpreting the poet's attempts to bridge the gap between the two. As I will later demonstrate at length, "Tintern Abbey" contains profound correspon-dences to descriptions of mystical experiences but no elements of or-thodox belief. By contrast, while in both The Prelude and The Excursion Wordsworth continues to endorse a naturalistic monism based in private mystical or quasi-mystical experience, he downplays the experiences themselves, and also introduces references to orthodox belief and doctrine that conflict with the naturalistic epistemology associated with mystical experience in his poetry. Because private experience thus exacerbates the conflict between the epistemological results of quasi-mystical experience and orthodox religion, Words-worth's late *Ecclesiastical Sonnets* exhibit an extraordinary drive to-ward religious conformity, demonstrating an alignment of ordinary and extraordinary modes of perception and eschewing the value of private experience. Yet although the sonnets are the most seemingly orthodox of Wordsworth's poems, they are curiously secular, focusing on neither religious experience nor orthodox belief and dogma. Finally, in its focus on exemplary historical Anglican figures, *Ecclesiastical Sonnets* reveals the poet's intense desire for a personal identity defined by an existing social institution—put differently, for a marriage of public and private selves—rather than a convincing psychological and spiritual conversion to orthodox Anglicanism.[38]

The problem of what constitutes religion in romantic poetry is com-plicated by the suggestion that aesthetic forms, which over the course of human history have become increasingly secular and plural, can serve a religious function.[39] It has become something of a critical commonplace, more often implied than overtly stated, that beginning with the romantics and continuing through the nineteenth century—continuing, indeed, well into the twentieth—art itself solves the meta-physical crisis of modern culture by replacing religion. But what does it mean to speak of literature as substitute religion? How can, for example, poems, isolate individual aesthetic constructions, replace reli-gion, particularly in the social sense? As I intend to illustrate through-out this book, such a proposition is psychologically and logically questionable for modern cultures where religion and art serve funda-mentally different functions. Whereas primitive cultures most likely enjoyed a high degree of integration between aesthetic practices and ritual beliefs, modern cultures generally distinguish between the imaginary realm of the aesthetic and the forms of human experience and behavior identified as participation in reality.

This last question indicates a distinction between my investigation of the conflicting definitions of religion at work in Wordsworth's poetry and efforts to reaffirm and renovate religion through philo-sophical speculation. Romantic philosophy, which endeavors to recon-struct theology through the rationalistic modes of thought largely responsible for discrediting previous orthodoxies, is indeed beset with its own series of paradoxes.[40] But generally speaking, philosophical discourse seeks primarily to explain, while literature offers highly spe-cific examples of imaginative experience that enable both reader and writer to address the real by removing themselves from it.[41] Words-worth's poetry, like most modern art, therefore presupposes what most nineteenth-century philosophy forthrightly sought to resolve, the ambiguous nature of reality, and when the artist directs himself away from the recreation of the world's complexity and toward a comprehensive explanation of reality, he no longer writes poetry. Since sincere religious belief implies a stabilized concept of reality, the religious striving of romantic poetry is in one respect a case of art working against itself, an instance of the effort to fix the nature of reality in forms that are generated and survive because of their proximate but unpredictable relationship to the world out there.

Hence, the tension that results from a conflict between religious and aesthetic aims separates Wordsworth from the philosophers of his day in a fundamental way. Wordsworth was by no means fully conscious of his own attempts to recreate religion, and it is the partial consciousness of the conflict between metaphysical striving and creative writing that results in some of the distinctive stylistic and formal innovations of romanticism. But my sense of what we would now call the limited self-awareness of this poet is not intended to deny the self-consciousness of his artistry or to attribute a more than average degree of human blindness to the poet. It is based in one of the most valuable things that modern psychology has given us, the awareness of human limitation. As Freud, whose general theoretics often belie his truer insights into behavioral dynamics, says, "In general [,] men experience the present naively, so to speak, without being able to estimate its content; they must first place it at a distance, i.e. the present must have become the past before one can win from it points of vantage from which to gauge the future."[42] A realistic conception of the writer at work therefore assumes that, like any other person, he is incapable of an objective analysis of his present task, of every possible fact that impinges upon his immediate project and motives. Thus an author's stated intentions are an important but unavoidably partial explanation of the possible meanings of a work of art. And the psychologically realistic view insists that, an artist's talents notwithstanding, he or she be understood in his or her fully human proportions. Meanings inhere in life and in language which we cannot at all times grasp, and conscious intentions neither consistently arrest nor control what Henry James, one of our most careful observers of the human mind, calls "the beautiful circuit and subterfuge of our thought and our desire."[43] Beginning with romanticism, modern literature rests in the discovery of this circuit and subterfuge, and to appreciate the mind's windings we must first engage sympathetically with the needs and desires the poet shares with the men of his day. Romanticism is, as we have been told, a dark and daemonic ground, but its modes of melancholy are many.

"Religious melancholy," says William James, "is not disposed of by a simple flourish of the word insanity. The absolute things, the last things, are the true philosophic concerns; all superior minds feel seriously about them, and the mind with the shortest views is simply the mind of the more shallow man."[44] Writing and lecturing after the turn of the twentieth century, James thus addresses an anxiety that had been emerging into consciousness for the better part of a century. In both *Pragmatism* and *The Varieties of Religious Experience*,[45] James achieves a comprehension and clarity of expression that is a kind of culmination of the nineteenth-century struggle with faith, sympathizing with the underlying human need for explanations without necessarily endorsing the means of its fulfillment. Because he speaks from this pivotal juncture between the nineteenth and twentieth centuries, James's analysis of religion provides an illuminating point of departure and a consistent though qualified frame of reference for the consideration of poetic religion.

The romantic poets themselves, living in and through the first period of profound religious melancholy, hardly had the benefit of James's long view backward, his access to a century of lived solutions to the doubtful quest for absolute and last things. Since the romantic effort to understand the true philosophic concerns was in the deepest sense existential, straining away from but also necessarily clinging to the relatively clear conceptual explanations of the past, the poetry that embodies religious melancholy dramatizes a grasping toward linguistic and formal clarity that nevertheless recedes in the accumulating consciousness of doubt. The tension between a maze of conflicting emotional and intellectual demands and the desire to both express and solve one's religious crisis results aesthetically in some extraordinary poetry and, culturally, over the long term, in a dichotomous view of art and language as man's salvation and his curse.

Today we are very apt to find the phrase *religious melancholy* rather ponderous, even histrionic, for the urge to discover meaningful explanations for life has been held in check with increasing embarrassment since the Enlightenment. Commenting on the split between studies of religion and of literature in America, James Benziger says, "Few writers of either variety are quite at home in the borderland between a humanistic poetic imagination and a more traditional faith. Yet some such land is the Romantic locus."[46] Indeed, we are uncomfortable there because it is our locus as well. If the crisis of existence first addressed by the romantics took nearly a century to be formulated in the analyses of a keen psychological observer like William James, it took almost another entire century to dismiss it as a frivolous question. Now, almost a century after James wrote *Pragmatism,* the desire to comprehend the absolute and last things is, for intellectual men and women, more of an embarrassment than ever, hidden both unwittingly and intentionally from the cogitating selves that increasingly proclaim such yearnings fruitless or dismiss them as the inheritance of a false and destructive culture. No doubt James would have deplored the enthusiastic cry of meaninglessness so recently issuing from beneath the aegis of deconstruction, convicting it not so much for its claim to truth as for its enthusiasm. To submit man's loss of order—personal, social, cosmic—may meet pragmatism's criterion for a valid hypothesis, but it is a possible truth that, if embraced, offers only the certainty of psychological destruction. Surely, a strong sense of the psychic and social jeopardy of nihilism underlies the "will to value" that Laurence Lockridge has recently identified as the dominant ethical direction of British romanticism.[47]

"Our interest in religious metaphysics," says James, "arises in the fact that our empirical future feels to us unsafe, and needs some higher guarantee."[48] As a proposition that defines the origin of religious belief, James's remark is perhaps inadequate, but as a precise statement about the genesis of religious melancholy for modern man, it is entirely correct. By the end of the eighteenth century, the Enlightenment faith in nature as a moral order operating according to discernible laws had collapsed, exposing the incompatibility of nature and orthodox religion as alternate sources of revelation and essentially discrediting either as a legitimate source of belief. Newton, who had faith in science and in religious orthodoxy, felt safe in both the empirical moment *and* the potential afterlife, while the romantic feels—and knows, because science has shown him—the precariousness of existence, what Lionel Trilling calls the hard paradox of organic growth, man's development toward death.[49] Thus, religious melancholy may include a desire to retrieve a discredited orthodoxy, a supernatural order compatible with the natural order, but it is not rooted in social and theological anachronisms. Its basis is, in fact, scientific intelligence, the human consciousness of the organic paradox, and it is an embodiment of the survivor's urge to allay his insecurity and adapt to his environment.

Consistent with this, both the historical and psychological study of religion emerge in the nineteenth century because it is obvious that traditional religious institutions have become unsatisfactory. Beliefs, no longer assumed, become the object of conscious study and of personal preoccupation. As Morse Peckham notes,

> To the degree a culture becomes secularized, to that degree it becomes more and not less concerned with religion. Religion becomes more widespread, more pervasive through the culture as religion proper becomes

less pervasive. Secularization means, more or less, the disappearance of institutionalized occasions and symbols for the religious experience, but it does not mean the religious function has vanished from culture, or is even weaker. It is probably stronger.[50]

Peckham, as something more of a behaviorist than myself, uses the term *religious function* because he is stressing the powerful force of institutional religion in controlling human action.[51] I am stressing the emotional motivation for all-encompassing belief. Our emphases are different but our points are not really separable: only because there is a strong human yearning for explanation can orthodoxies exert such powerful social control. The strict behaviorist would take issue with this and suggest that such a desire is learned and not organic, that it assures the reinforcement of such social controls. But the question of what is merely a learned response and what is an exfoliation of our natural needs and desires has yet to be answered in anything approximating full detail, and the point of contention within modern psychology is in fact a later, more fully articulated scientific attempt to explore the identical central uncertainties that the romantic poet finds himself discovering.

The growth in the currency of the word *religion* during the nineteenth century attests to the accuracy of Peckham's remarks, indicating the concern of a society shaken in its traditional beliefs as well as its struggle to define what it has lost. The word today admits of various uses and is a matter for some debate. Reflecting the predominant sociological concern with man's organization into groups, G. K. Nelson applies the term *religion* to the institutionalization of man's spiritual needs.[52] Religion, in this sense, applies to an organizational hierarchy, a body of beliefs and laws, and a conceptual structure that delineates the character and power of deity and the rituals of worship. In contrast to such a sociological circumscription of religion as a social form with a proscribed set of beliefs, the psychologist applies the adjective *religious* to a unique kind of emotional experience, regardless of the association of that experience with institutional practices. Thus, the psychologist defines as religious any experience treated by the subject as such, whether it is induced by traditional religious service, private meditation, hallucinogenic drugs, or any other means.

The psychological definition derives from the affective tradition in the study and philosophy of religion, established in the writings of the German romantic philosopher Friedrich Schleiermacher at the turn of the nineteenth century.[53] Schleiermacher took as his task the separation of inner religious experience from church ritual and authority, insisting on the pure ontological status of the former and the secondary and symbolic nature of the later. Hence religion came to be defined as a core of feeling not necessarily attached to a body of beliefs and practices. William James approaches religion from within the affective tradition established by Schleiermacher, and for this reason he tends to analyze states of mind irrespective of the institutional practices of his subjects.

James's own definition of religion, in fact, provides a pointed example of the modern difficulty of defining this concept: "Religion, therefore, as I now ask you arbitrarily to take it, shall mean for us the *feelings, acts, and experiences of men in their solitude, so far as they apprehend themselves to stand in relation to whatever they may consider the divine.*"[54] Broad as this preliminary definition is, it identifies an emotional component, an object of worship, and a pattern of actions and behaviors. Traditionally, religion retains all three of these elements. But the definition poses some problems for the man of the late nineteenth century, and hence James offers a second definition that redirects itself toward the affective aspect:

> Religion, whatever it is, is man's total reaction upon life, so why not say that any total reaction upon life is a religion? Total reactions are different from casual reactions, and total attitudes are different from usual or professional attitudes. To get at them you must go behind the foreground of existence and reach down to that curious sense of the whole residual cosmos as an everlasting presence, intimate or alien, terrible or amusing, lovable or odious, which in some degree everyone possesses.[55]

Religion, then, is man's passionate and comprehensive embrace of experience, one that includes a perception of metaphysical presence.

In the text between his initial definition of religion and this modification of it, James discusses the problem posed by the word *divine.* Using the example of Emersonian transcendentalism, James notes the replacement of the Christian anthropomorphic deity with the Oversoul, a sort of spiritual essence. Thus a transcendent, anthropomorphic god is replaced with what is more appropriately termed a quality. Is this a divine being? The same question arises in Wordsworth's poetry with respect to the ambiguous conception of the deity. Although Wordsworth employs the traditional term *God,* as a term of reference *God* is almost as unspecific as Emerson's Oversoul, particularly in Wordsworth's early poetry. *God* loses its traditional determinate status in Wordsworth's poetry because, first, it is sparsely used, and second, it essentially competes with other words awarded honorific status that are used with similar if not greater frequency: *nature, mind,* and *human life,* for example. Hence, in view of both James's example and the apparently equivocal status of the deity in Wordsworth's major poetry, religion seems no longer to require a visualizable godhead or defined ritual structure, so the emotional character of the believer becomes the crux of the definition. Yet this is surely another paradox. Strong and persistent emotions have objects, but in this case, emotion not only continues but intensifies in the face of a dissipating object. Moreover, the fact that it is nature that inspires a Words-worthian "total reaction" aggravates rather than solves the imbalance of unambiguous emotions and ambiguous belief, for nature intuitively perceived becomes less and less a divine object; it becomes increasingly continuous with the conditions and limitations of human life. It is this contradiction between so great an emotion and so problematical an object that defines and confirms rather than assuages Wordsworth's religious melancholy.

Doubt itself intensifies faith, as Tennyson was wont to point out. But can this be so if that faith lies in no shared dogmas and practices? Tennyson's assertion may serve for a man of later date than the roman-tic, a man more fully aware of the nature of his doubt and of his deviation from religious orthodoxy. The problem which James begins to trace between forms (doctrine, deity, and ritual) and private experi-ence makes it as likely that the faith deepened by uncertainty is apt to produce, in turn, a correspondingly reinforced doubt. For when the term *religion* and its appropriate feeling are divorced from a stable form of worship and its attendant conceptual clarity and social rein-forcement, the believer begins to suspect the veracity of either or both his feelings and his concept of the divine. Thrown back on strictly subjective resources, he begins to suspect, in short, that his apprehen-sion of God is a product of his imagination.

According to Abrams, the romantic poet created a successful rein-terpretation of Judeo-Christian myth, adopting the metaphors of mar-riage, fall, and redemption and placing the imagination in the role of the redeemer. But for all the overt romantic rhetoric glorifying the imagination, the covert movement of much romantic poetry indicates deep distress about the nature and function of imaginative experience. As Gerald Graff has cogently noted,

> The concept of an autonomous creative imagination, which fabricates the forms of order, meaning, and value which men no longer thought they could find in external nature, implicitly—if not necessarily intentionally— concedes that artistic meaning is a fiction, without any corresponding object in the extra-artistic world. In this respect the doctrine of the crea-tive imagination contained within itself the premises of its refutation.[56]

In "Tintern Abbey," Wordsworth describes and attempts to validate an apparently authentic mystical experience, but since the sociocultu-

ral structures that typically confirm such an experience are insufficient, the poet relies on the subjective resources of poetry. In the
process of poetic creation, Wordsworth begins to recognize that his
words neither fit the orthodox categories nor adequately express his
internal experience, and comes to understand that through artistic
creation he is attempting to build what individual works of art can
never offer, a statement of belief with the authority of cultural orthodoxy. While the complicated religious nature of the romantic poem
never rises to full consciousness in the period, the fear that his deepest
commitments are merely a bundle of lies, fabrications of the self-
serving mind—or the imagination—accounts for the extraordinary
tension of much romantic poetry that addresses metaphysical questions and experiences.

Modes of Transcendence and the Limits of Poetry

The romantic lyric to which I will soon turn is religious, then, in
this particularly modern sense: it dramatically asserts authentic religious experience while simultaneously raising doubts about the genesis, ontological status, and social value of the experience. "Tintern
Abbey," like Coleridge's "Eolian Harp" and Shelley's "Mount Blanc,"
adopts religious language and rhetoric and a cumulative structure that
mimics psychological development toward religious belief. But at the
same time, the conceptualization and communication of a transcendent
experience that is no longer circumscribed by a relatively stable religious orthodoxy tends paradoxically to foreground doubt by introduc-
ing the epistemological crisis into consciousness. Words, expected to
serve at first an explanatory and finally a ritual function, can do
neither in a satisfactory fashion.

Three separate and often conflicting aspects of religion are therefore
at large in "Tintern Abbey," and a proper understanding of them rests
on separate and sometimes conflicting psychological analyses. I will
address these concerns in turn, beginning with an exposition of the
phenomena of religious experience and proceeding to the question of
their interpretation (which encompasses doubts about their origin and
relationship to orthodoxies), and the problem of the psychological
analogy between religion and art. James's *Varieties of Religious Experience* provides the appropriate starting point, since it is still the seminal
study in religious psychology, and many of the characteristics James
describes are clearly analogous to the psychology underlying some
romantic poetry.

James's definition of religion, as we have seen, stresses its passionate
nature and its totalizing impulse while minimizing the significance of

ritual and conceptual structure. It is "the feelings, acts, and experiences of men *in their solitude,* so far as they apprehend themselves to stand in relation to whatever they consider the divine."[57] Despite the breadth of this definition, it is still more precise than some others of James's day. James distinguishes his concept of religion from Havelock Ellis's, which relates religion to all happiness, and from that proposed by J. R. Seeley, from whom religious feeling becomes equated somewhat generally with strong and constant admiration. In differing with Ellis, James is careful to say that religion, whose driving impulse is the acceptance of the universe, is not essentially a feeling of escape, and against Seeley's conception James insists that religion entails sacrifice and submission. In short, even though James defines religion primarily as a private form of experience, that privacy itself is contingent upon an apprehension of life beyond the self—social, natural, and supernatural.

Insofar as this definition applies to the religious ethos of Wordsworth and other British romantic poets—educated post-Enlightenment Englishmen raised within various Protestant denominations—the emphasis on submission, sacrifice, and the moral imperative of accepting the universe is especially relevant. Spirituality, in this sense, is part of a person's dynamic relationship with others and with the material universe, not an end in itself. Indeed, James's primary justification of religion is on the grounds of its social value, its capacity to adjust man to the circumstances and uncertainties of existence. The conception that a full spiritual life feeds the social good is characteristically Western and distinguishes James's definition of religion from oriental spiritual practices that cultivate states of higher consciousness for what we might term their escape value precisely because the material world is considered unredeemable.[58] Additionally, James's perception that transcendent experience ultimately serves social interests stands in contrast to the Freudian view that such states constitute regression to infantile narcissism (a hypothesized state that is, to be sure, especially asocial) and is instead consistent with recent developmental research. Tracing the source of such states, like Freud, to the mother-child dyad, theorists including Erik Erikson, Stern, and John Bowlby nonetheless offer a contrasting interpretation.[59] Insisting that the primary bond with the mother fosters the need for attachment, developmental theorists maintain that this primary bond is crucial for the later development of social relations and language.

In the past thirty years, most analyses of the transcendent moments in romantic poetry, whether celebrating such experiences as interludes of rejuvenating consciousness or identifying them as episodes of repression or sociopolitical false consciousness, have overlooked the traditional relationship between spiritual enlightenment and social commitment. As a result, literary scholars tend to treat transcendence as an isolated phenomenon, divorced from a larger context of practices, beliefs, and intentions; interpretations of the meaning and outcome of such experiences concentrate almost exclusively on the poet's *self*— its preservation, augmentation, delusion, and so on. But an understanding of how transcendent experience within the Western tradition is one component of an interactive process directed toward spiritual clarity *and* ethical engagement drastically modifies this perceived antagonism between subjective insight and social participation. The habit of seeing antagonism between the private and public aspects of human life may well reflect our specifically American heritage, with its strong claims for the self and its suspicion that conformity to social norms diminishes the individual.[60]

Following this, I disagree with James Twitchell's assertion that "cosmic consciousness" is a secular phenomenon within romantic poetry, even while Twitchell does not disparage transcendence as do more recent materialist critics. Twitchell contends that the Western world's distrust of heightened mental states is a result of "treating expanded consciousness as a religious phenomenon. It is not. It is a shift in consciousness that occurs, as Blake said, 'only when the doors of perception are cleansed.'"[61] Clearly, whether we define these experiences as religious depends in part on how we parse that term, and it is perhaps most accurate to say they are neither fully religious nor manifestly secular. But as the poet's rendering and interpretation of his own experiences crucially demonstrates, the system of values which circumscribes them and may, in fact, be their source differs significantly from the celebration of altered consciousness characteristic of the counterculture and the New Age. It matters little, given our current knowledge, whether such experiences refer to a higher spiritual order, this being undetermined as a matter of fact. What is important is that the romantic poet strives to understand these experiences in ways fully characteristic of James's definition of religion, and to insist that he does not is merely to project contemporary consciousness backward onto a period far less enured to metaphysical doubt. The poet being under a moral compulsion to accept the universe, the mystical experience cannot merely provide an escape from everyday consciousness, but must instead be understood as part of a dynamic relationship between the self and all of reality, visible and invisible.

In his definition of religious personality, James distinguishes two religious types, the once-born and the twice-born, and it is the second that primarily concerns him. Again, this emphasis on the fragmented self and the movement toward rebirth, on faith as a process of loss

and repossession of belief, describes a religious psychology far more
common to post-Enlightenment persons than to those of earlier date,
who had less occasion to doubt their initial metaphysical unities. "The
psychological basis of the twice-born character," James tells us, "seems
to be a certain discordancy or heterogeneity in the native temperament
of the subject, an incompletely unified moral and intellectual constitu-
tion."[62] This divided self seeks unification, and the process of religious
conversion and rebirth is a potential means of realizing the impulse
toward order and unity. James's point of view is consistently psychological in its stress on the healing potential of conversion; conversion
is a possible but certainly not an exclusive means of overcoming pathological depression.

Numerous literary scholars, including David Perkins, M. H. Abrams, Frank McConnell, and Stephen Prickett, have noted the similarity between the pattern of development in romantic poetry and either
the conversion experience or its ritual corollary, the testimonial (or
Protestant confessional) form.[63] At times certain poems of this period,
particularly Wordsworth's, do almost read like a mapping of the standard conversion experience. But what makes the difference for these
poets is that the emotional pattern of conversion is carried out beyond
the limits of orthodox religious ritual, where any substitute religion
is certainly problematical. Most crucially, how is it possible to speak
of conversion when there is nothing definite to be converted to? Studies from social psychology in the function of religious testimonial tend
to highlight the dilemma of the poet whose conversion is removed
from a shared ritual and lacking a dogma- or object of worship. The
practice of including accounts of conversion in the religious service is
in fact extraordinarily effective in ensuring the faithfulness of the
congregation, because it recognizes individuality by prescribing its
proper function.[64] Through a structured practice that dictates the
length and occasion for personal statements and supplies a familiar
audience (or congregation) that will respond in a predictable fashion,
giving testimony as part of a religious ritual fulfills both the need for
individual recognition as well as the necessity to belong to a human
community.

Adopting the categories outlined by E. D. Starbuck in *The Psychology of Religion*, James says that conversion can be either willed or
achieved through self-surrender, but often includes a combination of
the two, involving subliminal cerebration. Notably, chroniclers of religious experience both before and since James's day insist that some
degree of self-surrender is imperative for successful conversion. The
resulting faith-state or state of assurance is characterized by a loss of
worry, a perception of new truths, and a rejuvenated perception of

external reality. Once again, conversion is defined not as a means of escape from reality but as a mode of renewing the subject's connection with it; by unifying the subject's intellectual and emotional impulses, religious belief reduces the conflicts that alienate the subject from reality by altering his picture of it.

Because self-surrender means a temporary falling off of self-consciousness in the subject's perception of a larger order of being, the phenomenon of conversion involves a quasi- or proto-mystical experience. Mysticism represents an extremity in states of higher consciousness, and its various characteristics therefore provide the paradigm for identifying extrarational states. In James's scheme, mystical states have four major characteristics: ineffability, noetic quality, transiency, and passivity; thus they are inexpressible at the same time that they lay claim to special insight and knowledge, they are of short duration, and they are selfless in the most literal sense of the word. Mystical states, as James points out, are frequently defined in negative terms, because all of their characteristics rest on some paradox: they are inexpressible, yet they are an experience of absolute being; they offer new knowledge that cannot be communicated; they are fleeting but absolute; they are passive but produce a fundamental change in the subject.

Since mysticism is by definition characterized as an extrarational form of consciousness, efforts at literal description of such states are bound to fail. "In mystical literature," says James, "such self-contradictory phrases as 'dazzling obscurity,' 'whispering silence,' 'teeming desert,' are continually met with. They prove that not conceptual speech, but music rather, is the element through which we are best spoken to by mystical truth. Many mystical scriptures are indeed little more than musical compositions."[65]

Insofar as we accept James's definition, any accurate description of mystical experience—as opposed to an explanation of its meaning—is a logical impossibility. That mystical states are by definition inexpressible presents no particular problem for the traditional mystic, whose transport is explained by a set of unified beliefs. In fact, the inexpressibility of the mystical state constitutes a great part of its appeal for the orthodox believer, reinforcing a sense of mystery that is at once private, shared, and completely other. Mystical writings, for the orthodox believer, serve an incantatory function, and any trance-state induced by them is later interpreted according to an already accepted set of beliefs. By contrast, for the individual straying from orthodoxy who feels compelled to relate his experience and thus place it in a social and spiritual context, the paradoxical and ineffable nature of the experience threatens to undermine communication, and with it the value of the experience itself. An explanatory as well as an imitative language is required to make sense of the experience, even though the terms of the experience dictate that accurate conceptualization of an extrarational experience is a logical impossibility. This represents the first dimension of the romantic poet's difficulty in selecting adequate language for his experience.

At one point James says that he equates mystical states with all faith-states, but elsewhere he is careful to acknowledge that his description is not the result of a comprehensive study of modes of heightened consciousness within all religions, and is therefore probably limited in its accuracy. More recent researchers in this are indeed exploring the varieties rather than the similarities of religious and supernatural experiences. As David Hufford points out, use of traditional terminology in describing supernatural experiences tends unwittingly to connect heterogeneous experiences to each other and to a single tradition.[66]

In an article entitled "A Typology of Religious Experience," Robert D. Margolis and Kirk W. Elifson distinguish four kinds of higher religious consciousness, thus expanding on the initial description given by James.[67] (All of the sixty-nine subjects selected for the study, it should be noted, were tested for and selected on the basis of sound mental health.) Corresponding to the classical mystical state, the transcendental state is characterized by metaphysical contact and a change in the subject's perception of reality, whereas the vertigo experience involves disorientation and a fear of loss of control. The life-change experience is defined as difficult to express, but results in a change in perception of self or of God. Finally, visionary states are, as one might suspect, characterized by visions and voices. Although this last kind of experience often occurs during a dream, it is considered religious because the subject interprets it as contact with the divine.

Elifson and Margolis thus make distinctions between the nature, emotion, and, in the visionary instance, physiological condition involved in these states. For instance, conversion or life change, which for James corresponds to the mystical experience of an established believer, is here rather distinct from the transcendental state. The breakdown seems to suggest that a change in perception of self or of God does not imply a change in the perception of external reality. If these two phenomena do not appear sharply distinguished, however, the vertigo experience is psychologically of an entirely different order than the faith-state James describes. The result is apt to be greater insecurity and self-consciousness rather than self-unification. Finally, the visionary state is distinguished by its conceptual order, either visual or narrative, and its appearance in sub- versus supraconsciousness.

Within literary studies, the terms *vision* and *visionary*—along with the word *sublime*—admit of an extraordinary broad usage that is, nevertheless, understandable in view of their use within theology. Two of the states that Elifson and Margolis are careful to distinguish, the transcendent and the visionary, here are easily confused under the generalized application of these terms. As Hufford explains it:

> The term *intellectual vision,* of which St. Teresa did not know the source, and which may have a confusing sound to the modern ear, was coined by St. Augustine (A.D. 354–430) to describe what he considered one of the three basic forms of vision, speaking of ordinary as well as extraordinary vision. He used the term to refer to a "reality which can be perceived by the intellect alone" (*The Essential Augustine,* p. 95). In this he is distinguishing intellectual vision from visionary sensations and images. Always concerned with distinguishing the real from the illusory and the divine from the deceptive, mystics have generally regarded the intellectual vision as more real and more trustworthy than those visions in which images are seen, words are heard, and so forth. This is an interesting element in the mystical consensus since, to those of us who have never had such an experience, there is at first a tendency to assume that a "sense of presence" must be more vague and possess less impact than an experience in which one believes one sees someone nearby and hears him speak. But among those who have had the experience the reverse is true.[68]

Intellectual vision, then, corresponds to what James, Elifson, and Margolis call the classical mystical state. By contrast, if we entertain the possibility that, say, the Book of Revelations or the prophecies of Blake relate acts of supernatural sight, we understand them to describe an entirely different order of religious experience. As Hufford moreover points out, the term *visionary* elides the perceived values of these experiences as well as their distinct natures. Hufford's findings regarding the value placed on these experiences also correlates with James's; intellectual vision or the mystical state represents the pinnacle of religious experience, while the phenomenon of visualizing supernatural figures or events, akin to hallucination, is considered a secondary form of religious "sight." And precisely because such visionary experience engages conceptual understanding in a way that mystical experience does not, it is more plausibly a product of the human mind and therefore has been treated with greater skepticism throughout religious history.

The descriptions of religious experience from James forward suggest a particular orientation within psychological research, one that Hufford calls experience-centered, and justifies in these words: "The primary theoretical statement of the approach might be roughly summed

up as follows: some significant portion of traditional supernatural belief is associated with accurate observation interpreted rationally. This
does not mean that *all* such belief has this association."[69] Hufford's
statement is based on his own substantial research, which indicates
cross-cultural similarities in supernatural experiences that cannot be
explained by traditions within the cultures. However, the orientation
within religious psychology that concerns itself with the problematical
nature of the relationship between experience and interpretation is,
given our current psychological knowledge, equally valid.

Like Hufford, Proudfoot supports an experience-centered approach
to religious psychology, but proceeds under a conviction that social
influences, including religious doctrines and practices as well as common values, are the probable source of most religious experience, an
approach Hufford refers to as the cultural source hypothesis. Thus
the concepts governing thought are said to be formative of the experience, rather than vice versa. Proudfoot's position rests fundamentally
on a conception of the human mind as an interpretive organ. If one
acknowledges, as nearly all modern psychology does, the Kantian
precept that the mind is active during perception, all cognition is
understood as some species of interpretation. The capacity for interpretation, in turn, involves concepts. The description of a transcendent experience in a shared language is a further interpretive
refinement of the initial experience, and the researcher's analysis represents yet a third interpretive remove from the initial experience.
This being the case, what are the concepts governing thought at the
moment of apparent supernatural perception, or during the conscious
description of this event to a researcher? Then, what are the concepts
governing the analyst's interpretation of the experience? As Proudfoot
explains in his lucid discussion of this problem, "Any attempt to differentiate a core [of experience] from its interpretations, then, results in
the loss of the very experience one is trying to analyze . . . One cannot
attain Nirvana by accident. This is a logical matter, not just a contingent fact."[70]

Two major difficulties arise from this ambiguous situation. The first
concerns the experience itself. What is its genuine character? The
second concerns its origin. Does a mystical experience merely demonstrate the power of suggestion, the enormous force of orthodox rituals
in inducing a faith-state? And if in fact religious institutions shape
private experience, how can any of the states described by James,
Elifson, and Margolis be understood outside of a set of theological
concepts and rituals that quite probably induce the experiences
themselves?

These questions are of course rhetorical, for we are hardly more equipped to answer them than the romantics were. But they are now familiar to us, becoming concerns, as far as possible, of objective study, whereas for the romantic poet they are largely subliminal. In his renderings of transcendent experience, Wordsworth tries to be at once the outside observer and the religious mystic. Hence, the interpretive struggle of religious psychology determines the second dimension of an anxiety about language. In effect, is it the case that the mind, operating through the medium of language, merely interprets as otherworldly experiences that are really nothing other than the effects of culturally generated beliefs? Paradoxically enough, the linguistic limits to the expression of belief seem to generate doubt about the validity of human interpretations of reality.

The third and final dimension of the problem of language and belief is an outgrowth of the other two and originates as a possible solution: if language cannot render religious experience, and if, indeed, such experience may be nothing more than a product of language, then the enormously constructive powers of language must be put to use to replace destabilized religion. In "Tintern Abbey," Wordsworth tries to resolve doubt by grounding belief in the literary process but, in so doing, he actually heightens the discrepancy between the ground of religion and the ground of art, proving that private language cannot offer public redemption and spiritual transformation.

This last of the problems with language faced by the romantic poet is also the least recognized in academe today, for the mystification of art is still remarkably prevalent in literary culture. And the tendency of literary critics to see art as a substitute for religion parallels the tendency in psychology to propound a close analogy between the two. But art and religion do not really represent alternative activities, psychic experiences, and social functions, and the habit of seeing them as such stands as the limitation of an exclusively pragmatic psychological view. Relying on D. W. Winnicott's speculation that art and religion function for adults as play does for the child by providing a mediating psychological space between the self and reality (the transitional realm), Paul Pruyser asserts that both are crafts characterized by practice and ritual, that their sphere is imagination, and their ontological status illusion. "As each form of art 'takes a stab' at expressing ineffable truth, each religion can be seen as a special way of probing, and communicating, the transcendent that seems to escape logical formulation."[71] The psychological point, that religion and art both help us to adjust to reality by exploring experiential unknowns, is legitimate as far as it goes. But it is a little too neat. The artist can easily believe his work to operate on these terms, but the religious believer who is capable of doing so professes to a religion that has been subsumed by aesthetics. Contrary to Pruyser's assertion, the transcendent does not at all escape logical formulation for most ortho- dox believers: for most contemporary Christians, Christ is not a sym- bol for human possibility, he *is* at once human and supernatural, and God is an all-powerful divine being. As Proudfoot puts it:

> To experience God or his providential activity is not, from the subject's point of view, to entertain a possible world in which there is a God and he governs events in the world, nor is it to entertain a concept that permits one to externalize certain hopes and fears by projecting them onto another plane. One might suspect that the proper explanation of religious belief and experience would be found along these lines, but it is not the account that would be given by the believer. The experience has a noetic quality for the subject and is taken to reveal something about the world beyond the individual self. In this way, it is similar to the experience of actually skiing down [a] slope, as contrasted with that of thinking about skiing down [a] slope.[72]

The poet in the act of writing knows he is creating something artificial and hypothetical, no matter how realistic or autobiographical the de- tails of his work are; as Wordsworth's revisions of his own life in *The Prelude* indicate, he put creative purpose before factual accuracy. Likewise, the reader of the poem shares in the distillation and unique formalization of experience, and he understands this experience to be illusory. In opposition to this, the religious believer understands his heightened consciousness to be occurring not in a sphere of illusion but in an absolute reality that transcends the actual world of human observation. For the devout, religious experience has the force of truth; it is not an access to different kinds of human experience or ways of perception. This difference explains why a religious person can participate in the same rituals over and over again, while writers and readers move on to new projects and entertainments.

I recognize that my distinction between the domain of religion and that of art is particularly modern, and must insist that its value rests not on a claim to total truth but rather on its ability to explain a sensible uneasiness in "religious" romantic poetry because it corre- sponds to a discrimination already available to nineteenth-century consciousness. The romantic lyric thus works toward a reorganization of modes of knowing and forms of behavior that the poets are just beginning to perceive as inevitably separate. The anthropologist Johan Huizinga claims that, in early culture, there is a lack of distinction between art and religion, play and seriousness, which become polar- ized with the progress of civilization. Referring to the archaic poet- vates, Huizinga writes, "the possessed, the God-smitten, the raving one ... Gradually the poet-seer splits up into the figures of the prophet, the priest, the soothsayer, the mystagogue, and the poet as we know him."[73] Notwithstanding all their wishful claims for the prophetic power of the poet, the romantics lived late enough in history to perceive that the poet-vates was an irretrievable anachronism. Much as these poets might have wished to resolve religious doubt through art, their lyrics ultimately attest to the psychological impossibility of unifying art and religion within modern culture.

"The standard account of the dramatic monologue," Robert Langbaum tells us, "is that Browning and Tennyson conceived it as a reaction against the confessional style."[74] Indeed the reaction to confessional form begins before the Victorian era, in romanticism itself. Abrams has rightly, I think, announced the importance of the romantic lyric as a formal innovation, yet the relative scarcity of these poems seems curious in the face of their generic significance. And yet, perhaps not so curious: the discursive mode of reasoning encouraged by an irregular blank verse form tends to multiply questions and hypotheses, tends, in the case of a poem that probes metaphysical questions, to explore every possible implication of those questions. Thus the philosophical wish to solve the problem of reality and the creative desire to explore its ambiguities generate enormous tension within the form.

As the result of confronting spiritual crisis in creative form, Wordsworth is forced to recognize the limits of language—its relative ability to convey experience and to lead man toward knowledge and its complete inability to transform reality. In the next chapter, I will demonstrate how, in "Tintern Abbey," Wordsworth's experimentation with poetic form as both a vehicle for communicating religious experience and a structure to contain and stabilize it reveals the problematic nature of that very enterprise. In the following two chapters, I will show how Wordsworth attempts to resolve this conflict. First, in *The Prelude,* Wordsworth deemphasizes religious experience per se and instead elaborates a monistic conception of reality which is the characteristic result of mystical experience. In no longer attempting the pure renderings of spiritual states exemplified in "Tintern Abbey," Wordsworth finds a partial but ultimately inadequate solution to the paradoxical attempt to describe and to frame an experience with absolute authority within the syntactic and semantic limitations of private language. Next, in the *Ecclesiastical Sonnets,* Wordsworth ultimately abandons the conflicts arising from the need to explain intense religious experience by eliminating the spiritual and experiential dimension of religion from his poetry altogether. The poet's spiritual consciousness, formerly aroused and reinforced by nature, is literally reformed to an orthodox perspective that disciplines the contradictions arising from private experience. As Wordsworth moves toward acceptance of institutional religion and therefore toward a systematic social structure that should stabilize mystical experiences, the private spiritual experiences that served as the impulse toward belief must paradoxically be abandoned. Throughout these selected works of Wordsworth's, then, there is an inverse relationship between the representation of valued religious consciousness and the elements of orthodox Anglicanism, a phenomenon that suggests that art cannot mediate between individual spiritual commitments and perceptions and the affirmations of socially shared beliefs.

2

Intellectual Vision and Self-Qualifying Structure in "Tintern Abbey"

> Only the very greatest art invigorates without consoling, and defeats our attempts, in W. H. Auden's words, to use it as magic.
> —Iris Murdoch, "Against Dryness"

IN THE PREVIOUS CHAPTER, I SUGGESTED THAT THE WORD *RELIGION* comes into use and that vigorous debate about what in fact religion is begins only when orthodox beliefs become generally unstable. Hence, the persistent discussion of religion since the nineteenth century attests not to a stable concept thus defined but to a rift between spirituality and traditional forms of worship: intense conviction and/or intuition of the existence of a divine being or higher order within the universe is not sufficiently strengthened, explained, or justified by orthodox ritual and dogma. But since it appears generally true in human life that stable faith is maintained (and perhaps even established) by individual and group rituals, including meditation, prayer, and worship, the lack of a creed and of rituals that ostensibly offer objective verification and thus confirm the reality of subjective religious experience is apt to lead to doubt about the authenticity of the experience.[1] Any attempt to communicate the experience through poetry as a means of supplying the missing verification and validation traditionally provided by social forms would tend, paradoxically, to reinforce doubt. There are two reasons for this. First, the highest order of religious experience is by definition extraconceptual, and therefore extralinguistic, and second, attempts to recreate such states highlight the interpretive and creative capabilities of human consciousness, undermining the claim of ecstatic states to absolute reality.

The effort to stabilize religious belief from the ground of individual experience and writing is, then, a psychologically contradictory enterprise that results in increased ambiguity about the nature and authenticity of the experience, as well as new ambivalence about language and creativity. Thus, a poetry that endeavors both to express religious experience and to erect the forms of belief relies increasingly on the metaphoric and suggestive capacities of language, effectively denying the public form that it otherwise sought to establish. Inasmuch as the kind of total structure of metaphysical and cultural beliefs sought by the poet must emanate from communal values and intentions to be perceived as truth rather than the creative individual's imaginative illusion, the desire to assert a privately intuited supernatural order will, inevitably, be fraught with doubt. Hence, one by-product of a quest for stable objective forms through creative enterprise is that an apologetic or even distrustful attitude toward both artist and artistic creation persists throughout the poetry of the romantic period, not-withstanding explicit claims for the superhuman potentialities of both creator and artwork and thus for his fitness for the task of reunifying reality. In consequence, not only is the purportedly religious poetry of this period rarely religious in a consistent way, but the ambitions of romantic religion are counterbalanced by poems that minimize or refute high claims to art.

"Tintern Abbey" is the type of romantic poem that attempts to balance intense religious feeling with formal embodiment as I have described above. Yet while this poem dramatizes the highest level of religious experience, it is ultimately most equivocal, among Words-worth's poems, about creed and the system or structure that contains the experience. In composing "Tintern Abbey," Wordsworth selects and exploits an indeterminate form, the English blank verse ode, to counter his own efforts at structuring experience. In this sense, the poem is not typical of Wordsworth's contemporaneous lyrics. As the final poem in the first edition of Lyrical Ballads, "Tintern Abbey" is an odd conclusion to that volume and remains so in the face of Wordsworth's subsequent volumes of lyrics, Poems, in Two Volumes, 1807. It is the only Wordsworth poem in blank verse in the first edition of Lyrical Ballads; those added to the second (1800) edition balance the formal indeterminacy of blank verse with subject matter that is either more minimally occasional or expressly narrative. And although "Tintern Abbey" affirms experience per se and the particular religious experiences it dramatizes, the poem remains formally and metaphysically perhaps the most inconclusive of Wordsworth's poems. This is to suggest that "Tintern Abbey," a poem we view as quintes-sentially Wordsworthian, is in some respects an anomalous poem, that as an experiment in generating religious forms through aesthetic considerations it reveals the disparate nature of religious and aes-thetic experience.

The point that inconclusiveness, both in "Tintern Abbey" and other poems of the period, is in fact the result of preoccupation with structure rather than a devaluation of form requires some stressing.[2] In the long-famous phrase from the Preface to the *Lyrical Ballads,* a phrase that is too frequently divorced from its relevant contexts—textual, biographical, and sociohistorical—Wordsworth informs us that "all good poetry is the spontaneous overflow of powerful feelings" (*Lyrical Ballads,* 744. 102–4). Criticism has tended to import later statements celebrating an expressivist aesthetic back onto Wordsworth's claim, and as a result find in the Preface a more or less Manichean divide between feeling and conceptual thought (and it attendant orders, including poetic form), with our poet as a vocal spokesman for feeling. John Stuart Mill insists that "when [the poet] turns round and addresses himself to another person; when the act of utterance is not itself an end, but a means to an end—viz. by the feelings he himself expresses, to work upon the feelings, or upon the belief, or will, of another,—when the expression of his emotions, or of his thoughts tinged with his emotions, is tinged also by that purpose, by that desire of making an impression upon another mind, then it ceases to be poetry, and becomes eloquence"; in these words, Mill makes the argument for a fictive language of feeling opposed to Wordsworth's real language of men, and thus for a subjectivism that Wordsworth sought at all moments to avoid.[3] Poetry, for Wordsworth, is an act of communication that demands a self-conscious effort toward common words and forms. What Wordsworth repeatedly emphasizes in the "Preface" is just the kind of deliberative, meditative consciousness directly antithetical to vulgar emotionalism: the chief attributes of the poet are to be exceptional sensibility and the capacities for long and deep thought and sustained recollection.

Among other factors, Wordsworth's use of the word *feeling* in the Preface is misleading to contemporary minds, since we treat this word as a synonym for emotion or affect and thus distinguish it from rational or intellectual thought. But Wordsworth's use derives from David Hartley's associationist psychology, which places both sensations and ideas under the rubric of "internal feelings of the mind."[4] For Hartley, the opposition between affection and understanding corresponds to our distinction between feeling/emotion/affect and intellect.

In keeping with this, what Wordsworth's statement attests to is not the glorification of affect over intellect, but the necessity of thinking about and refining emotion. Emotion and intellect are therefore conceived as cognitively separate, yet not existing in polar opposition: "I have said that Poetry is the spontaneous overflow of powerful feelings: it takes its origin from emotion recollected in tranquillity: the emotion is contemplated till by a species of reaction the tranquillity gradually disappears, and an emotion, similar to that which was before the subject of contemplation, is gradually produced, and does itself actually exist in the mind" (*Lyrical Ballads,* 756. 537–41). Poetic composition, then, reunifies intellect and affect, which exist in a roughly progressive, dialectical arrangement, into "powerful feelings."

Indeed, Wordsworth's admittedly mechanical adoption of associationism (an admittedly mechanistic school of psychology) and its rhetoric seemingly construes poetical composition as a foreordained series of chain reactions and consequently belies the underlying importance of his theoretical statement. But the field of psychology has been simultaneously enabled and limited by mechanical metaphors for centuries, a fact that has not obviated all inquiry in that discipline; one must simply look beyond the limitations of the metaphors.[5] Wordsworth's conception of poetical composition is less rigid than it seems, the poet's principle point here being that literary creation emerges as a process of shaping the data of psychological experience. Far from granting a release from formal constraints, then, poetic creation for Wordsworth is an exercise in integrating cognitive experience, and of producing, in consequence, a more genuine aesthetic object through the interaction of emotion and conceptual thought. And the body of Wordsworth's poetry, so obsessively revised during his lifetime that it will forever present us with bibliographical dilemmas, exemplifies, as one critic notes, "a continuous discipline of art on the behalf of truth."[6] Precisely because the romantic poets reconceptualize the notion of form itself in an effort to find the ideal structure for their poetic subjects, they are preoccupied with the question of form as no one before them.[7]

But while the breakdown of established forms in turn opens up an entire new range of artistic possibilities, it also introduces a new range of constraints, the first of which is, paradoxically, an excess of freedom. Given a heightened awareness of the mind as actively engaged in experience, as interpreting and to some extent shaping it, the poet is obligated to know the experience fully as he formalizes and thereby establishes its meaning. The comprehension that incorrect interpretation is a likely by-product of man's creative relationship to actuality results in a confirmed sense of the fictiveness of poetic enterprise, and the counterpart of a persistent preoccupation with form is an ambivalence about whether such forms correspond to orders within reality or serve a self-delusive human need to believe that such orders exist and can be intuited by the human mind. The amazing fact of "Tintern Abbey" is not that it announces a revolutionary expressivist aesthetic to replace a traditionally mimetic one, but that it aspires, at the outset, to a form that will encompass the two, merging a state of mind that defies expression with a verbal order that strives to articulate the complex structure of reality.

"Tintern Abbey" is consistently quoted in scholarship that argues the religious nature of romantic poetry in general and of Wordsworth's poetry in particular. In fact, Wordsworth is frequently an important source for scholars outside of the literary specializations who wish to press an analogy between religion and art; the psychologist Pruyser refers to "Tintern Abbey" as corroboration of his argument that religion and art are similar crafts, and F. C. Happold includes Wordsworth in his chapter on nature mysticism.[8] The two key passages from the poem which have served to exemplify Wordsworth's religious consciousness are by now so familiar that quotation seems almost superfluous here, but, as Wordsworth himself would probably be the first to suggest, repetition serves no small epistemological function. The first crucial passage is contained within the second half of the second verse paragraph of the poem, in which Wordsworth recalls "forms of beauty" that contribute to

> that serene and blessed mood,
> In which the affections gently lead us on,
> Until, the breath of this corporeal frame,
> And even the motion of our human blood
> Almost suspended, we are laid asleep
> In body, and become a living soul:
> While with an eye made quiet by the power
> Of harmony, and the deep power of joy,
> We see into the life of things.
>
> (42–49)

The second passage is centrally located in the fourth verse paragraph, and follows the recognition that youthful, spontaneous pleasure in nature has been subdued yet deepened by the knowledge of human suffering:

> And I have felt
> A presence that disturbs me with the joy
> Of elevated thoughts; a sense sublime
> Of something far more deeply interfused,
> Whose dwelling is the light of setting suns,
> And the round ocean, and the living air,
> And the blue sky, and in the mind of man,
> A motion and a spirit, that impels

> All thinking things, all objects of all thought,
> And rolls through all things.

(94–104)

While there is some difference of opinion about which of these passages conveys the greater degree of religious spirit and is therefore relatively more profound, literary scholars consistently identify these passages with an extraordinary mode of consciousness, or with its direct counterpart, the illusion of an extraordinary mode of consciousness, created through the agency of the self-deceptive imagination.[9] Since the second strain of interpretation reflects an atheistic bias that therefore cannot entertain the possibility that the poem refigures an authentic experience, I will focus on the first critical orientation, which seeks to characterize the state of mind dramatized in the poem. Thus, I will look first at one of the twin aspects that comprise a complete definition of religion, that beginning with Schleiermacher and continuing in modern psychology, which stresses the inner, experiential character of religion.

In 1908, Solomon Gingerich called the first of these passages "the completest expression of the highest stage of [pure mystical experience]".[10] Other critics since that time have not only reiterated the specifically mystical character of these passages but made passing reference to James's study for the paradigm for mystical experience. In a predictable countermovement, critics of atheistic orientation have offered other explanations of these passages, or simply hastened to deny that they or anything else in the body of Wordsworth's poetry exemplifies or attests to mystical experience.[11]

One of the dilemmas for criticism regarding this matter has been the assumed need to confirm or disconfirm paranormal experience as a fact of Wordsworth's life. It seems to me an error to stake claims about whether Wordsworth himself was or was not a mystic on the evidence of his poetry, since it is clear that Wordsworth took extensive liberties with biographical facts in the interest of his artistic aims. While I will proceed to demonstrate that there are indeed overwhelming similarities between these passages and the highest order of religious experience, identified in chapter 1 by the analogous terms *intellectual vision* and *the mystical state*, I make no claims whatsoever for the reality of mystical experience in Wordsworth's life. On the one hand, it seems unlikely that Wordsworth did not experience something at least akin to intellectual vision; on the other, and perhaps more important, it is certain that he valued such a state of consciousness to the point of attempting the impossible, representing a definitionally ineffable state in language. If, then, the state is an imaginative construction and not, in fact, derived from Wordsworth's mental state as he wandered the environs of Tintern Abbey, it is still imagined and presented in the poem as an ideal ontological state. Furthermore, that the poet himself never mentioned mysticism neither proves nor disproves his mystical bent, for mysticism is not defined as a purely orthodox endeavor in the literature that describes it.[12]

These passages do in fact display enormous consistency with the phenomenon of mystical experience, both of a traditional and of a nontraditional kind. To recall the earlier overview of the psychological literature on religious experience, James's definition gives four predominant characteristics of mystical experience: ineffability, noetic quality, transiency, and passivity. And because the experience of encounter with the divine is manifest in an otherworldly mode of consciousness, nonconceptual and consequently extralinguistic, paradox of expression is one of the fundamental characteristics of mystical writing. Thus, the attempt to grasp (or to enforce) the ineffability of the experience is realized through a sometimes systematic disorganization of logical modes of expression. In keeping with this, mystical writings that attempt a description of the state generally move from relative concreteness to a high level of abstraction.

Several of the images in both passages echo the paradoxical language of mystical writings, and thus convey the ineffability and passivity of mystical states. In the first passage, the governing image in lines 44–49 is of temporary physical death that enables greater spiritual life. The expression *living soul* is especially oxymoronic, since the word *life* has significance for biological organisms precisely because they are mortal, while the word *soul* usually suggests a belief in an immortal essence or spirit. The contradiction therefore implies that mortal life is the abstraction and spirit the material thing, and the movement from "corporeal frame" to "living soul" is thus from the concrete to the conceptually incomprehensible, from suspension of life in the human organism to mortality comprehended in immortality. The assertion of "an eye made quiet" confounds the human senses and reinforces the perception that this experience takes place outside of physical as well as psychical self-consciousness. The figure additionally underscores the passive nature of the experience, conveyed originally through the images of suspended circulation and bodily rest. Moreover, the coalescence of sight, hearing, and speech suggests the unifying aspect of the experience, as perception has become so fully cooperative that there remains no intelligible distinction between the senses.

The images employed in this passage to describe the process of attaining the mystical state also bear a striking resemblance to those used by orthodox Christian mystics. St. Teresa, for instance, describes contact with God as follows:

> In the orison of union . . . the soul is fully awake as regards God, but wholly asleep as regards things of this world and in respect of herself. During the short time the union lasts, she is as it were deprived of every feeling, and even if she would, she could not think of any single thing. Thus she needs to employ no artifice in order to arrest the use of her understanding: it remains so stricken with inactivity that she neither knows what she loves, nor in what manner she loves, nor what she wills. In short, she is utterly dead to the things of the world and lives solely in God . . . I do not even know whether in this state she has enough life left to breathe. It seems to me she has not; or at least that if she does breathe, she is unaware of it. Her intellect would fain understand something of what is going on within her, but it has so little force now that it can act in no way whatsoever. So a person who falls into a deep faint appears as if dead . . .
>
> Thus does God, when he raises a soul to union with himself, suspend the natural action of her faculties. She neither sees, hears, nor understands, so long as she is united with God. But this time is always short, and it seems even shorter than it is.[13]

Wordsworth's description shares the central features of St. Teresa's: the image of a personified soul, living while normal respiration appears suspended and the physical body remains in a sleep akin to death, and the trope of an analogous sensory paradox, arrested bodily perception whose counterpart is an abstract union or vision.[14]

The second of the two passages from "Tintern Abbey" also abounds in the characteristics of mystical experience. The rendering of such experience seems here, if anything, more complete than the first description, the increased level of paradox resulting in an intensified sense of contact with the divine. The sensation Wordsworth recalls in lines 94–104 is at once more apparently concrete and more fully paradoxical than the previous description of mystical unconsciousness in paragraph two. Thus, the description of the state includes a series of images of paradox in unity. And whereas the earlier description follows a more linear development, partially describing the process that leads to intellectual vision, the second passage is paratactic in structure; the repeated use of the coordinating conjunction *and* links descriptive elements without establishing logical or causal priority. Thus connecting images in a seemingly arbitrary pattern, Wordsworth mimes the static and passive nature of mystical experience. Moreover, the abundance of images, as opposed to the single trope of the first passage, suggests the insufficiency of any single image to convey the experience. The denotative meanings of words are thus undermined, so that they effectively allude to an endless series of paradoxical images beyond the poem, suggesting a metaphysical reality coextensive with nature.

Once again, consciousness is projected into "things," but here some of them are specified. "[T]he light of setting suns," both intensely bright and evanescent, is imagined as a place of eternal unity, evoking both the transience of the mystical moment and its paradoxical effect of continuity. Additionally, the images "round ocean" and "living air" cannot be rationally understood—the ocean is not round and air supports life but is not itself alive—yet the images correspond, respectively, to the mystic's sense of wholeness and of life in absence. The penultimate image in the series, "the blue sky," seemingly undercuts the paradox embedded in the previous images by its mundane coherence, but the subsequent emphasis on "the mind of man" underlines the essentially figurative aspect of all these images. With this final image, Wordsworth's intentional disregard for parallelism places disproportionate emphasis on the preposition *in,* consequently incorporating even "the blue sky" into an eternal mind. Hence, a superior consciousness ("a sense sublime / Of something far more deeply interfused") has been projected into objects which are, as well, objects of consciousness, and lines 102–4 iterate the sameness of concrete and abstract, material and spiritual, "things." What has been achieved is not so much a tyranny of mind over matter, as our romantic critical tradition tends to conclude, but a fusion of the material and spiritual in a temporary monistic apprehension of reality.

If the first mystical passage reflects the traditional mystical consciousness of St. Teresa, the second, in its consistent conflations of natural imagery, recalls the experience of many nonpracticing mystics. Frequently such experiences take place outdoors; as Andrew Greeley comments, "The moments of ecstasy can come in strange places— particularly for Englishmen it seems—drab rooms, African landscapes, and even on a cricket field."[15] (To my knowledge, no one has speculated about the reason for the preponderance of such phenomena among the English, although it seems quite possible that the actual experiences are no more frequent than in other nations or cultures, but simply more often recorded.)

Now mystical experiences that take place outdoors are by no means decisively unorthodox. Practicing mystics are those who consciously engage in established meditative disciplines in an effort to attain heightened consciousness, but such states are sometimes achieved by persons of very different religious convictions, including atheists, agnostics, and conventional believers who are not vocational mystics.

Respect and love for God's creation are no sure signs of natural religion, having always had their place in revealed religion, and, as Richard Brantley points out, enthusiasm for nature was particularly
common among the Evangelical Anglicans.[16] This denomination lies
midway between traditional Anglicanism and the dissenters of Wordsworth's day. In keeping with this, a deep and abiding enthusiasm for
nature, and a profound spiritual experience in the presence of nature,
do not of themselves indicate pantheistic beliefs. In sum, although one
of the passages shows more correspondence to the rhetoric of Christian tradition and the other to nature mysticism, they are not, removed
from the larger context of the poem, necessarily in conflict either with
each other or with Anglican doctrine. However, when these passages
are considered in relation to the entirety of "Tintern Abbey"—that
is to say, in their proper context—they are problematic as evidence of
either Christian faith or an easily defined naturalism.

In addition to its correspondences with James's delineation of mystical experience, the second passage includes two elements that recent
commentators suggest are overwhelmingly prevalent in contemporary
descriptions of mystical phenomena experienced within Christian or
other God-centered traditions. The first is a distinct sense of presence,
frequently described, according to Hufford's account, as the sense of
a person nearby. In Wordsworth's second description, the presence
precedes the fuller description of the experience; while not necessarily
the cause of the unusual state of knowledge and feeling, the presence
is fundamental and integral to the entire experience. The second element is a perception of light; Greeley remarks that "An amazing number of the mystics I have interviewed personally report the light
phenomenon. It is always of the same colors—pale, diffused blue or
rose. It is worth noting, incidentally, that these are precisely the colors
that Eliade describes in *Patterns in Comparative Religion*."[17] Wordsworth's second description implicitly suggests this kind of glow, the
presence being inseparable from the light of late sun and the expanse
of ocean and sky.

The special knowledge that results from such experiences, its noetic
quality, is implicit in the holistic effect of the oxymoronic images, but
is also explicitly summarized after each of the two passages. The "serene and blessed mood" of the first passage enables all those who enjoy
it to "see into the life of things," and the import of the second experience is summarized at the end of the verse paragraph, with what
appears to be an overwhelmingly confident credal assertion of the
profound knowledge offered by the experience. Wordsworth finds, as
he tells us,

> In nature and the language of the sense,
> The anchor of my purest thoughts, the nurse,
> The guide, the guardian of my heart, and soul
> Of all my moral being.
>
> (109–12)

The comprehensiveness with which nature unifies human life here indicates unqualified affirmation, but it is important to remember that such robust faith is nowhere anticipated in the beginning of the poem. If it is true, as Stephen Gill claims, that "never again was [Wordsworth] to express with such assurance the faith on which everything—his poetry, his sense of self, his awareness of vocation—was now grounded," it seems just as valid to hold that, while The Prelude asserts community, "Tintern Abbey" pleads for it.[18]

How assured is the profession of faith in "Tintern Abbey"? This question engages with the central, overarching controversy in Wordsworth studies: Does the poet's work attest to an unshakable wholeness of personal character, poetic vision, and religious belief, or does it conversely demonstrate deep, abiding, and even pathological selfdivision?[19] As is nearly always the case, the truth lies somewhere between these two extremes. Indeed, following the recollection of an experience whose supernatural power seems irrefutable, the confirmed assertion that nature is "the guardian of my heart, and soul / Of all my moral being" lays deceptive claim for an unalterable faith. But the claim is nonetheless deceptive. For if one of the principal characteristics of mystical experiences is their transiency, one of the crucial functions of a belief system is to maintain a continuous sense of the significance of such illuminating moments. Alternately, one of the recurrent residual phenomena of such experiences outside of an orthodox belief structure is doubt about their authenticity. Most studies of mysticism agree fundamentally with James regarding the evanescence of mystical experience, as well as its unpredictability:

> Mystical states cannot be sustained for long. Except in rare instances, half an hour, or at most an hour or two, seems to be the limit beyond which they fade into the light of common day. Often, when faded, their quality can but imperfectly be reproduced in memory; but when they recur it is recognized; and from one recurrence to another it is susceptible of continuous development in what is felt as inner richness and importance.[20]

In quoting the last sentence of this passage from James, Greeley makes this comment: "There is, then, some kind of continuity between such experiences, though when one is not immediately involved in the experience, the thread of continuity seems lost; in fact, it is there, though unrecognized."[21] This "thread of continuity," however, is more likely to be lost or to go undetected when no explanation for the experience is forthcoming from a belief system.

The question, then, of how the individual is to incorporate the moral and spiritual knowledge of this experience into his or her life when that knowledge is nonconceptual becomes critical when, as for Wordsworth speaking in "Tintern Abbey," the supersensible experience is not an aspect of faith but the foundation of it. For the traditional mystic, verbal interpretation of the experience is neither necessary nor in fact desired, because intellectual vision is already understood according to the terms of a conceptual system that defines such experience as ineffable, inscrutable contact with the divine. Thus, if the particular feel of intellectual vision is lost after the interval has passed, its importance is continually reinforced by the institutional beliefs of the individual. The perception of the state's transience itself reinforces faith, for that quality further establishes the correspondence between the individual episode and the orthodox paradigm.

Similarly, in speaking of conversion, which certainly involves some perception of divine contact and can involve mystical experience, James addresses the question of the permanence of new-found faith. Drawing on statistics from E. D. Starbuck's research, he observes that converts continuously identify with the new commitment.[22] But again, this research reflects the continuity of belief within self-described religious communities, whose dogmas and rituals repeatedly ground the subjective experience of communion with God in an established religion. Hence an entire community validates and celebrates the individual's spiritual rebirth. The same cannot be said of either any nature mysticism that appears to contradict orthodox creeds or any experience had by an individual who is not a member of an established faith. For instance, after describing his moment of unexpected transcendence on the cricket field, characterized by the loss of a sense of self and a unified, heightened perception of the world, Happold concludes:

> Nothing more can be said about the experience, it brought no accession of knowledge about anything except, very obscurely, the knower and his way of knowing. After a few minutes there was a "return to normalcy." The event made a deep impression on me at the time; but, because it did not fit into any of the thought patterns—religious, philosophical, scientific—with which, as a boy of fifteen, I was familiar, it came to seem more and more anomalous, more and more irrelevant to "real life," and was finally forgotten.[23]

There is an explicitly causal relationship between the incompatibility of this experience with all available explanations and Happold's ultimate sense of its irrelevance. It is both inconsistent with his own previous experience and unaccounted for by systems of thought that might possibly explain such anomalies. Thus, an ongoing sense of the importance of a mystical or conversion experience normally if not always requires some explanation or support in the form of communal consensus—an established religion or a theoretical formulation; individuals to whom such explanations are unavailable will typically discount them or minimize their significance rather than vainly spin in the void.

And, with all due acknowledgment that awe for and celebration of God's creation is often part of a devout Christian perspective, it cannot in the final analysis be said that Wordsworth establishes the security of his faith in "Tintern Abbey" by interpreting his experience in terms of Christian orthodoxy. If, in and of themselves, the experiences in the poem are not irreconcilable with orthodox Christianity, there is certainly no attempt to give them a specifically Christian meaning. Because Christian theology teaches the coinherence of matter and spirit, and thus allows for God to be both simultaneously immanent and transcendent, it is *logically* possible to claim that the apparent worship of nature in this poem is completely in keeping with orthodox teachings, but in another respect such justification of Wordsworth's faith seems to argue the limits of logical explanation.[24] For the choices that Wordsworth makes in circumscribing these experiences are significantly divergent, both in form and function, from the religious traditions proscribing individual expression of belief and from the poetic forms that are an extension of meditative practices.

In one sense, there are substantial correspondences between "Tintern Abbey" and *The Prelude* on the one hand and the forms to which they have traditionally been compared, confessional autobiography, testimony, and meditative poetry on the other; all reflect the drive toward psychic unity and an attendant need to found restored self-perception within a human community of shared beliefs and values.[25] All this conforms to the psychological pattern of the twice-born personality, but, as James points out, this psychological make-up, while characteristic of religious believers, is not limited to them. Unlike romantic poems, confessional autobiography, testimony, and metaphysical meditative poetry are ancillary to a structured social explanation for man's existence. All of these forms, whether literary or performative, refer to a set of beliefs and an institution organized for the explicit purpose of fostering and perpetuating individual commitment to the belief system. By enabling individuals to express the difficulties of maintaining faith, these forms increase the sense of triumph for the individual who returns to or discovers God. Within traditional Christianity, therefore, these forms both increase the incentive for faith and enhance the humanism of that faith by ritualizing personal expression. In essence, these forms do not merely depend on a belief system but exist quite simply because of it. And "Tintern Abbey," by contrast, exists not to fortify existing faith, but to find a creed.

One need only refer to the first few paragraphs of St. Augustine's *Confessions* to understand the purpose of his writing:

> *Can any praise be worthy of the Lord's majesty? How magnificent his strength! How inscrutable his wisdom!* Man is one of your creatures, Lord, and his instinct is to praise you. He bears about him the mark of death, the sign of his own sin, to remind him that you *thwart the proud*. But still, since he is a part of your creation, he wishes to praise you. The thought of you stirs him so deeply that he cannot be content unless he praises you, because you made us for yourself and our hearts find no peace until they rest in you.
>
> Grant me, Lord, to know and understand whether a man is first to pray to you for help or to praise you, and whether he must know you before he can call you to his aid. If he does not know you, how can he pray to you?[26]

In Augustine's version of reality, the Lord is absolute in his mystery and sublimity, and the problem for the believer is not whether to believe, but whether one is worthy to praise the Lord, and how one sorts the true path of devotion from all the likely false ones. Faith in a Christian God is given; what is problematic is the proper procedure for carrying out this difficult relationship between mortal (and, in Augustine's version, lustful and ever-sinning) man and divine being. By enacting the difficulties of this relationship, Augustine's *Confessions* demonstrates its worth as an example to other struggling believers and thereby reaffirms Christian faith.

If anything, Christian testimonial or confessional forms have become more systematic from the time of Augustine onward. Explaining that testimonial is especially important for the cohesion of religious groups in a heterogeneous society, Ingram notes that "because individuality in religious experience is one of the collective representations, individualism is less problematic than it might otherwise be."[27] This statement is supported historically by the assimilation of confession to Catholicism. After the Reformation, the loss of this personal element in religious life combined with (and to a great extent caused by) the determinism of Calvinism fostered hopelessness and a sense of alienation from God. In consequence, congregational confession or testimony (what we might call witnessing) became an important part of Evangelical Protestantism, a means of reinstituting the significance of the individual's personal experience. Ingram's study, which focuses on contemporary Evangelicalism, details the function of testimony and the forms it might take. Of great importance is the identification of auditor to speaker, which serves as a stimulus for identification with Christ. With this aim, testimony generally follows three thematic patterns, focusing on common experience, vicarious deprivation (or stigma), or secular achievement. While the last of these does not have the same bonding effect between speaker and auditors as the first two, final value in the narrative is habitually placed on the common experience of shared faith: "In a testimony of this type, the speaker recounts his/her achievements or advantages, discounts them, and proceeds to exalt the conversion experience."[28] As this makes clear, testimony as an aspect of religious service follows an intentional pattern that typically reinforces faith by mediating between the experience of the speaker and that of the congregation.

Likewise, the word *meditative,* when applied to seventeenth-century religious poetry, does not merely mean *thoughtful*; it ties that poetry to a discipline of religious devotion with the reaffirmation of orthodox Christianity as its aim. Wordsworth's poetry, by contrast, is meditative in a quintessentially modern sense—discursively probing, alternately circling about and questioning the nature of human existence and the possible meanings of things beyond it. The religious poetry of the metaphysical poets derives from the private devotions of the Counter-Reformation, and therefore from a method of preparing the self for God. As with confessional autobiography and testimony, meditational devotions and the poetry connected to these devotions turn to the self with the purpose of recognizing human successes and failures within the larger necessity of self-abnegation before God. As Louis Martz says, "Self analysis, then, becomes a way of taking up arms on the side of God."[29] Like testimonial, meditative practices often follow a suggested (but not obligatory) outline, the threefold way, which includes visualization of the subject followed by analysis and concluded with a colloquy or petition to God. This process respectively engages the three powers of the soul—the memory, the understanding, and the will—and ideally corresponds to three modes of consciousness—meditation, contemplation, and infused contemplation (mystical experience), although the last of these is in general only accessible to vocational mystics. By exercising the three aspects of his soul, the man or woman unifies the trinity within himself and so reflects the Holy Trinity. Thus, like confessional autobiography and testimony, religious meditation has devotion as its aim, and it likewise emphasizes the necessity of self-discipline in the service of religious faith.

And while the poetry that arises alongside seventeenth-century meditative practice dramatizes the difficulty of belief in a culture torn by the controversies of the Reformation and Counter-Reformation, it never questions the truth of Christianity. Like the forms of ritual that institutionalize individualism, this poetry is essentially conservative in the generic sense of that term: it recounts fallen man's struggle for faith and in so doing reaffirms the magnificence and inscrutability of God.

In fact, Martz's provocative suggestion that this poetry evolved out of note-taking on meditative practices (a recommended procedure) points toward a need to receive communal corroboration for even the most private experiences of religious life. If, in the processes of confession, admission of doubt leads to the control of doubt, so profession of spiritual joy may well magnify that joy and establish continuity between transient ecstatic moments.

In view of the contrast in "Tintern Abbey" between its unorthodox relationship to established religious forms designed to account for and guide the individual on the one hand and the need to recover and relate transcendent states of mind on the other, why not accept the position that it demonstrates an agnostic attempt to attain higher consciousness? Quite simply, although the poem does not share the teleological function of those forms, it is generated out of a rhetoric of doubt and a contingent need to recover, reinterpret, and communicate the value of mystical experience. Because the poem dramatizes the "discordancy and heterogeneity" of what James calls the twice-born character and because it seeks restored self-unity through recuperated mystical experience that includes a total vision of reality, the motivating force behind "Tintern Abbey" is significantly religious in the psychological sense of that word. The problematic and imperative need for a stabilized mediating center—between self and sister, visible and transcendent realities, and past and present—is not merely a characteristic of the poem but its larger theme and purpose, and it is the spiritual necessity of devising a whole from these diverse realities that attests to a psychological urgency toward form not reducible to experimentation in altered states of consciousness.

In organized religion, this mediatory function is served by the belief system, of which discursive forms like confessional autobiography and practices like testimony and confession are extensions, and which produces the effect of continuity for the individual between disjunct experiences.[30] Since the system is structured in accordance with particular values and beliefs and has as its aim their perpetuation, its forms remain relatively stable. And because belief systems prescribe the general content and the orientation of discursive and ritual practices, orthodoxies perform institutionally structured mediation that delivers consistent interpretation. By contrast, there is no belief system in "Tintern Abbey," although there is, eventually, a credal statement ("In nature and the language of the sense . . . "). But the potential assuredness and dogmatism of this statement are undercut because it does not mediate either intersubjectively or intrasubjectively; it is itself *produced* by the dramatic action of the poem. Poetic utterance itself stands in the place of the belief system; but since poetic utterance depends upon flexible linguistic structures of no inherent religious value or significance, it is by nature unlike the stable forms of orthodox mediation. Therefore, as Wordsworth strives in "Tintern Abbey" to establish through poetic utterance the thread of continuity normally supplied by a belief system, he rediscovers and exposes the impermanent and problematic nature of belief.

The motivating force behind the impulse to institutionalize religious experience is to a large extent the product of Western culture and religion, with its emphasis on the social dimension of experience. Hence, while "Tintern Abbey" fits no neat doctrinal patterns, the driving impulse toward a community of shared beliefs, experiences, and values aligns it with the traditional Christian dynamics of such experiences. Robley Whitson points to the unanimous agreement of mystics on the need to invest the experience with meaning:

> Like any man the mystic is an integrated entity and cannot tolerate dismemberment. If he could not find meaning for the mystical act—necessarily intellectual, conceptual meaning—the mystical process would be one of annihilation as far as the Christian would be concerned. The Christian, then, relates the sign of the extrarational process to conceptual knowledge, and analyzes the *effect* the experience of Presence has had on him interiorly. The result is at least a knowledge of contrasts. From this the mystic grasps something of the significance the mystical act should have for his total existence. In this he integrates the experience with his religious tradition.[31]

For the mystic who operates within an organized religion, therefore, the experience is contained within and given meaning through received concepts of deity and the order of the universe. The belief system, in other words, mediates by defining the experience as one of privileged vision, as opposed to a lapse in sanity or a neurological disorder, for example. Within this context, the extrarational experience, despite its apparent solitariness, validates the mystic's sense of unity with all adherents of his religion. Mystical experience consequently gains its significance in a socially defined context of shared beliefs and values; without a mediating belief system, sufficient expla-nation for the experience is lacking, and the holistic character of the experience is undermined by a return to heightened self-consciousness and doubt once the experience has ended. For Wordsworth, to share or embody the experience with others through the form of the poem becomes, therefore, an approximation of belief that validates the ex-perience, but it is an act perpetually and necessarily hampered by the inadequacies of language to convey nonconceptual experience, by the attendant fear of undermining the experience through rational inter-pretation, and by the demand that subjective creative utterance medi-ate, on both the personal and interpersonal levels, in place of an established belief system. As Abrams remarks, Wordsworth's imagina-tion, "without violence to the truth of perception, operates as myth in process rather than as myth in being"; but it is the incipient aware-ness that faith to perception and to language commands this paradoxi-cal phenomenon—*myth in process*—and thus countermands the poem's drive toward stability that results, simultaneously, in the enor-mous drive toward communication and resistance to it.[32]

In "Tintern Abbey," the resistance to communication is implicit in general characteristics of the poem's style and form. While in the bulk of *Lyrical Ballads* Wordsworth exploits or inverts the structural and metrical limitations of ballad forms to offer compressed reflection about common life or to parody the standard uses of such forms, in "Tintern Abbey" he exploits the structural indeterminacy of the blank verse ode. Initially—and deceptively—the language establishes a tone of repose and leisurely meditation: the long, grammatically loose sen-tences of enjambed blank verse and the seemingly casual movement in and out of memory lend the poem a discursive, almost prosaic, character, suggesting, paradoxically, an inattention to structure in a poem all about formalizing experience. As Geoffrey Hartman has noted,

[In the first lines of the poem] . . . a countervailing movement is felt at once. It is expressed by a peculiar type of redundance and indicates resist-ance to abrupt progression. The feminine caesurae (winters, waters, mur-mur) plus echoing sound enrich our sense of inwardness and continuity. It is no single means that produces the lingering or "lengthening" effect . . . I am tempted to say that in the opening verses of "Tintern Abbey," as well as in other sections, there is a *wave effect* of rhythm whose characteris-tic is that while there is internal acceleration, the feeling of climax is avoided.[33]

Although this "wave effect" does establish a surface continuity of mood in its resistance to statement—the caesurae create the effect of sentences dying off and flowing into one another, of grammatically and logically complete statements whose integrity is undercut by aural elisions—its persistence in the first verse paragraph, combined with repetitions and qualifications of word and phrase, emphasizes the "wave effect" as a pattern in which the structuring of language rests on hesitation and on unwillingness to assume normative structures.

As Hartman suggests, what manifests itself as a simultaneously progressive and retrogressive movement is not attributable to one specific metrical or linguistic technique. It is partly the product of the hovering effects of persistently enjambed blank verse, which undermine expectations of conceptual closure within the line unit.[34] In addition to this, a complex and asymmetrical syntax overlays the blank verse pattern, on the one hand prolonging units of meaning and on the other adding unanticipated grammatical breaks to the predictable breaks supplied by line endings. Linguistic and grammatical repetitions tend to suggest hesitation and difficulty in expression while simultaneously implying an urgency toward communication. Finally, through repetition and placement, common words come to have expanded significance but no consistent or determinate meaning; common nouns, as J. P. Ward points out, function metonymically, retaining their stable and mundane meanings but signaling something larger and inexpressible, and implicitly far more important, beyond the poem.[35]

This combination of linguistic, prosodic, and grammatical techniques engenders a form whose overriding principle is self-qualification, and is accordingly in direct contrast with the rhetoric of religion. Questioning the purpose of ritual language that frequently repeats what the community already knows and agrees upon, Ninian Smart points to the fundamentally performative aspect of the language of worship: "[the function of these descriptions] is celebratory. In telling God at Easter that he has raised his Son up from the dead, the worshipper is not reminding God or the congregation, but re-presenting the event . . . By the principle of likeness . . . they come to share in the power of the primary event and thus their use in the celebration reactivates the power of the primary event."[36] While confessional autobiography and testimony do, unlike the language of worship, focus on the experiences of individual believers, they include celebratory discourse and, more crucially, are intentionally structured to return both speaker and auditor to the belief centered in this discourse.

In "Tintern Abbey," the larger units of the ode, whose formal logic entails an unresolved dialectical progression, partake of this characteristic self-qualification no less than the more specific units of utterance.[37] If enjambed blank verse undermines a traditional mathematics of poetic form, the temporal disjunctions signaled by the verse paragraph transitions subvert the expectation of linear narrative and with it the simple structure for communicating and interpreting experience that Wordsworth seems, at the outset, prepared to employ. It is only through an enlarging field of memory, achieved through the repeated disruption of straightforward conceptual orders, that Wordsworth can affirm the experience of intellectual vision. But the enlarging field of memory highlights the fundamentally constructive nature of poetic language, as opposed to the mediating, performative, and directed language of orthodox belief systems. Thus the contradictory functions of the poem—to describe a religious experience and to offer a system of explanation for it—resolve themselves in language that moves progressively toward the ineffability characteristic of the language of intellectual vision.

Through progressive reliance on memory and on a shift away from the denotative value of utterance, Wordsworth tests and ultimately deconstructs (as it were) the desire for a permanent system of belief. The first paragraph of the poem attempts to describe an objective relationship between speaker and scene which is overturned not by the memory anticipated in the first paragraph, but by a memory of that memory. The third paragraph interrupts the movement out of time with an expression of present doubt. Paragraphs four and five repeat this movement from present to past and back again and finally expand into the future. Thus, memory enfolds the present in successive movements, undermining the reality of the present; when the movement is repeated, the past once again enfolds the present, but this time the repeated subversion of linearity enables Wordsworth to assimilate the experience into a unified perception. The chronological disjunctions that appear to work against the act of communication ultimately free the poet from the fear of speaking in a too-reductive language by rendering his expressions increasingly metaphorical; while they progress away from exactness and toward abstraction and paradox, and thus toward language evocative of mystical experience, they firmly establish human consciousness as the mediating center of the poem.

Throughout the first verse paragraph, Wordsworth's complex self-qualifying technique works in opposition to his simultaneous efforts to establish a linear, historical narrative. Information about date, location, and occasion appear in the poem's subtitle, a factual specificity that ironically suggests the mode of the occasional poem. But although the poet's first utterance is apparently an attempt to define more clearly the sense of time and place, the anticipated balancing of past and present events is quickly subverted:

> Five years have passed; five summers, with the length
> Of five long winters! and again I hear
> These waters, rolling from their mountain-springs
> With a sweet inland murmur.—Once again
> Do I behold these steep and lofty cliffs,
> Which on a wild secluded scene impress
> Thoughts of more deep seclusion; and connect
> The landscape with the quiet of the sky.
> The day is come when I again repose
> Here, under this dark sycamore, and view
> These plots of cottage-ground, these orchard-tufts,
> Which, at this season, with their unripe fruits,
> Among the woods and copses lose themselves,
> Nor, with their green and simple hue, disturb
> The wild green landscape. Once again I see
> These hedge-rows, hardly hedge-rows, little lines
> Of sportive wood run wild; these pastoral farms
> Green to the very door; and wreathes of smoke
> Sent up, in silence, from among the trees,
> With some uncertain notice, as might seem,
> Of vagrant dwellers in the houseless woods,
> Or of some hermit's cave, where by his fire
> The hermit sits alone.
>
> (1–22)

Thus, the opening clause of the poem initiates a narrative simplicity and directness that is, however, immediately imploded. Instead of offering the information that clarifies the relation of present to past, Wordsworth qualifies "five years" with "five summers, with the length / Of five long winters!" (1–2). Logically, the passage of the seasons has already been inferred in "five years," so the poet's insistence on specifying what any reader would assume merely dramatizes discomfort about the capacity of objective, linear narrative to convey the experiential significance of this temporal span. In consequence, the repetition of "five" is essentially ironic, revealing that the poet wants but is unable to perceive himself in a chronological relation to that past moment, and the disparity between psychological time and chronological time is further emphasized by the iterated length of the winters, an emphasis that suggests the winters are proportionately longer than the "years." In lines 4, 9, and 15, the poet "once again" tries to place himself in the present by recapturing the scene of five years earlier, but the declarative openings are lost in a landscape that seems to alter shape as Wordsworth observes it. The logical question aroused by the opening clause of the poem—"five years since what?"—dissolves in the poet's preoccupation with the shifting landscape.

The dislocation of the speaker in this passage, reflected in the repetitions and qualifications that create an unsettled scene, are in striking contrast to the preparatory composition of place in meditative poetry. Martz explains the importance of this aspect of religious poetry as it resembles the practice of the meditative discipline:

> St. Ignatius directs that one must also use the image-forming faculty to provide a concrete and vivid setting for a meditation on invisible things; for example, in meditation upon sins, he says, "the composition will be to see with the eyes of the imagination and to consider that my soul is imprisoned in this corruptible body, and my whole self in this vale of misery, as it were in exile among brute beasts" (pp. 20–1). We must attempt, says the Jesuit Puente,

> "to procure with the imagination to forme within our selves some figure, or image of the things wee intende to meditate with the greatest vivacity, and propriety that wee are able. If I am to thinke upon hell, I will imagine some place like an obscure, straight, and horrible dungeon full of fier, and the soules therin burning in the middest of those flames. And if I am to meditate [on] the birth of Christ, I will forme the figure of some open place without shelter, and a childe wrapped in swadling cloutes, layed in a manger: and so in the rest (I, 23)."[38]

As both St. Ignatius and Puente make clear, the specific religious subject of the meditation is determined prior to the selection of a fitting concrete image frequently associated with Christian typological or allegorical traditions.[39] By contrast, "Tintern Abbey" begins with a simultaneous effort to find both subject and image, an effort in which the one object in the scene that might plausibly serve to direct the poet's meditations ironically augments the somber mood: the "steep and lofty cliffs" do not act as the phenomenological focus for Wordsworth's meditation, but seem, paradoxically, to substantiate wildness and seclusion as the overarching structure of reality. The forms of nature—notice that the supposedly talismanic word *nature* is not actually used here—do not then offer the thread of continuity between mystical experience and present doubt, but lead ironically toward the temporary loss of all realities: the wreaths of smoke suggest a correlative isolation of vagrants and hermits, but the existence of these solitaries is posed hypothetically. Searching the scene for a meditational focus, the poetic imagination leads not out of isolation but into doubts about the efficacy of personal alienation itself.

The second verse paragraph announces the turn inward toward memory, and thus toward subjective experience and away from the initial attempt at linear narrative undermined in paragraph one. As Curran remarks, "The transitions of 'Tintern Abbey' are sudden, sharp, self-advertising"[40]: while the poet's opening apostrophe to the "forms of beauty" refers grammatically to the nature of paragraph one, its logical and psychological referents have not as yet been described in the poem. The "forms of beauty" are still emerging in the creating consciousness of the poet and are neither in the disquieting and lonely scene he has been observing nor in the "lonely rooms . . . 'mid the din / Of towns and cities" (26–27). Like the creed that will emerge only in paragraph four, the focus of meditation, selected prior to the exercise in orthodox meditational practice, is still evolving in the poem.

Wordsworth's strategies of self-qualification mask the unexpectedness of the shifts between verse paragraphs but, on the whole, render them more rather than less sudden, displacing the scene within a tone of casual continuity. Moreover, whereas the nearly compulsive effort to establish time in the first verse paragraph has the paradoxical effect of stopping time and thus undermining linear narrative, the confounding of time in paragraph two enables a fluid progression from one memory into another, from the acknowledged value of transcendent experience to language suggestive of it that temporarily threatens to move beyond language as the poet recovers the mystical experience itself.

As the poet slides out of time and place and begins to recover his past mystical moment, his language tends toward the abstraction and paradox characteristic of mystical experience, and "the resistance to abrupt progression" inherent in the rhythms and sounds of the verse is matched by images only conceivable in suspended time. For instance, Wordsworth's recognition that he owes to the aspect of nature "feelings . . . / of unremembered pleasure" begins the drift toward a less rational, increasingly elusive use of language. The paradox of "unremembered pleasure" foreshadows the evocation of the "serene and blessed mood," the first mystical moment rendered in the poem, both as a linguistic structure common to such experiences and as a descriptive characteristic of them. For while the experience is undoubtedly remembered in the literal sense of that word (otherwise, Wordsworth could not recall its pleasurable quality), it is "unremembered" as all true mystical experiences are: the perception of contact with the divine is transient, beyond the capacities of human description, and impossible to repeat at will. It is only through this progressive disruption of the literal capacities of language that Wordsworth can describe the "serene and blessed mood."

Wordsworth's rendering of the serene and blessed mood suggests that, like all mystical moments, the "unremembered pleasure" has been fundamentally transformative, yet contains a meaning that cannot be fully articulated. Indeed, the transition into verse paragraph three identifies doubt as the result of the reductions of language and points to the insufficiency of poetic utterance as a mediating system for religious belief. Because the description of the experience lacks reference to an existing belief system, the assertion that "we see into the life of things" is both inadequate as a description of intellectual vision and as an explanation of its value. As I noted before, the vague and paradoxical language of mystical experience is distinctly advantageous in reinforcing orthodox faith; man cannot express what is beyond his powers of mind and spirit. Within the orthodox scheme, such vagueness thus corroborates a preexisting definition of God's omnipotence and superiority to men. Wordsworth's vision, by contrast, does not fit such a conceptual system, and its ungraspable character thus evokes doubts about the reality of the experience itself. Accordingly, the poet's attempt to verify the experience by sharing it reveals instead the reductive qualities of language, enforcing the perception that such experience is anomalous, subjective, and quite possibly apocryphal rather than transcendent. The tenuous reimagining of the mystical moment consequently results in an even more explicit and urgent sense of futility than that implied in the repetitions and qualifications of the first paragraph, and the third verse paragraph begins with an abrupt transition into doubt:

> If this
> Be but a vain belief, yet, oh! how oft,
> In darkness, and amid the many shapes
> Of joyless day-light; when the fretful stir
> Unprofitable, and the fever of the world,
> Have hung upon the beatings of my heart,
> How oft, in spirit, have I turned to thee
> O sylvan Wye! Thou wanderer through the woods,
> How often has my spirit turned to thee!

(50–58)

For the moment, intellect has consumed what it has attempted to embody, and the poet fears his self-unifying experiences are illusion and "vain belief" (50). But Wordsworth breaks off what initially poses as a balanced expression of doubt and its consequences (If this . . . then this) as abruptly as he introduces this statement. No logical answer to the problem ensues. Rather, it is the frequency (how oft ... how oft ... how oft) of the Wye as a source in memory and imagination of consolation and faith that assuages doubt. The focus of meditation has been found, not in a prior image suitable to a selected subject of meditation, and not in the scene before him, but in the memory of repeated recollections of the Wye.

Temporarily, Wordsworth's first attempt to communicate transcendent experience seems to end in failure, casting suspicion on the experience and simultaneously exacerbating self-division. But with the turn inward to memory and creative consciousness that begins in paragraph three and continues throughout paragraph four, time and landscape take on a more metaphorical function than in paragraph one, and the poet is able to offer both a more precise account of transcendent experience and a more expansive sense of it. This time, as I suggested in my earlier discussion of the second mystical passage, the partial reimagining of intellectual vision is both more reminiscent of mystical language and less reductive of the experience it relates. And because the value finally attributed to the experience is highly personal, the description does not threaten immediately to reduce meaning; by contrast, it is the more integrated centering of these experiences in the poet's perceptions that supersedes the tensions between the conceptual and nonconceptual and leads to a temporary affirmation of religious experience. However, since this affirmation rests on the paradox that transcendent experience has been subjectively mediated and that the mediatory mode is creative, the experience is redeemed only through the implicit recognition that poetic language cannot offer a systematic explanatory basis for such an experience.

Whereas the repetitions of "five years" and "once again" in the first verse paragraph reveal an effort to establish an objective ordering of experience, time indicators in the opening lines of verse paragraph four insist on the value of present to future, but without the numerical specificity of paragraph one:

> And now, with gleams of half-extinguish'd thought,
> With many recognitions dim and faint,
> And somewhat of a sad perplexity,
> The picture of the mind revives again:
> While here I stand, not with the sense
> Of present pleasure, but with pleasing thoughts
> That in this moment there is life and food
> For future years.
>
> (59–66)

In this passage, the poet's insistence on "now," "present pleasure," and "this moment" produce irony that works to opposite effect of that in paragraph one (59, 64, 65). The insistence on "now" suggests, in its lack of chronological specificity, relative rather than absolute time, just as "future years" designates a period of undefined length and distance from "now." As a result, these varying designations empha-size the poet's perception of fluid and expansive time, rather than discrete moments irrevocably finished; "now" is simultaneously the transient moment on the banks of the Wye and the recurrent remem-brance of the river. Similarly, his assertion that, in remembering his boyhood love of nature, "I cannot paint / What then I was" (76–77) and the repetitions of *then* as a market of time past are to some degree undercut by the description of nature evoking unconscious joy in lines 77–86, which seems to do exactly this. The unconscious enjoyments of childhood have, in this language, been assimilated to adult experi-ence. And the ordering of experience, so earnestly sought in paragraph one, has been recovered through the restored objects of memory. The lesson that leads to the second, triumphant mystical moment rests firmly on the interpretation and reordering of developmental experi-ence, and thus grounds faith in the mutually qualifying phenomena of mutable experience and self-preserving consciousness. It is only by thus implicitly acknowledging the creative circumstances of his utterance that Wordsworth can describe the second mystical experi-ence in language fully suggestive of transcendence, of a sense sublime both fully "in the mind of man" and completely unifying with all of reality.

Only after reimaging the transcendent experience through paradoxi-cal language that defies its own concreteness can the poet articulate its meaning without fear of reducing it. Wordsworth concludes his description of "the sense sublime" with the credal statement whose affirmative, even overtly dogmatic, rhetoric self-consciously exploits the gap between celebratory language and the impermanent, paradoxi-cal language on which it is founded:

> Therefore am I still
> A lover of the meadows and the woods,
> And mountains; and of all that we behold
> From this green earth; of all the mighty world
> Of eye and ear, both what they half-create,
> And what perceive; well pleased to recognize
> In nature and the language of the sense,
> The anchor of my purest thoughts, the nurse,

The guide, the guardian of my heart, and soul
Of all my moral being.

(103–12)

The crucial term in this creed, *nature,* soon to greet us as a proper
noun in paragraph four, has transformed in meaning several times
throughout the poem. Added to Wordsworth's progressively suggestive or metonymic use of language in the poem, *nature* gradually aspires to the ambiguity of mystical terminology itself. As in all
Wordsworth's best poems that revert to the language of direct statement, meaning in "Tintern Abbey" seems most obvious when it is
actually least so. As an implicit term in paragraphs one through three,
nature refers first to the physical landscape and then to the mental
image of the Wye, definitions that for the time being remain mutually
exclusive. In the first lines of paragraph four, the nature that leads
the boy "more like a man / Flying from something that he dreads" is
both the animal responsiveness of the young boy and the forms of the
physical world (71–72). In these final lines of paragraph four, yet another nature emerges, one that has been redeemed and humanized by
the perceptions of the adult. For the moment, creative consciousness
is both an extension of and a maker of nature, one that redeems the
poet's interfused experience. But since this nature has, in fact, been
several times reconstituted in the poem, the naturalistic, seemingly
dogmatic credal statement is more than half-created by the poem, and,
as an object of belief, nature lacks the conceptual clarity required of
godhead in an explanatory belief system.

The transition to the final paragraph advertises the instability of the
credal statement through Wordsworth's anticipation of the potential
circumstances of doubt. Faith is tacitly acknowledged as resting on a
unique combination of experience and mental power, and, barring
such conditions, the saving possibility for spiritual integrity is human
communion. In keeping with the further humanization of belief, nature—now Nature—already personified in the credal statement, is
described in her active engagement in human life:

'tis her privilege,
Through all the years of this our life, to lead
From joy to joy: for she can so inform
The mind that is within us, so impress
With quietness and beauty, and so feed
With lofty thoughts, that neither evil tongues,
Rash judgments, nor the sneers of selfish men,
Nor greetings where no kindness is, nor all
The dreary intercourse of daily life,

> Shall e'er prevail against us, or disturb
> Our chearful faith that all which we behold
> Is full of blessings.
>
> (124–35)

Nature, half-created and half-perceived, now fulfills the functions of nurse, guide, and guardian, and, in this final transformation, apparently attains the status of deity. It is here, as Abrams notes, that the language of the poem becomes overtly theological: Wordsworth, now a self-proclaimed "worshiper of Nature," has returned to the scene with "holier love" and now offers this prayer for Dorothy.[41] But because Nature only gains divine status through progressive humanization and through the progressive realization that godhead is a human creation, the explicitly religious language is subtly but decidedly ironic. The condition of faith becomes Dorothy's presence, in which the poet sees the resemblance between her experience and his own, a resemblance that signifies the efficacy of human nature.

Easy as it is to see why Fairchild deplored Wordsworth as a prideful self-worshiper, such an interpretation finally limits the meaning of nature in a way not consistent with its expansion throughout the poem. Contrary interpretations that describe Wordsworth as a pantheist or a worshiper of art likewise offer a single solution to the question of belief in "Tintern Abbey," solutions Wordsworth himself, in this poem at least, ultimately rejects. When Wordsworth delivers his final benediction, the vestiges of the religion of nature and the religion of man become indistinguishable from the creative mediating function of poetic language, incorporating human creativity into the expanding significance of nature:

> Therefore let the moon
> Shine on thee in thy solitary walk;
> And let the misty mountain winds be free
> To blow against thee: and in after years,
> When these wild ecstasies shall be matured
> Into a sober pleasure, when thy mind
> Shall be a mansion for all lovely forms,
> Thy memory be as a dwelling-place
> For all sweet sounds and harmonies; Oh! then,
> If solitude, or fear, or pain, or grief,
> Should be thy portion, with what healing thoughts
> Of tender joy wilt thou remember me,
> And these my exhortations!
>
> (135–47)

The poet is only entitled to offer this benediction when he realizes that his creativity is yet another permutation of nature; thus, he speaks both *for* and *as* the nature he has embodied in the poem. In this, there is the implicit acknowledgment that man cannot mediate between personal experience and the larger structures of reality without creating the forms of his own comprehension, and that man's participation in nature mitigates the construction of an enduring system of belief. In the final lines of the poem, Wordsworth speaks in the past tense, tacitly recognizing the impermanence of his utterance, and predicting Dorothy's future recollection of the scene:

> Nor wilt thou forget,
> That after many wanderings, many years
> Of absence, these steep woods and lofty cliffs,
> And this green pastoral landscape, were to me
> More dear, both for themselves, and for thy sake.
>
> (155–60)

With his implicit acknowledgment of the periodic nature of belief, Wordsworth places the continuity of human experience not in individual life but in the repeated process of growth and development throughout the species. By focusing on Dorothy, Wordsworth ends the poem in the self-reflexive recognition that the hope literature restores is in the creative fact of human life, a hope inevitably grounded in the knowledge of impermanence and individual mortality.

It is not by accident that, as the full title of the poem specifies, we are some miles from the abbey and have not, in the end, moved a step closer to it. Wordsworth is uncompromising in this poem, detailing, through a dramatic recreation of his own experience, the inevitable discrepancy between the human need for order, explanation, and sense and the limited cohesion of human experience, which is only redeemed by our own tireless reshapings of it. In this particular poem, Wordsworth identifies the self-saving function of creativity, but does so in the final recognition that absolutes must be abandoned, that consciousness of the function of imagination, far from offering a divine replacement for God, precludes the entire system on which such static concepts are founded. It is because this poem first acknowledges and addresses our yearnings for religious security and then refuses to offer solace that it is both illuminating and troublesome to read. It is easier to find in Wordsworth a heretic, a pantheist, or a weak philosopher than an unrelentingly complex and honest poet who refuses to debase his art with false consolations.

3

Self-Qualification and Naturalistic Monism in *The Prelude*

> ... for in the end naiveté lies at the bottom of being, all being,
> even the most conscious and complicated.
> —Thomas Mann, *Dr. Faustus*

In the preceding chapter, I discussed at length the relationship between forms of religious discourse and the belief systems to which they refer in order to underscore the progressively questioning nature of "Tintern Abbey." While "Tintern Abbey" shares the psychodynamics of conversion and therefore some of the formal and literary qualities of spiritual autobiography and conversion narrative, including techniques of personal address and circular structure, it is finally only by undermining the teleology of traditional conversion that Wordsworth can assert psychic wholeness in the poem. Typically in religious experience, including conversion, the focus of meditation and the forms of meditation lie outside the individual and are consistent with the conventional symbols, roles, doctrines, and rituals of the particular orthodoxy; it is the interplay between individual experience and social institution that strengthens belief and maintains its consistency. But in "Tintern Abbey," all the functional aspects of traditional worship and ritual devolve upon individual mind: the closest equivalent to a meditational focus in the poem is a memory of the Wye, and the nearest equivalent to a mediating center is the poet's individual consciousness. Paradoxically, though, the replacement of institutional with individual explanation enables an otherwise impossible psychic integration; but given the conflict between the poet's intuitive knowledge of nature and Christian belief systems, this psychic unity is necessarily temporary. However, for the moment, the final resolution of the poem in a personally expressed naturalism brings radically into question the need for religious institutions that exemplify and explain man's ultimate relation to the universe.

78

Wordsworth's final refusal of credal explanations is dramatized by the increasingly figurative quality of the language in "Tintern Abbey," most importantly signified in the progressive expansion of the word *nature* in the poem. If, in the initial paragraphs, Wordsworth tries to reconcile past mystical experiences to a rationalist apprehension of nature as a discrete object outside of and apart from himself, by the end of the poem he has asserted the epistemological and psychological limits of such terms. "Nature" is not simply a conglomeration of anonymous rocks and trees; it is an entity that encompasses and extends beyond humanity and the physical world. Wordsworth's refusal of creed is therefore a refusal to accept the view that dualist thought offers an accurate conceptualization of reality. Within the concluding perspective of "Tintern Abbey," the fear that a lack of creed damns man to isolation and escapism becomes immaterial and even false; man is quite literally *by nature* part of a community that exists prior to himself and exceeds his powers of explanation.

Yet Wordsworth's belief in a nature whose forms and purposes exceed human understanding is both profound and psychically destabilizing, for it rests in the knowledge of mankind's ambiguous place in reality over and against the clarity provided by social institutions, especially belief systems and rituals. Traditional Christianity defines reality as an organized whole in which persons have a specific place and function; orthodoxies thus supply answers to questions about both the concerns of individual life and the larger structure of reality. By contrast, the evolutionary and developmental view that lies implicit in "Tintern Abbey" and *The Prelude* offers slight consolation to the individual. It is enormously hard for the single human being, faced with the implications of his inevitable losses and his own mortality, to maintain a consistent faith in a reality that exceeds his comprehension, and he moves back and forth between two contradictory perceptions. In the broader view, he apprehends the continuity of life of which he is a part; in the narrower view, he desires that his own particular successes and losses have an eternal significance. And because pragmatic insight into nature necessitates that the individual adopt these two perspectives and try to resolve the tension between them, such insight furthermore increases the ambiguity that it is the distinct purpose of belief systems to resolve.[1] Under the constraint of his concern for his personal survival, it is enormously difficult for a person to reject the belief in a god who, in ordering and controlling creation, offers individual immortality. In sum, the self-abnegation implicit in Wordsworth's expanded sense of nature entails a continuous struggle against the interests of self, and an almost impossible willingness to admit uncertainty.

The paradox that knowledge of our lives in nature leads toward uncertainty rather than greater certainty—that, in other words, epistemological success entails psychological instability—underlies *The Prelude* and is responsible for the ultimately contradictory nature of the beliefs described in the poem. On the one hand, both the thematic focus on nature and its relationship to human development and the technical emphasis on repetition, qualification, and embellishment of language, image, and incident provide a dramatic extension of the naturalistic monism of "Tintern Abbey"; on the other, the persistence of an orthodox frame of reference within the poem cannot be entirely explained or explained away, particularly in the concluding book of the poem. The predominant emphasis of *The Prelude* is to draw out and develop the implications of the knowledge that human beings live in nature by tracing the origins of human creativity to its source in the natural love of parent for child. As in "Tintern Abbey," nature, of which the human self is a recognized part, is the "object" of emotion and is responsible for the ultimate continuity of the poet's perception of reality.[2] Simultaneously, however, references to God and Christian tradition seem at times to accommodate orthodoxy to nature, at others to establish the legitimacy of orthodox belief.

While the poem offers two competing philosophies, it presents no experiences so definitionally similar to religious states of consciousness as the passages in "Tintern Abbey." The experiences at the Simplon Pass and on Snowdon, which critics have singled out as visionary,[3] are not strictly either mystical or visionary according to the paradigms of religious experience presented in chapter 1. Instead, Wordsworth modifies the idea of supersensible experience to his aesthetic and didactic purpose of demonstrating the continuity of reality. Thus, although passages in *The Prelude* exhibit traces of religious forms of experience and expression, including mystical, vertigo, and visionary experiences, nothing in the poem directly mimics the qualities of transiency, passivity, ineffability, and extraconceptual knowledge characteristic of the mystical state as do the "Tintern Abbey" passages.[4] By contrast, the moments of extraordinary perception in *The Prelude* operate rhetorically, as analogues to rather than representations of religious experience. In this sense, the difficulty of describing heightened modes of consciousness becomes emblematic of the difficulties of human epistemology and expression.

Any assessment of why Wordsworth moved away from renderings of mystical states is admittedly speculative, but a number of different theories, by no means mutually exclusive, can account for this fact. Gingerich offers this explanation:

We have seen that [Wordsworth], for the most part, renounced the purely mystical, that he dispensed with the pleasure of building charming abstractions through concrete images of the outer world, and from seeing "into the life of things." We shall now see that he renounced the pleasure of the pure mystic because of artistic purposes, because his deepest impulse of life was the artistic impulse. "Faith," says E. Recejac, "identifies mind with its object in a way that artistic reflection can never do. When we reflect we find that we get the feeling of love, joy of being, from within, and then we picture them as belonging to all sorts of things: but in the mystic state, the consciousness and the world meet directly in a world that transcends them both—in God who at once contains them and carries the sense of their affinities to the highest point. It is this meeting of the inner life of the spirit and the outer life which leaves behind every aesthetic effect." In the purely mystic consciousness, then, the inner and outer life meet in such close affinity that the artist, who must work in concrete imagery, pictures, colors, etc., in order to be effective, cannot find expression for the purely mystical experience. The pure mystic may indeed be able to "see into the life of things," as he says, but it does not help the artist, for he has no way of representing what he sees, and, as has just been said, representation is essential to the artist.[5]

First, then, as Gingerich indicates, representing mystical experience entails a logical and aesthetic problem, one that Wordsworth probably recognized after his experiments in "Tintern Abbey." Thus, Gingerich correctly points to the contradiction inherent in describing a definitionally ineffable state. However, as we have seen in "Tintern Abbey," it is true that an approximate rendering of such a state is possible through the exploitation of paradoxical expression, a technique that undermines the denotative and symbolic properties of individual words and things. But as Gingerich reminds us, the enterprise itself severely constrains aesthetic choice; whether Wordsworth's decision was a conscious one or not, it seems clear that he realized on some level that further poetic renderings of intellectual vision would result, ironically, in poetry of a repetitive, mechanical, and peculiarly uninsightful cast, for creating an image of the ineffable would have necessitated a repetition of the same techniques.

Second, in addition to the constraint that rendering such experiences puts on artistic freedom, the attempt to render such states tends to destabilize rather stabilize the subject's faith in that experience. Like the nature mystic who has no structure or philosophy to explain such experiences, Wordsworth may have come to feel that transcendent experiences were not real, were the product of imaginative excess.[6] However, even if the poet believed in the validity of such experiences, he was certainly aware that the lack of an explanatory system means

such experiences are potentially solipsistic and escapist, and that therefore their significance should be deemphasized. In *The Prelude*, Wordsworth does this both by describing extraordinary experience as
something that takes place in this world and by integrating such experiences in an elaborate context of ordinary experiences.[7]

Third, Wordsworth learned that the problem of expressing an extraconceptual state of consciousness can serve as a useful paradigm for
the individual struggle to make sense of life and to give it shape
through language. In *The Prelude*, Wordsworth exploits the lesson he
has learned in "Tintern Abbey": that a self-qualifying and metaphorical use of language mimics the way the human mind revises and reas-
sembles any particular experience to make it consistent with an
operative conception of reality, and thus to give it meaning and value.

While I would suggest that all of these reasons are to some degree
responsible for Wordsworth's movement away from the direct expression of transcendent experience, it is also not true, as Gingerich suggests, that poetry and mystical consciousness are inherently
incompatible. As I have argued, there are many kinds and degrees of
mysticism, and it is likely that only extreme followers of a particular
"way" who practice a severe asceticism and aspire to a constant state
of beatitude would experience the sort of conflict Gingerich mentions.
Such persons, solely preoccupied with otherworldly considerations,
would probably not be interested in writing poetry. In contrast, the
aesthetic and didactic questions for Wordsworth, at the time of writing *The Prelude*, correlate with the moral and spiritual concerns of a
mysticism of action. And indeed, such moral and spiritual concerns
may find an invigorating reward in mystical insight, for although the
incidents themselves defy description, there is a consistent tendency
to adopt either a monistic or optimistic philosophical perspective as
the result of such experiences.[8] What becomes important for Wordsworth in *The Prelude*, then, is not dramatizing and legitimating the
mystical experience itself, but illustrating a vision of reality that corresponds to the aftereffect, the sense of knowledge or what James calls
the noetic quality, of mystical encounter—the sustained and sus-
taining knowledge of unity amidst the seeming disorder of experience.

But again, how does one render the noetic quality of this state, the
knowledge beyond words that is the residue of an experience beyond
words? On the one hand, the mystic gains a knowledge that can be
neatly summarized: reality is a whole. On the other hand, the exact
nature of this wholeness, like the mystical experience itself, is extraconceptual and therefore exceeds his powers of explanation, and thus
engages with one of the central problems of explaining mystical experience. The self-qualifying techniques that Wordsworth developed in

"Tintern Abbey" function at a much higher level of complexity within *The Prelude,* enabling Wordsworth to unify diverse experiences while simultaneously mimicking the infinite complexity of reality. Self-qualification operates on many different stylistic and thematic levels in the poem—through association, resemblance, and repetition—and thus creates a system of cross-reference that moves backwards and forwards across the poem's temporal and chronological dimensions, elaborating a continuity within existence that is simultaneously conceived in and transcendent of temporal existence. Wordsworth thus develops an aesthetic correlative for his intensely monistic vision which enables him to demonstrate that *The Prelude* itself is not only metonymic of his philosophical perspective but also, because language emerges from human existence in nature, a contribution to the reality in which he believes.[9]

It is therefore the comprehensiveness of self-qualification and association within *The Prelude* that constitutes a dense but irreducible holism within the poem, and, because self-qualification operates across the scale of magnitude, it is ultimately impossible to trace with any thoroughness. On the purely linguistic level, diverse episodes are sometimes linked by the repetition of specific words or word groups, thus creating the echo effect that Ferguson and Sykes Davies have noted. Significantly, many of these repeated terms are abstract or tend toward abstraction. On the imagistic level, there is a consistent and intentional figurative pattern, one that has been much discussed in criticism of the past forty years.[10] The primary figures include breeze and breath, river and other water imagery, islands and solitaries, mist, and the like. While these images sometimes occur as distinctly isolated figures of speech, at other times they are simply aspects of the literal scene, and at still others they blur in outline and assume an equivocal position between trope and referent. By thus obscuring the status of aesthetic image and concrete object, Wordsworth compels the reader to feel how the mind inheres in nature. On the narrative level, patterns tend to repeat, invert, or modify previous patterns. The relationship between the Simplon Pass and the Snowdon episodes is often cited in this regard.[11] Finally, there is the pattern of repetition within key episodes that is similar to the use of repetition in "Tintern Abbey": as Lindenberger notes, this feature of Wordsworth's verse suggests that the struggle toward definition is more important than definition itself.[12] In fact, the impossibility of full definition is implied extensively throughout the poem, as the techniques I have mentioned, and probably others I have neglected to mention, blend into one another, connect and refine disparate aspects of the text.

While the complexity of associations in the poem suggests the interconnectedness of events and perceptions, and hence the difficulty of establishing their ultimate significance in view of a reality the poet cannot absolutely know, Wordsworth's technique does not imply a radical deferral of meaning. In Susan Wolfson's words, "Indeterminacy is more often than not a consequence of Romantic inquiry rather than a premise: if questioning implies vacancy, absence, or intractable mystery beyond the world of language, it also expresses a longing for presence and intelligibility."[13] In *The Prelude,* meanings do not cancel one another, but tend, instead, to proliferate, and in so doing to underscore the reflexive realization that language is *by nature* approximate and human. Since Wordsworth recognizes that man is a participant in natural and social life, and cannot step out of this perspective into a purely objective relationship with the universe, the ultimate or absolute meaning of any particular experience is finally not available to him, and therefore not relevant to the monistic vision of *The Prelude.* Rather, it is the capacity to see relationships between experiences and to notice resemblances in the world that itself has meaning. Indeed, Wordsworth seems to intuit what is only now central to much social and developmental psychology, that meaning-making is a centrally important human activity.[14]

The use of self-qualification and association within *The Prelude* also raises interesting questions about the poem's organization. Lindenberger points to three overlapping structural patterns in the poem—chronology, Judeo-Christian cycle, and repetition—and J. T. Ogden details the psychological pattern that contains all these as a specific structuring of imaginative experience.[15] While Wordsworth employs these various means of organizing the poem in an effort to show how humans use diverse and mutually qualifying patterns to reconstruct their experiences in time, what he ultimately wants to illustrate is that the knowledge we gain in time is not bound by temporality. Hence, the complex associations within the poem act as a corrective to the chronological and cyclical organizations, qualifying patterned means of organization with an irreducible particularity. Self-qualification builds in complexity as the poem progresses and consequently becomes a means of organizing Wordsworth's philosophical vision while simultaneously disorganizing the necessary and standard means by which the individual structures his experience through time. Thus, the patterns of association that emerge as the poem progresses indicate that the growth in importance of the individual in time depends, ironically, on his increasing intuitive perception of the universe beyond himself. As the speaker in the poem, Wordsworth gains stature correspondingly with his growing consciousness of himself as a part of nature, and it is the unique capacity for this level of consciousness that both distinguishes humanity and reaffirms its inclusion within the whole of reality.[16]

Within this perspective, the fundamental importance of the "vision-ary" experience in the Ravine of Gondo below the Simplon Pass in-heres not so much in its immediate, apocalyptic force but in its function as a test to the poet's ability to describe the continuity of reality. Neither the poet's knowledge of reality nor of any philosophi-cal system can entirely account for the extraordinary impression the scene makes on him, and, like the mystical and vertigo experiences with which it has something in common, the experience threatens to be annihilating if left unexplained.

> The brook and road
> Were fellow-travellers in this gloomy Pass,
> And with them did we journey several hours
> At a slow step. The immeasurable height
> Of woods decaying, never to be decay'd,
> The stationary blasts of waterfalls,
> And every where along the hollow rent
> Winds thwarting winds, bewilder'd and forlorn,
> The torrents shooting from the clear blue sky,
> The rocks that mutter'd close upon our ears,
> Black drizzling crags that spake by the way-side
> As if a voice were in them, the sick sight
> And giddy prospect of the raving stream,
> The unfetter'd clouds, and region of the heavens,
> Tumult and peace, the darkness and the light
> Were all like workings of one mind, the features
> Of the same face, blossoms upon one tree,
> Characters of the great Apocalyps,
> The types and symbols of eternity,
> Of first and last, and midst, and without end.
>
> (VI. 553–72)

This passage shares with those in "Tintern Abbey" the primary fea-tures of descriptions of mystical experience, paradoxical expression and progression from relative concreteness to abstraction. But whereas the paradoxical expressions in "Tintern Abbey," such as "round ocean" and "living air," suggest stasis and motion simultaneously be-cause of the seemingly arbitrary manner in which one image follows the next, those in *The Prelude* passage suggest the same effect through an intense focus on the specific scene. Thus, the apprehension of unity inheres in the recognition of the process of decay and the force of natural elements. The waterfalls, rushing with such force that the human eye cannot perceive their action, are "stationary," just as the evidence of decaying woods ensures reforestation. Through focus on a specific scene rather than the seemingly random selection of natural images which Wordsworth employs in "Tintern Abbey," then, the coinherence of the temporal and the eternal is located within a particular memory of a natural scene.

If, then, the visual intensity of lines 551–61 recalls the experiences of intellectual vision in "Tintern Abbey," it also firmly grounds such perception in the physical scene itself. In grounding his experience in the physical scene, Wordsworth underscores the belief that extraordinary experience is a dimension of ordinary experience. But at the same time, by condensing and fusing many of the stylistic techniques that arise gradually in "Tintern Abbey," Wordsworth demonstrates that ordinary experience is also extraordinary and consequently not reducible to materialist or rationalist explanation. The passage progresses from the descriptive level to clearly anthropomorphic language, then to language of excessive generality, then to similes that appear to be linked arbitrarily, and finally, to overt borrowings of orthodox rhetoric. These compressed effects give the passage distinctly religious overtones, and hence suggest that the impact of the scene cannot simply be explained by its physical force.

Although the condensation of these effects seems to imply a unity in the poet's perceptions akin to the holistic feeling of mystical experience, certain aspects of Wordsworth's description convey a contrary sense of disorientation and fear that are entirely lacking in "Tintern Abbey." For instance, the imputation of human characteristics to the scene has an effect quite the opposite of the same technique in "Tintern Abbey," where anthropomorphism and personification emphasize nature's role as a place of nurture, thus insisting on the positive continuity between man and nature. In the Ravine of Gondo, by contrast, the anthropomorphized features of the scene act as alienating reminders of the pervasively nonhuman impression it makes—the winds become bewildered and forlorn and the rocks mutter. Thus, in a few brief lines, what seems like an emblem of eternity becomes an image of man and nature inevitably bound together but working at cross-purposes with each other and themselves.

However, while the relationship of man to nature in the Ravine of Gondo is demonstrably uneasy, Wordsworth repeats the movement toward greater inclusiveness characteristic of "Tintern Abbey" and thus reinforces the sense of unity without resolving the conflicting emotions the scene evokes. What is most importantly missing from this passage is the relatively distinct dialectic between past and present experience that exists in "Tintern Abbey," for it becomes increasingly clear that the movement toward inclusiveness is a function of the present poetic consciousness, that the language that seems to shade off into mystical experience expresses a feeling of unity not at the moment of the experience but in the recreation of the event. The last lines of the verse paragraph move further and further away from specific imagery and thus toward inclusiveness rather than contain-ment and reconciliation of the opposed perceptions. As a result, the series of similes that concludes the paragraph suggests and links the spiritual, human, and organic aspects of the scene without prioritizing them. First, the chasm is likened to "workings of one great mind, the features / Of the same face," an analogy that identifies the natural scene with both God and man. Second, the chasm is compared to "blossoms upon one tree," an image of picturesque naturalness logi-cally antithetical to the sublime incomprehensibility of the Alps scene. Finally, the elements of the scene are compared to "[t]he types and symbols of Eternity," and thus to Christian myth. The stylistic device of piling qualifier upon qualifier in an effort to convey the impact of the scene ironically emphasizes the effect of inclusiveness, for the similes, added to what begins as a naturalistic description of the scene, seem actually to be part of an extended description rather than tropes indicative of resemblance. Wordsworth paradoxically approaches definition by dramatizing indefiniteness. Ultimately, there is no dis-tinction between the eternity "[o]f first and last, and midst, and with-out end" and the chasm, for the scene partakes of these characteristics in addition to resembling them. Human myth is placed on a continuum with nature at its most forceful and physical.

Although the initial "sick sight" is ameliorated by the series of similes indicative of the reflecting poet's ability to place the chaotic scene in a larger perspective, the immediate psychological impact of this scene for the young travelers is one of deadness and dehumaniza-tion. Wordsworth offers a description of their resting place that night which further qualifies the impression of unity he creates in his de-scription of the chasm:

> A dreary Mansion, large beyond all need,
> With high and spacious rooms, deafen'd and stunn'd
> By noise of waters, making innocent Sleep
> Lie melancholy among weary bones.
>
> (VI. 577–80)

The battering of the streams heightens the consciousness of destruc-tive forces called up earlier by the waterfall in the Ravine, and the human travelers are reduced to the insentience of "weary bones." The smallness of the humans is reinforced by the shortness of the verse

paragraph, which reflects the ennervation, diminution, and disappointment the travelers feel. And the apparent grammatical logic of
the sentence, which anthropomorphizes the inn as "deafen'd and
stunn'd / By noise of waters," reduces the human participants to a
state of temporary nonentity. Here, the participial phrase "making
innocent Sleep / Lie melancholy among weary bones" refers, by logic
and association, to both the noise of waters and the dreary mansion.
As in the attribution of human characteristics to the chasm, the anthropomorphism of the mansion and of sleep seems to occur at the cost
(or for the purpose) of dehumanizing the travelers, now imagistically
reduced to their stripped-down physical forms.

Both the experience in the Ravine of Gondo and its immediate
aftereffect have more in common with the disorientation and fear of
loss of control that Margolis and Elifson describe as characteristic of
vertigo experience than they do with classical mystical experience.[17]
Whereas the poet's present memory of the chasm leads to the inclusiveness of mystical language and an impression of intense unity, both
the immediate force and result of the experience emphasize its negative, annihilating impact. Wordsworth gives this experience contradictory characteristics to dramatize the difficult process of bringing
such an experience into relationship with the rest of reality. As a first
step in the realignment of experience with conception, the description
suggests a tentative and fragile unity that retains the tension of disin-
tegrating impressions within itself. For the mutual accommodation of
conceptual structures to experiences is a prolonged process; the chasm
scene must first be incorporated in the immediate scene of writing
before it can be qualified by further remembered events that enable
the poet to contextualize and recontextualize it within an enlarging
picture of reality.

Thus, the disorienting feature of this episode only predominates
when the passage is scrutinized outside of its several important contexts, the first of which is the chronological narrative. Within the
chronology of Wordsworth's story, the two previous paragraphs relate
first the abortive crossing of the Alps and then the recognition of the
power of imagination. What links these two paragraphs to the descent
into the Ravine of Gondo is a thematic and psychological concern for
the significance of accident and chance, and the mutually qualifying
relationship between chance and the potential for spiritual illumination and psychic integration. Like spiritual encounters that are unpredictable when not consciously cultivated, the scene in the chasm
unsettles only because it appears, at the moment, inconsistent with
and inexplicable in terms of prior experience. But Wordsworth takes
pains to illustrate in this part of the poem that the unexpected is to

be expected, that, in the broader view, fragmentation, inconsistency, and surprise are in fact consistent characteristics of human existence. Furthermore, Wordsworth relies on the reader's ability to exercise her retrospective consciousness to connect the unpredictable impression of the poet's past episode in the chasm with the present, unpredicted recognition of imagination.

The first in this series of passages that leads up to and includes the chasm scene describes the anticlimactic crossing of the Alps, relating the events through straightforward narrative. After questioning the peasant and learning that they have crossed the Alps without knowing it, Wordsworth recalls:

> Hard of Belief, we questioned him again,
> And all the answers which the Man return'd
> To our inquiries, in their sense and substance,
> Translated by the feelings which we had,
> Ended in this, that we had cross'd the Alps.
>
> (VI. 520–24)

Expecting an awe-inspiring, sublime scene, the travelers are surprised and disappointed to have already begun their descent. At this point, the famous paragraph on imagination interrupts the chronology of past events and in so doing corroborates the unity of the writing poet's perspective. This passage represents a chance, spontaneous reve-lation in the mind of the creating Wordsworth that explains the rela-tionship between failed vision and unexpected vision by dramatically demonstrating and repeating the function of accident:

> Imagination! lifting up itself
> Before the eye and progress of my Song
> Like an unfather'd vapour; here that Power,
> In all the might of its endowments, came
> Athwart me; I was lost as in a cloud,
> Halted without a struggle to break through,
> And now, recovering, to my soul I say
> I recognize thy glory; in such strength
> Of usurpation, in such visitings
> Of awful promise, when the light of sense
> Goes out in flashes that have shewn to us
> The invisible world, doth Greatness make abode,
> There harbours whether we be young or old.
> Our destiny, our nature, and our home,
> Is with infinitude, and only there;
> With hope it is, hope that can never die,

Effort, and expectation, and desire,
And something evermore about to be.

(VI. 525–42)

The first eight lines of this paragraph stress the importance of events and perceptions whose significance eludes us during the moment of their temporal occurrence, and the specific focus is on the paradoxical function of imagination in both past and present. Imagination comes "athwart" the poet in two different senses at two different times; in both cases, it comes near the poet, adumbrating vision, and in both cases the initial effect of this is an obstruction or thwarting of the poet's imaginative expectations. Vision is obstructed during the crossing of the Alps, and later, in a paradoxical reversal, the verbal expression of disappointment is obstructed by the envisioning of imagination, which usurps the writing poet's narrative account. Thus Wordsworth dramatically illustrates the dependency of imaginative vision, unity, and verbal ability on feelings and experiences of incapacity, alienation, and speechlessness.[18] The expectation of vision and imaginative power in the presence of a typical sublime scene, an expectation that was virtually a cliché of Wordsworth's culture, must be disappointed so that the poet may ultimately achieve a more profound understanding of vision and imagination.

Moreover, in the long run, the compounded effect of the consciousness of human insignificance and speechlessness has the salutary result of reminding Wordsworth that individual acts of perception and creation attest to the larger creative powers within the universe by virtue of their very human limitation. Hence, in lines 531–36, during a moment that seems most to prove the failure of individual imagination, Wordsworth returns to the rhetoric of mystical experience. When Wordsworth says that "the light of sense / Goes out in flashes that have shewn to us / The invisible world," he adopts once again the rhetoric of traditional mystical encounter characteristic of the first mystical passage in "Tintern Abbey." Like those earlier lines, these depict a mode of consciousness in which suspension of bodily perception—and, perhaps, even normal bodily processes of all kinds, given a plausibly expanded definition of the word *sense*—enables extrasensory sight. But three things differentiate Wordsworth's rendering of this mode of experience in *The Prelude* from that in "Tintern Abbey": first, the description of the experience is much briefer than that in "Tintern Abbey"; second, it results from and fuses with the experience of disappointment; and third, it is directly linked with imaginative experience. Thus, the disappointment attendant upon crossing the Alps and the corresponding inability to describe that disappointment

are causally connected to an experience of extraordinary consciousness. The "strength / Of usurpation" and the "visitings / Of awful
promise" refer backward to the uninspired inarticulateness attendant
upon the anticlimactic crossing of the Alps and forward to a quasi-
mystical apprehension beyond language in the Ravine, and in this
juxtaposition provide a verbal link between two nonverbal modes
of experience. The uniquely human ability to see and express the
relationship between these episodes becomes much more significant
than the individual experiences of alienation and enlightenment themselves. That the meaning of these experiences ultimately transcends
the poet's singular existence and his limited capacity for comprehension is emphasized by the shift to the third-person plural, a shift that
augments the holistic vision that follows the union of the disparate
states: "Our destiny, our nature, and our home / Is with infinitude,
and only there."[19] These lines raise the interdependence of events to
the level of universal principle in which the chief characteristics of
human life—effort, expectation, and desire—those qualities felt by
Wordsworth crossing the Alps, which seem so preeminently to mark
our finite existence, themselves partake of the infinite.

The seeming intrusion of this passage on the narrative—the "accident" of this realization in the moment of writing the poem, so to
speak—places the preceding and subsequent paragraphs in a broader
perspective than mere chronology allows, even while acknowledging
that this broader perspective can be achieved only through temporal
experience and retrospective contemplation. In this light, the descent
into the Ravine of Gondo both exemplifies and corrects the vision of
unity in the preceding paragraph. The decaying woods and powerful
force of the waterfalls seem a naturalistic corollary to the abstract
statement that infinitude contains within itself human desire and
hope; conversely, however, the enigmatic, disorienting, and dehumanizing effects of the scene suggest that the wholeness of nature is antithetical to the survival of man. The negative characteristics of this
encounter serve as a reminder, first, that, within the sequence of nar-
rated events, the perspective of the preceding paragraph has not, in
fact, been achieved. The apparent sense of finality and wholeness in
the chasm therefore rests not in the moment of past insight, but in the
mature consciousness of the adult poet. In this sense, the perception of
negative force in the scene iterates the relationship between expectation, desire, and disappointment. Second, the interruptive character
of the experience recalls the interruptive realization of the previous
paragraph, and the significance of this experience is superseded by the
intuitive realization that unexpected or accidental illumination is a
general characteristic of reality that identifies disappointment, poetic

inspiration, and disorientation with one another across time, suggesting a cohesion that transcends any given moment—or, indeed, any
given life.[20]

Thus Wordsworth demonstrates that the human significance of religious or quasi-religious experience and its analogues rests on an irony
about language: while language, being inadequate to description of
the extraconceptual, threatens to undermine the extraordinary experience, it is only through language that the significance of the extraconceptual can be recognized and, in some way, known. The inadequacy
of language, then, which seemed such a threat in the opening paragraphs of "Tintern Abbey," accedes to its greater adequacy: in enabling complex thought and conceptualization, it allows us to draw
infinite relationships, to see the interrelatedness of disparate facts and
experiences, and so to perceive a fundamental wholeness within reality. In Wordsworth's apprehension, it is not the core moment of experience that is ultimately most valuable, but the uniquely human
ability to see and express that moment's relative significance, and thus
to enhance one's grasp of the unity of existing things.

Accidental illumination, moreover, occurs one final time in Book
VI, and, in this specific rendering, reinforces the implication that significant levels of illumination occur through fairly ordinary types of
perception, and therefore place experiences of apocalytic force—the
inward apprehension of imagination and the visual apprehension of
the chasm—on a continuum with more ordinary levels of experience.
Wordsworth narrates the experience of mistakenly rising too early in
the hope of watching the dawn over Lake Como:

> The second night,
> In eagerness, and by report misled
> Of those Italian clocks that speak the time
> In fashion different from ours, we rose
> By moonshine, doubting not that day was near,
> And that, meanwhile, coasting the Water's edge
> As hitherto, and with as plain a track
> To be our guide, we might behold the scene
> In its most deep repose.—We left the Town
> Of Gravedona with this hope; but soon
> Were lost, bewilder'd among woods immense,
> Where, having wander'd for a while, we stopp'd
> And on a rock sate down, to wait for day.
> An open place it was, and overlook'd
> From high the sullen water underneath,
> On which a dull red image of the moon
> Lay bedded, changing oftentimes its form

Like an uneasy snake: long time we sate,
For scarcely more than one hour of the night,
Such was our error, had been gone, when we
Renew'd our journey. On the rock we lay,
And wish'd to sleep but could not for the stings
Of insects, which with noise like that of noon
Fill'd all the woods: the cry of unknown birds,
The mountains, more by darkness visible
And their own size than any outward light,
The breathless wilderness of clouds, the clock
That told with unintelligible voice
The widely-parted hours, the noise of streams
And sometimes rustling motions nigh at hand
Which did not leave us free from personal fear,
And lastly the withdrawing Moon that set
Before us while she still was high in heaven,
These were our food; and such a summer night
Did to that pair of golden days succeed,
With now and then a doze and snatch of sleep,
On Como's Banks, the same delicious Lake.

(VI. 621–57)

Unlike the passage recalling the descent into the Ravine of Gondo, this one never quite departs from the tone of straightforward narrative that provides temporal continuity throughout the poem, and it correspondingly lacks the rhetoric of religious experience which marks the two earlier passages. Yet neither is this passage simply a mundane summary of events, like the paragraph that describes the disappointment attendant on crossing the Alps. Rather, this paragraph fuses the relationship between ordinary and extraordinary perception by combining straightforward narrative with naturalistic description of a disorienting scene. It is thus linked to the Gondo scene in several ways: chronologically, it describes a final impression during this Alps adventure; emotionally, it indicates a less intense but certainly noticeable disorientation; and intellectually, its significance exceeds the poet's powers of explanation. The fusion of the inexplicable with the mundane—the snakelike moon and dark mountains are counterbalanced by the stings of insects, cries of birds, and rustling foliage—results in a paradoxical sense of peacefulness combined with unrest and disappointment, consequently confirming while modifying the earlier feelings of disorientation and disappointment. Moreover, this peacefulness exists not in spite of but because of the slightly threatening aspect of nature. Like mystical experience in "Tintern Abbey," like the quasi-religious experience in the Ravine, the ultimate meaning of this experience is beyond explanation. But as it combines the seemingly opposed experiences of crossing the Alps and of descending into the Ravine by offering the travelers, notwithstanding the darkness, a broader visual perspective, it intimates the cohesiveness of diverse forms of experience. As an episode that echoes and qualifies the feelings attendant on crossing the Simplon Pass and descending into the Ravine, the night on the shores of Lake Como establishes the underlying continuity of experience and points chronologically toward (while alluding narratively backward to) the recognition that "Our destiny, our nature, and our home / [are] with infinitude." And because the passage itself enacts the integration of experience, it emphasizes the fact that the links between disparate moments, although not consciously perceived, existed at the time of the tour of the Alps.

Thus, within its specific context in Book VI, an experience with spiritual overtones is repeatedly contextualized to stress its importance in the developing power of intuition. Paradoxically, then, the exceptional nature of such episodes, and an attendant sense of individual power and privilege, is available only to the person who perceives the continuity between these and more common forms of experience.

Wordsworth's perception that extraordinary experience truly becomes extraordinary only when it can be brought into relation with common experience is reasserted in the passage which most conspicuously echoes the Lake Como passage, the recounting of the ascent of Snowdon in Book XIII. Like the paragraph describing the moon over Lake Como, this one is narrative and naturalistically descriptive; and while the grandeur of the scene recalls the moments in the Ravine of Gondo, Wordsworth does not employ techniques of religious description—the movement toward vagueness and abstraction, accumulations of metaphors or similes, paradox—that tend to emphasize the special and extrasensory qualities of heightened consciousness. Instead, the experiences that seem to offset one another during the tour of the Alps—profound disappointment, profound insight, and uneasy peace—are modified and reordered in rhetoric that stresses continuity of feeling and of responsiveness to the external universe.[21]

> It was a Summer's night, a close warm night,
> Wan, dull and glaring, with a dripping mist
> Low-hung and thick that cover'd all the sky,
> Half-threatening storm and rain: but on we went
> Uncheck'd, being full of heart and having faith
> In our tried Pilot. Little could we see,
> Hemm'd round on every side with fog and damp,
> And, after ordinary Travellers' chat

With our Conductor, silently we sunk
Each into commerce with his private thoughts . . .

(XIII. 10–19)

The beginning of this description recalls the mood and atmosphere of
the night spent on the shore of Lake Como: warmth, darkness, silence,
and the threat of rain contribute to a sense of uneasiness and physical
discomfort. At the same time, the inwardness of the climbers mirrors
Wordsworth's earlier inwardness during the climb of the Alps that
proved so disappointing. In addition to the unpromising weather,
which seems to offer little hope for a sublime view, the description of
the dog unearthing the hedgehog dulls rather than sharpens expectation, seemingly heightening the uneventfulness of the climb:

> Thus did we breast the ascent, and by myself
> Was nothing either seen or heard the while
> Which took me from my musings, save that once
> The Shepherd's Cur did to his own great joy
> Unearth a hedge-hog in the mountain crags
> Round which he made a barking turbulent.

(XIII. 20–25)

But in fact, this unpromising beginning does not at all dull the anticipation of the travelers, who continue on "with eager pace, and no less
eager thoughts" (32), and the climb leads toward a vision of immense
wholeness, one that juxtaposes and combines the visual aspects of the
various episodes in the Alps. Thus the supreme experience of vision
in *The Prelude*, which entails seeing reality as an undivided whole,
both emerges from and depends upon mundane perception and experience: the dog's joy, while apparently deadening expectations of the
extraordinary, foreshadows the poet's own revelation:[22]

> I panted up
> With eager pace, and no less eager thoughts;
> Thus might we wear perhaps an hour away,
> Ascending at loose distance each from each,
> And I, as chanced, the foremost of the Band—
> When at my feet the ground appear'd to brighten,
> And with a step or two seem'd brighter still,
> Nor had I time to ask the cause of this,
> For instantly a Light upon the turf
> Fell like a flash. I looked about, and lo!
> The Moon stood naked in the Heavens at height
> Immense above my head, and on the shore
> I found myself of a huge sea of mist,

Which meek and silent, rested at my feet:
A hundred hills their dusky backs upheaved
All over this still Ocean, and beyond,
Far, far beyond, the vapours shot themselves,
In headlands, tongues, and promontory shapes
into the Sea, the real Sea, that seem'd
To dwindle and give up its majesty,
Usurp'd upon as far as sight could reach.
Meanwhile the Moon look'd down upon this shew
In single glory, and we stood, the mist
Touching our very feet: and from the shore
At distance not the third part of a mile
Was a blue chasm, a fracture in the vapour,
A deep and gloomy breathing-place thro' which
Mounted the roar of waters, torrents, streams
Innumerable, roaring with one voice.
The universal spectacle throughout
Was shaped for admiration and delight,
Grand in itself alone, but in that breach
Through which the homeless voice of waters rose,
That dark deep thorough-fare, had Nature lodg'd
The Soul, the Imagination of the whole.

(XIII. 31–65)

What is crucially significant about the "vision" on Snowdon is that
it is simultaneously and inseparably a *view* of the physical world; while
the moment in the Ravine seems to require a discovery of meaning
for which human language is inadequate, the significance of the insight
on Snowdon is inseparable from the scene itself. The knowledge of
wholeness that heightened consciousness brings can thus be artisti-
cally embodied because it is perceptually recognized in the actual
world; the mists and vapors connect travelers, hills, sea, and chasm
in one continuous panorama. Moreover, in the last few lines of this
verse paragraph, Wordsworth explicitly indicates that the unity he
perceives in the scene includes the spiritual and intellectual qualities
that he has sought; asserting that "soul" and "imagination" have been
placed *by nature* in the scene, Wordsworth establishes an inclusive,
continuous conception of reality which defies the separation of matter
and spirit.

The Ravine of Gondo episode in Book VI, seemingly absolute and
unsurpassable as a kind of sublime experience, becomes, retrospec-
tively, an important stage in the development of a monistic apprehension of reality which transcends distinctions between man, nature,
and imagination in a greater knowledge of their unity. Thus, the Ravine experience, and implicitly, the kinds of heightened states of con-

sciousness which it suggests, is ultimately interpreted within the context of the poem as a means to an end. It is the capacity of such experiences to disrupt the teleology of human thought, and with it the standard forms of explanation, that reawakens the human mind toward the reality in which it lives. In enabling understanding as a creative process, therefore, extraordinary perception points back toward the ordinary, redirecting the poet's attention to the significance of the mundane. It is only in this functional capacity that the experience becomes truly sublime.

It is no simple accident, then, that while the Gondo scene is rendered in language that typically indicates a struggle toward expression, the Snowdon scene unfolds more gradually, and in progressive and coherent detail. In the Gondo scene, the use of paradox, the movement toward abstraction, and the proliferation of tropes reveal a struggle to articulate meaning through language. Literal description is, at that moment and in that place, insufficient to the poet's purpose. By contrast, the scene on Snowdon is at once more consistently literal and figurative. The various components of the scene—bodies of water, mists, mountains, wind—have been repeated with such frequency throughout the poem that they carry an emotional and intellectual weight far greater than the direct material realities they represent. Moreover, the disposition of these elements into a single continuous scene suggests the attainment of a higher level of symbolic awareness. But while Wordsworth thus enacts this growth in symbolic awareness, he does so through description that remains faithful to the literal qualities of the scene. Thus, the view from Snowdon dramatizes a high point in the poet's progress: the human attempt to symbolize perceived realities beyond the physical world ultimately leads to the recognition that such realities coinhere with the physical world. Analogy, and its aesthetic embodiment in metaphor and symbol, serves a crucial epistemological function, enabling both the discovery and communication of the wholeness of reality; however, it ultimately gives way to a more comprehensive unity. In keeping with this, the vision on Snowdon is an adequate symbol for Wordsworth's monistic vision precisely because it is part of it. Within the necessarily reductive structures of human cognition, the symbol apparently mirrors a greater order, but that perception of resemblance, as an important fact of human learning, proves to be only a step toward recognizing the continuous nature of reality.

In short, literal and figurative language become indistinguishable in *The Prelude* as a stylistic corollary to the insight that, given the limitations of human knowledge, the concept of literalism itself is a kind of illusion. To believe in a distinct separation of literal and figurative language presupposes a distinct separation of the real and the imaginary. For Wordsworth, it would not only be presumptuous to suppose that we can make such a distinction, it would also be empirically false, since the act of creation is fundamental to the reality we know. While given aspects of reality may have specific meanings within a given temporal and experiential framework, nothing, ultimately, is reducible to its literal terms. In Wordsworth's conception, the significance of objects is always changing as we strive to know them as part of a reality we can never completely know, and it is our creative ability to qualify and redefine, as well as our interest in the mysterious fact of our lives in nature, that constitutes our special status within nature as human beings.

Hence, Wordsworth's habit of merging literal and figurative language, of superimposing the imaginary on the actual and vice versa, elaborates his underlying philosophical outlook. But since Wordsworth must convey his monism by relationship and elaboration—for to explain it as a systematic philosophy would contradict and therefore undermine the belief itself—his aesthetic practice has been variously interpreted.[23] Paul de Man, for instance, offers a very different interpretation from my own:

> At times, romantic thought and romantic poetry seem to come so close to giving in completely to the nostalgia for the object that it becomes difficult to distinguish between object and image, between imagination and perception, between an expressive or constitutive and a mimetic or literal language. This may well be the case in some passages of Wordsworth and Goethe, of Baudelaire and Rimbaud, where the vision almost seems to become a real landscape . . .

When tropes are not drawn from a category or plane of experience distinct from the things represented, as is frequently the case in romantic poetry—naturalistic metaphors in Wordsworth represent mental experience at the same time that the world is described naturalistically—the line between imaginative fabrication and actuality becomes ambiguous. For de Man, this is indicative of the poet's desire to escape or deny material reality. In this context, the passage on imagination in Book VI signifies "a possibility for consciousness to exist entirely by and for itself, independently of all relationship with the outside world, without being moved by an intent aimed at a part of this world."[24]

But de Man's analysis is itself based in a confidence in language that emerges from a rationalist belief in the objective integrity of human conceptual structures which Wordsworth did not share. What de Man ignores here is that the image of imagination as a disembodied entity reflects a temporary perception, not a static conception of a supposed mental faculty. Rather, the passage on imagination which de Man cites constitutes an interruptive moment at midpoint in *The Prelude;* in Book XIII, as we have seen, Wordsworth describes imagination as continuous with nature in what surely is meant to be a more comprehensive reflection of mature "vision." Correspondingly, it is in no way clear that imagination is an exclusively human term to Wordsworth, as de Man assumes it is. In fact, *imagination* for Wordsworth is a rather vague and protean term, suggesting something like a universal creative principle that man embodies and extends. In this sense, it is a permutation of the expansive nature of both "Tintern Abbey" and *The Prelude.* During the Simplon Pass episode, imagination is perceived as an entity outside the poet which comes upon him; in the Snowdon episode, by contrast, imagination is lodged in the scene, having been placed there as a part of the whole by nature. The important relationship between these two episodes does not lie in a particular definition or philosophical conception of imagination, but in what Lockridge refers to as the "struggle for coordination"—that is, in the progression from the poet's perception of separate forces and realities to that of their mutual integration.[25] Thus, the initial recognition of imagination as a separate and significant power demonstrates the ability to distinguish modes of experience and categories of perception upon which a later sense of their subtle integration rests. In contrast to de Man, then, Wordsworth works through a dualist perspective toward a monistic one, gradually realizing in the process that categories of mind and matter attest not to fixed realities but to the activity of human perception and cognition in its relationship to reality.

In fact, quite early in *The Prelude,* Wordsworth explicitly identifies categorization as a fact of human perception which should not be taken as the ultimate truth about reality. Addressing Coleridge directly in this passage, Wordsworth declares:

> Thou art no slave
> Of that false secondary power, by which,
> In weakness we create distinctions, then
> Deem our puny boundaries are things
> Which we perceive, and not which we have made.
> To thee, unblinded by these outward shows
> The unity of all has been reveal'd
> And thou wilt doubt with me, less aptly skill'd
> Than many are to class the cabinet
> Of their sensations, and, in voluable phrase,
> Run through the history and birth of each,

> As of a single independent thing.
> Hard task to analyse a soul, in which,
> Not only general habits and desires,
> But each most obvious and particular thought,
> Not in a mystical and idle sense,
> But in the words of reason deeply weigh'd
> Hath no beginning.
>
> (II. 220–37)

Wordsworthian statement is sometimes very uncomplicated, and this particular passage happens to be a case in point. "Puny boundaries" are continually broken down in The Prelude and with them simple distinctions between literal and figurative language and physical and material reality. Thus *imagination* in The Prelude, like *nature* in "Tintern Abbey," cannot be given a specific definition because Wordsworth revises and expands his conception of it as the poem progresses.

This point about terminology brings us to a crucial question about The Prelude: In what sense is it a philosophical poem? Attempts to discern an intellectually coherent explanatory system within the poem generally seem to eradicate the underlying complexity that gives the poem its coherence and appeal; in Sheats's words, "The very act of applying a philosophical nomenclature to Wordsworth's poetry constitutes a radical departure from the realm of discourse in which his poetry claims authority."[26] Writing to George Beaumont on 3 June 1805, shortly after both his brother's death and the completion of the poem, Wordsworth himself certainly does not appear to find the solace in the poem which systematic explanation brings:

> I have the pleasure to say that I finished my Poem about a fortnight ago, I had looked forward to the day as a most happy one; and I was indeed grateful to God for giving me life to complete the work, such as it is; but it was not a happy day for me I was dejected on many accounts; when I looked back upon the performance it seemed to have a dead weight about it, the reality so far short of expectation; it was the first long labour I had finished, and the doubt whether I should ever live to write the Recluse and the sense which I had of this Poem being so far below what I seem'd capable of executing, depressed me much: above all, many heavy thoughts of my poor departed Brother hung upon me . . . This work may be considered as a sort of portico to the Recluse, part of the same building, which I hope to be able erelong to begin with, in earnest.[27]

The pleasure, indeed, seems minimal, as does any solace the poem might provide for its author, and it is clear that Wordsworth still views The Prelude as prefatory to The Recluse, the planned philosophical poem.

Whether one deems *The Prelude* a philosophical poem depends, I
think, on how one understands that term, on whether one employs
philosophical to designate an outlook or a systematic explanation of
life and our place in it, an explanation that would either be based in
or replace religious orthodoxy. Ideally, of course, one's philosophical
outlook, one's intuitions about life, should be consistent with one's
system of explanation. But in *The Prelude,* the conflict between beliefs
based in and derived from experience on the one hand and available
forms of explanation on the other parallels the conflict between religious experience and orthodoxy in "Tintern Abbey." Because Wordsworth's outlook reflects a thoroughly naturalistic monism, basing
meaning in an understanding of our lives in nature, it reflects a pragmatic view of human epistemology and is therefore essentially antisys-
tematic. As we grow, reflect, and communicate, our conceptions—
like Wordsworth's conceptions of imagination and nature—grow, and
we improve our human understanding; thus it is only through our
understanding of knowledge as a process within human existence that
we acquire knowledge at all. But once knowledge is understood as a
process relative to the structures of human biology and experience, it
becomes enormously difficult to accept absolute truths and static systems of explanation. Belief systems, philosophical systems, and theories are perceived as modes of adaptation rather than revelations, and
truth is understood to evolve in and be revised in experience.[28] Correspondingly, since humans are by nature predisposed to construct and
reconstruct the reality in which they live for the purposes of survival,
creativity is essential to the capacity to know. Once modern man is
aware that imagination both facilitates and forestalls knowledge and
that ideas must thus be tested by observation, religions and abstract
philosophical systems, which are not amenable to empirical testing,
become inherently suspect, and consequently unstable as bases of
belief.

Precisely because Wordsworth's comprehensive use of self-
qualification throughout *The Prelude* therefore demonstrates a modern
conception of knowledge and, by implication, a corresponding belief
in the limitations of human knowledge, it gives truth-value to the
uncertainty of our existence and to the human experience of self-
division. This returns us to the point I made at the beginning of this
chapter, where I mentioned the tension between the broader philosophical outlook of pragmatism and the narrower individual view. In
the immediacy of our own particular losses and our own particular
progress toward death, the insight that reality is a whole that transcends our understanding does not satisfy our psychological need for
certainty. And what the final book of *The Prelude* indicates—what

certainly becomes unequivocal in Wordsworth's later writings—is that, faced with the loss of his brother and then his children, naturalistic monism was not enough.

It is perhaps the most striking paradox of *The Prelude* that the critical attempt to find a coherent religious philosophy within it reveals a poem simultaneously more secular and more orthodox than "Tintern Abbey." Certainly, the secular and pragmatic vision gains status as the poem progresses; the building and qualification of incidents mimics the developmental reality that leads toward pragmatism and monism, and the reassertion, in Book XIII, of the primacy of parental nurture grounds visionary meaning in physical existence. But conversely, the references to God and to a Christian scheme of belief, which throughout much of the poem seem to function in a nonorthodox or ambiguous fashion, become overtly orthodox at the end of the poem.

However, if Wordsworth ultimately insists on two incompatible ways of seeing the world, they are not equally convincing. Elaborating in full what it means to be human in nature, Wordsworth ultimately demonstrates that nature is the source of prophetic poetry, because the bond of love and trust from which emotional and linguistic development ensue is rooted in nature. It is Wordsworth's sense of the eternity of mutability, of the absolute value of our life within time and change, that is presented throughout the poem with consistently expanding breadth and depth, while the Christian references within the poem are neither much in evidence nor amenable to consistent interpretation.

As in "Tintern Abbey," Wordsworth shows scant interest in religion as an institution with established procedures and rituals. When, in Book III, Wordsworth protests enforced chapel attendance, his argument is neither theological nor traditionally moral:

> Was ever known
> The witless Shepherd who would drive his Flock
> With serious repetition to the pool
> Of which 'tis plain to sight they never taste?
> A weight must surely hang on days, begun
> And ended with worst mockery: be wise,
> Ye Presidents and Deans, and to your Bells
> Give seasonable rest; for 'tis a sound
> Hollow as ever vex'd the tranquil air;
> And your officious doings bring disgrace
> On the plain steeples of our English Church

> Whose worship 'mid remotest village trees
> Suffers for this.
>
> (III. 415–27)

This passage follows one in which Wordsworth compares his feeling of captivity at Cambridge to his earlier education in nature and is associated with it by an underlying concern that has nothing to do with Christian propriety. In Wordsworth's view, it is pointless to dictate that unwilling believers attend church for the same reason that his own attendance at Cambridge was pointless: it is unnatural. And far from being an offense against the beliefs and practices embodied in the Church of England, forced chapel attendance is a desecration of the country church itself, envisioned here as an aspect of nature. Indeed, the ambiguous syntax of lines 425–26, which conflates the physical building with the congregation of believers, suggests, strangely but appropriately, that the church itself is the object of worship. The church, protected and concealed by village trees, is treated with such reverence not because it symbolizes the endurance of Christianity but because it is such a consistent part of the landscape that Wordsworth associates it with the world of natural phenomena.[29]

In fact, Wordsworth's secularization of the physical church goes beyond this general identification of it with the natural world. In Book V, Wordsworth describes the graveyard where the Boy of Winander is buried and then depicts the church as a maternal presence:

> Even now, methinks, I have before my sight
> That self-same Village Church: I see her sit,
> The throned Lady spoken of erewhile,
> On her green hill; forgetful of this Boy
> Who slumbers at her feet, forgetful too,
> Of all her silent neighbourhood of graves,
> And listening only to the gladsome sounds,
> That, from the rural School ascending, play
> Beneath her, and about her. May she long
> Behold a race of young Ones like to those
> With whom I herded!
>
> (V. 423–33)

If the passage in Book III indicates that Wordsworth sees the country church as a kind of natural growth, as a part of the world of physical nature, this passage demonstrates that the church partakes of the enhanced conception of nature which includes human life. As a human creation that seems both to grow out of the scene and to be human itself, the church operates symbolically not to divide but to link man and nature. Personified as a mother whose perspective transcends the temporal uncertainties of the human life span, her forgetfulness of the boy and the other dead, far from revealing indifference and cruelty, attests to wisdom and love. As a symbolic embodiment of Words-worth's naturalistic monism rather than a symbol for church author-ity, she watches over an eternity of children, mediating between each individual death and the larger continuities of human existence. By implication, too, she is connected with the other maternal presences in the poem—including but not limited to the poet's mother, sister, and wife—sources of life and affection, all of whom are identified with the outward flow of love and poetry by the end of The Prelude.

Thus, the high value that Wordsworth places upon the country church has little to do with its traditional function as the house of worship. Instead, the country church's value arises from those things with which Wordsworth continually associates it: the unpretentious beauties of the natural world and the life-giving capacities of human beings. In depicting the church as a perpetual maternal presence, then, Wordsworth illustrates a conception of eternity singularly at variance with the traditional Christian concept. The Christian afterlife—what D. H. Lawrence saw as the postponed reward of that religion—is replaced by the natural wisdom that through temporal existence we not only participate in but also help constitute eternity.[30]

Just as the idea of the church itself is accommodated to the poem's philosophical outlook, which emphasizes the priority and ubiquity of nature rather than of God, many of Wordsworth's uses of religious language seem primarily rhetorical and literary rather than tradition-ally religious. For example, in the description of the Ravine of Gondo, Wordsworth refers to typology after he has dramatized how both descriptive and imagistic language offer only gropings toward the kind of experience he wishes to express. The "Characters of the great Apoc-alyps" and "The types and symbols of eternity" are placed within a context that esteems orthodox religion as a manifestation of an intu-ited higher reality and of the struggle to express it, rather than ascrib-ing a truth-function to the specific myths themselves. Moreover, Wordsworth's vague invocation of typology here stands in contrast to the extremely specific practice of typology in theology and meditative poetry, which explores relationships between Old and New Testament phenomena. While typology as a practice tends toward greater and greater concreteness of meaning, Wordsworth invokes typology in the process of expressing undiscoverable meaning.[31] In this case, Words-worth seems to have chosen religious language for its sanctifying prop-erties rather than its meaning within a religious tradition.

The significance of the word God is especially problematic in the

poem, sometimes serving, like the reference to typology and like the
words *imagination* and *nature,* as a metaphor that marks the limits of
language, sometimes distinctly referring to a Christian deity. In Book
VIII, Wordsworth recalls and recasts the lessons of London:

> Add also that among the multitudes
> Of that great City oftentimes was seen
> Affectingly set forth, more than elsewhere
> Is possible, the unity of man,
> One spirit over ignorance and vice
> Predominant, in good and evil hearts
> One sense for moral judgments, as one eye
> For the sun's light. When strongly breathed upon
> By this sensation, whencesoe'er it comes,
> Of union or communion, doth the soul
> Rejoice as in her highest joy; for there,
> There chiefly, hath she feeling whence she is,
> And passing through all nature, rests with God.
>
> (VIII. 824–36)

In this passage, as is typically the case, Wordsworth moves pragmati-
cally from experience to idealization. The seemingly miraculous realization of human community among the dismal scenes of London
becomes analogous to mystical experience, as the rhetoric of the passage indicates. As in the first of the mystical passages in "Tintern
Abbey," and as in St. Teresa's description of mystical experience,
Wordsworth emphasizes the awakening of the soul and the experience
of unification. While this description is perfectly compatible with
an orthodox reading, as we see when we compare it to St. Teresa's
description, there is no orthodox context to which the term *God*
refers. It is the general sparseness of Wordsworth's use of the term,
coupled with his lack of interest in doctrine and his extraordinary
attention to nature, that places the word *God* with his other fading
abstractions. *God* conjures up a sense of the intuited reality beyond
the limits of human expression, but it remains unclear whether the
idea of godhead has a particular conceptual significance to the poet.

By contrast, there are passages in the poem where "God" apparently
refers to a traditionally anthropomorphized being with supernatural
agency. For instance, in Book XI, describing his reaction to his father's
death, Wordsworth writes:

>   The event
> With all the sorrow which it brought appear'd
> A chastisement; and when I call'd to mind

> That day so lately pass'd, when from the crag
> I look'd in such anxiety of hope,
> With trite reflections of morality,
> Yet in the deepest passion, I bow'd low
> To God, who thus corrected my desires . . .
>
> (XI. 368–74)

This statement echoes the orthodox sentiments of Wordsworth's earlier description of his mother's beliefs, where he explains that she

> had virtual faith that he,
> Who fills the Mother's breasts with innocent milk,
> Doth also for our nobler part provide,
> Under his great correction and controul,
> As innocent instincts, and as innocent food.
>
> (V. 271–75)

Both passages, in emphasizing especially God's corrective powers, give
him the traditional attributes of the Christian deity: he is both creator
and controller of the world in which man lives, and he is the proper
object of worship. In the first of these passages, furthermore, the fact
that there seems no obvious reason why the young boy deserves the
rather harsh correction meted out by his father's death implies that
human beings in general require such correction, and thus reflects a
belief in human imperfection and humility consistent with the notion
of original sin.

Likewise, in Book VI, Wordsworth invokes the concept of an orthodox deity when he speaks of praying to him, "the Giver of all joy"
(VI. 614). Along with the above passages, then, this one reflects a
traditional concept of the relationship between God, nature, and man;
God, the sole source of power and creation, reveals himself to man
through nature. But the case is not so simple, for in other parts of the
poem Wordsworth also personifies nature and lavishes on her the
superlative terms applied to God. In Book V, for instance, after recounting the dream of the Arab, Wordsworth exclaims:

> Mighty indeed, supreme must be the power
> Of living Nature which could thus so long
> Detain me from the best of other thoughts!
>
> (V. 166–68)

In designating nature as a supreme power, Wordsworth contradicts
the traditional hierarchy he has elsewhere endorsed, establishing nature not as the medium through which God works but as a supreme

being in her own right. In Book IX, Wordsworth similarly speaks of "God and Nature's single sovereignty," once again treating them as equivalent powers.[32]

In sum, if we measure these statements about God and nature against one another, we will not arrive at a very convincing argument about a systematic theology containing coherent and stable definitions of its main terms underlying *The Prelude*. But to look for such consistency of thought in Wordsworth's poetry is to engage in an ultimately futile exercise, in which extracting such statements results in an evaluation of what is often the poet's least compelling poetry. For if we simply tally the orthodox sentiments against the unorthodox ones, we might conclude that the poet's Christian sentiments outweigh his naturalistic monism. Only we would be overlooking this significant fact about the poem: statements about God notwithstanding, in *The Prelude*, as in "Tintern Abbey," it is nature that invokes the psychological patterns typical of religious conversion and experience, and, in turn, it is nature—not God—toward which the poet directs strong emotion. In contrast to God, nature, conceived not as a particularized object or realm but as an expansive entity, is the focus of the poet's most intense emotions and ultimately provides the amelioration of uncertainty and self-division which enables a monistic view of reality.

Let us recall James's definition of religion, which I discussed in chapter 1. James wrestles with the problem of an overwhelming emotion—as he calls it, a "total reaction upon life"—that has become, with the breakup of the Enlightenment and the breakdown in orthodoxies—directed toward a vague object. Wordsworth's "God," much like Emerson's Oversoul, is thus in this sense typical of a modern deity; he seems to be, for the poet himself, an uneasy mixture of intuited reality and partially conceived idea. Now if what human beings are after in their perennial struggle toward belief is certainty, lavishing this fund of metaphysical love upon a notion rather than a concrete conception is apt to provide, at best, indifferent emotional results.

To be sure, there are students of religion who, taking up the question of religion from the perspective of a *purely* pragmatic psychology, would not make much of this inconsistency. The problem is akin to that which arises when religion and art are treated as direct analogues, a problem I addressed in chapter 1. For example, describing five modalities of religious belief that range from an elementary, primitivistic commitment to what is perceived by the believer as a truth system at the lowest level to a far more qualified commitment to particular creeds and rituals at the highest level, William Meissner asserts the

validity of a religious faith that views particular creeds as possibilities
of truth rather than certainties. Meissner says this:

> ... [in the fifth modality,] the religious belief system and its tradition are
> seen in increasingly realistic terms that affirm their inherent tensions and
> ambiguities and accept the relativity, partiality, and particularity of the
> beliefs, symbols, rituals, and ceremonials of the religious community.[33]

Within such a perspective, then, Meissner conceives of a believer for
whom a particular conception of the deity is understood by the believer to be an *attempt* at truth, not a literal description of a divine
being. While religious belief of this kind is not impossible and is surely
valid insofar as it works for any given individual, it requires an extraordinarily high degree of sophistication on the believer's part and
rests on an uncomfortable paradox. The believer is obliged, in practicing his or her religion, to embrace precisely those uncertainties that
religious institutions evolved to eradicate. Unlike a religion that offers
a specific conceptualization of God as an ultimate reality, the fifth
modality of religious belief offers only another possibility. If, as Rappaport argues, the function of ritual is to reduce ambiguity, once human
beings realize that religions are self-saving fictions, the primary function of belief is defeated. In fact, feelings of ontological insecurity may
well be exacerbated by the attempt to put faith in objects and systems
one cannot finally believe are real. A human being cannot make the
same emotional commitment to a possible object that he or she makes
to a real object, for such an investment involves a psychologically
perceived risk of being false and misdirected.

In Wordsworth's sketchily conceived God, I think, we see the effect
of the reintroduction of ambiguity into an orthodox system of belief.
The orthodox God and the attendant beliefs are still there, in some
sense, but God has become a metaphor for the ineffable, a thing beyond
the limits of human conceptualization, language, and emotion. By contrast, that personal relationship of the believer to his God so especially
characteristic of Protestantism is replaced by a personal relationship
to nature, which grows in complexity of conception throughout the
poem. In Book IV, Wordsworth speaks of returning to the lakes after
his first year at Cambridge and describes his feelings during long walks
in the countryside: "Gently did my soul / Put off her veil, and, self-
transmuted, stood / Naked as in the presence of her God" (IV. 140–
42). The small word *as* is of some significance here, for it makes the
lines a comparison between the present feeling and states of religious
awe, not a direct assertion that God is present. By contrast, in Book
VII, Wordsworth says, in explanation of his ability to survive the

soul-destroying scenes of London, "The Spirit of Nature was upon me here" (VII. 736). While God's presence is a possibility, nature's is a certainty.

In the last chapter, I spoke of how Wordsworth, in "Tintern Abbey," paradoxically deifies nature at the point in the poem at which he recognizes that he speaks both *for* and *as* nature; thus he addresses nature as a god-like being outside and above himself precisely when he realizes the significance of his participation in nature. Nature is represented as a supernatural figure when Wordsworth's naturalistic monism appears most manifestly to cancel such entities and the conceptual dualisms of which they are a part. Personifying nature, then, is a rhetorical means for Wordsworth to praise the force of life whose magnitude seems to defy words. This is perhaps even more true in *The Prelude* than in "Tintern Abbey," for the relationship between the physical and mental development of the poet and the changing conception of nature is drawn in thorough and elaborate detail. Moreover, the connection between nature, humanity, and poetry is reinforced by the poet's explicit connection of poetic productivity to the capacity for nurturing based in the human child's relationship to its mother.

Wordsworth unequivocally connects the creation of poetry with the source of human life within nature, for the passages stressing maternal influence and sympathy follow immediately the triumphant achievement of vision on Snowdon. Of the poet who can achieve imaginative powers like his own—in the specific interaction of the poem, of Coleridge—Wordsworth says:

> and he whose soul hath risen
> Up to the height of feeling intellect
> Shall want no humbler tenderness, his heart
> Be tender as a nursing Mother's heart,
> Of female softness shall his life be full,
> Of little loves and delicate desires,
> Mild interests and gentlest sympathies.
>
> (XIII. 204–10)

Just at the point where Wordsworth appears to have developed a metaphysical schema, a philosophical system that separates and assigns specific functions to man, mind, nature, and God, he describes the primary gifts of the successful poet as both the outgrowth and the individual reenactment of the reciprocal relationship of mother and child. Thus, while on the one hand nature, God, and imagination are hypostatized as differentiated objects of worship, on the other their coinherence within the processes of human life is underscored, and the artificiality of abstracting from the fundamental qualities of our physical existence is implicitly articulated. Paradoxically, then, basic human epistemological processes, the capacity for abstraction and simplification, confirm the sense of participation in a process that exceeds our understanding, and lead back to the origins of that process as both the source and the great culmination of life and poetry. What the poet has gained is an awareness of his participation, an awareness that confirms his monism. Wordsworth sees, at this moment, a universe in which the whole is greater than the sum of the parts that man can know.

Hartman claims that the paradox of Wordsworth's poetry is that the poet must pass through nature to imagination in what finally constitutes a denial of nature.[34] And when Wordsworth speaks of "the perfect image of a mighty Mind / Of one that feeds upon infinity," he does seem to be describing imagination as a power liberated from the claims of physical nature. But again, as with the paragraphs that provide the context for the Alps crossing and the descent into the Ravine of Gondo, the text that surrounds the image of disembodied mind qualifies it in crucial ways. For just at the moment that Wordsworth seems to suggest liberation from nature, he returns to the source of this power as the ultimate subject of the poet, although now he does not call it nature:

>   From love, for here
> Do we begin and end, all grandeur comes,
> All truth and beauty, from pervading love,
> That gone, we are as dust. Behold the fields
> In balmy spring-time, full of rising flowers
> And happy Creatures: see that Pair, the Lamb
> And the Lamb's Mother, and their tender ways
> Shall touch thee to the heart; in some green bower
> Rest and be not alone, but have thou there
> The One who is thy choice of all the world;
> There linger, lull'd, and lost, and rapt away,
> Be happy to thy fill: thou call'st this love,
> And so it is; but there is higher love
> Than this, a love that comes into the heart
> With awe and a diffuse sentiment . . .

>   (XIII. 149–64)

As the association of love with flowers and lambs makes clear, love begins in nature. In fact, Wordsworth makes this point more explicitly in the preceding book:

> There are who think that strong affections, love
> Known by whatever name, is falsely deem'd
> A gift, to use a term which they would use,
> Of vulgar Nature, that its growth requires
> Retirement, leisure, language purified
> By manners thoughtful and elaborate,
> That whoso feels such passion in excess
> Must live within the very light and air
> Of elegances that are made by man.
> True is it, where oppression worse than death
> Salutes the Being at his birth, where grace
> Of culture hath been utterly unknown
> And labour in excess and poverty
> From day to day preoccupy the ground
> Of the affections, and to Nature's self
> Oppose a deeper nature, there indeed
> Love cannot be; nor does it easily thrive
> In cities, where the human heart is sick,
> And the eye feeds it not, and cannot feed:
> Thus far, no further, is that inference good.

(XII. 185–204)

Love is a characteristic of nature but not an inevitable fact of human existence; adverse circumstances bring out "a deeper nature" in which the ability for affectionate exchange has been stunted. The capacity of adult imagination to acknowledge nature as a ground of value is therefore not an ordinary but an extraordinary achievement, because, as the numerous tales of disaster throughout the poem attest, there is no assurance that nature-as-love will win out. The irony of the mind that seemingly transcends nature is that it is only superior in its ability to know and articulate its place in nature. In his capacity for language, the poet can know and articulate the beauty of nature, but he also *adds to* nature, providing it with a distinctively human form. The indecision, guilt, and fear of the unproductive poet of Book I, who finds direction for his poem the moment he calls himself "a false Steward who hath much receiv'd / And renders nothing back" (I. 271–72), have been allayed and transcended by precisely those natural affections to which he feels such a debt.

Wordsworth's depiction of poetry as the triumph of love and nurture, and as, therefore, a supreme manifestation of the good he sees in nature, is extensive throughout the poem. While, in an essential sense, natural love is tied to the image of the nursing mother, the numerous images of nurture within the poem establish the mother as the paradigm for but not the exclusive source of human love and productivity. In learning the capacity for love and trust through maternal influences (in Wordsworth's outflowing vision, not necessarily limited to biological mothers or even women), both men and women are motivated to share that love and trust with others, and thus share in the production of human life. Notwithstanding those critics who insist that Wordsworth takes possession of (i.e., appropriates) the feminine and hoards it for his own purposes, his discovery is a developmentally accurate one: as Schapiro rightly points out, Wordsworth identifies maternal love as the source of the filial bond, and thus of all the love in the world.[35]

It is of no small significance, then, that Wordsworth, after describing the "female softness" of the achieved poet, once again turns to and addresses Dorothy:

> Child of my Parents, sister of my soul!
> Elsewhere have strains of gratitude been breath'd
> To thee for all the early tenderness
> Which I from thee imbibed. And true it is
> That later seasons owed to thee no less;
> For, spite of thy sweet influence and the touch
> Of other kindred hands that open'd out
> The springs of tender thought in infancy;
> And spite of all which singly I had watch'd
> Of elegance, and each minuter charm
> In nature or in life, still to the last,
> Even to the very going out of youth,
> The period which our Story now hath reach'd,
> I too exclusively esteem'd that love,
> And sought that beauty, which, as Milton sings,
> Hath terror in it. Thou didst soften down
> This over sternness: but for thee, sweet Friend,
> My soul, too reckless of mild grace, had been
> Far longer what by Nature it was framed,
> Longer retain'd its countenance severe,
> A rock with torrents roaring, with the clouds
> Familiar, and a favorite of the Stars:
> But thou didst plant its crevices with flowers,
> Hang it with shrubs that twinkle in the breeze,
> And teach the little birds to build their nests
> And warble in its chambers. At a time
> When Nature, destined to remain so long
> Foremost in my affections, had fallen back
> Into a second place, well pleased to be
> A Hand-maid to a nobler than herself,
> When every day brought with it some new sense
> Of exquisite regard for common things,

And all the earth was budding with these gifts
Of more refined humanity, thy breath,
Dear Sister, was a kind of gentler spring
That went before my steps.

(XIII. 211–46)

This passage adds to and embellishes the poet's address to Dorothy in the final verse paragraph of "Tintern Abbey." Whereas in "Tintern Abbey" Wordsworth predicts the continuation of his own existence through the insight that Dorothy, and others after her, will replace him by repeating the process of life-in-nature, in this passage Dorothy is recognized as one source of love and nurture for Wordsworth, and thus one source of his poetic ability. The gentler spring of Dorothy's breath links her with the gentle breeze of Book I, an image of inspiration for the entire poem (I. 1-4). By contrast, Wordsworth's description of his untamed soul as "a rock with torrents roaring" connects his psychological state with the scene in the Ravine of Gondo. Like that scene, which is placed on a continuum with scenes that echo and modify it, the figurative torrent of the mind is recontextualized within a broader view of the continuities of reality through Dorothy's nurturing influence. Just as Wordsworth has come to see, on top of Snowdon, that all aspects of nature participate in a larger whole, he identifies here, through analogy to the natural scene, a picture of humanity that transcends individual states of mind and being. And if the torrential impact of the sublime breaks up received concepts and is therefore crucial to an expanding vision, Wordsworth insists nonetheless that such states of mind are not only meaningless but clearly destructive outside of "exquisite regard for common things," our affectional link to the simple beauties of nature whose source in human life is the mutual responsiveness of mother and child and the pervading influence of that relationship.[36]

Wordsworth's final address to Coleridge, then, specifically draws the form and purpose of *The Prelude* into a fluid relationship with nature: that address, and implicitly the entire poem, grows out of the experience of human nurture and is a dramatic reenactment of the love the poet has learned. The capacity for nurture, nascent in the dependency of "the infant babe" in Book II, develops through the mutually compatible influences of the face of physical nature and the ministerings of an ever-expanding circle of human influences: the poet's mother, Ann Tyson, Dorothy, and Coleridge himself (II. 237). And the uniquely human ability to write poetry profoundly extends the magnitude of nature's benign influences, for it includes the readers within the circle of influence that Wordsworth has enacted and described. As Haney notes, readers share in this exemplary relationship and will reproduce it in "future ethical acts of love."[37] It is from this perspective that Wordsworth makes his final address to Coleridge in the concluding verse paragraph of the poem:

> Prophets of Nature, we to them speak
> A lasting inspiration, sanctified
> By reason and by truth: what we have loved
> Others will love, and we may teach them how,
> Instruct them how the mind of man becomes
> A thousand times more beautiful than the earth
> On which he dwells, above this Frame of things
> (Which 'mid all revolutions in the hopes
> And fears of men doth still remain unchanged)
> In beauty exalted, as it is itself
> Of substance and of fabric more divine.
>
> (XIII. 442–52)

Here, Wordsworth does not offer a view of the human mind and imagination released from the bonds of nature or from what we all most fear in it, our individual mortality. Those who will articulate human love through poetry are Prophets of Nature whose conscious knowledge, whose intellectual love, enables them to know that man's earthly dwelling place does not define the limits of nature. In their ability to know the benign influence of human love and generosity, such minds become more beautiful than the insentient face of the earth because, in producing poetry, they purposely create, and, in adding to human life, they contribute to the quantity of life within the universe.

Ultimately, then, to the very great extent to which Wordsworth deemphasizes transcendent experience and redistributes it within the terms of his experience in the known natural world, *The Prelude* is more secular than "Tintern Abbey." Whereas the initial passages in "Tintern Abbey" reveal a yearning for a poetic structure that would potentially replace institutional structures, *The Prelude* offers the pattern of human development and experience as the only known or knowable structure within existence. The sublime ability to see the unity of the universe emerges paradoxically from the ontological insecurity that organized religion seeks to alleviate. In the final book of the poem, therefore, it is not surprising that Wordsworth both reaffirms his naturalistic monism, in which loving the universe means loving not only one's own death, but also the innumerable losses inherent in the process of living, and reasserts an orthodox conception of "God and Man divided, as they ought / Between them the great

system of the world / Where Man is sphered, and which God ani-
mates" (XIII. 266–68). If the weight of belief falls toward nature
for the time being, Wordsworth's insistence on an orthodox frame
of reference hints at the eventual burdensomeness of naturalistic
monism.[38]

4

Too Much Liberty: The Sonnet and the Recompense of Institutions

Nuns fret not at their convent's narrow room;
And hermits are contented with their cells;
And students with their pensive citadels;
Maids at the wheel, the weaver at his loom,
Sit blithe and happy; bees that soar for bloom,
High as the highest Peak of Furness-fells,
Will murmur by the hour in foxglove bells:
In truth the prison, into which we doom
Ourselves, no prison is, and hence for me,
In sundry moods, 'twas pastime to be bound
Within the Sonnet's scanty plot of ground;
Pleased if some Souls (for such their needs must be)
Who have felt the weight of too much liberty,
Should find brief solace here, as I have found.
   —William Wordsworth, *Poems, in Two Volumes*

WHAT WORDSWORTH DISCOVERED IN HIS EXPLORATIONS OF SPIRIT-
ual experience in both "Tintern Abbey" and *The Prelude* was, in fact,
knowledge purchased at the price of one kind of power, perhaps the
most important kind from the human point of view: the power conse-
quent upon a systematic explanation of reality that delineates a secure
and purposive place for the individual within the universe. In contrast
to the certainties provided by stable belief systems, Wordsworth's
intuitive discovery of the magnitude and priority of nature presupposes the ontological insecurity of human beings, even while offering
them a clearer view of their own exceptional status, constituted in
the capacity for conscious awareness of their position in nature and
in their capacity for creation.

 The greatest irony is that Wordsworth's discovery of the priority
of nature begins in the desire to affirm the integrity of private experience and thus establish psychic wholeness, but leads toward a knowledge of reality that minimizes the claims of the individual; further, in

suggesting that alternation between the contradictory claims of the individual and those of generalized life is the inevitable mode our existence, Wordsworth's knowledge of the priority of nature presup' poses the very self-division that it initially set out to solve. The theory of the Preface, which describes poetry as spontaneous "feeling" pro' duced by the unification of affect and intellect, is perhaps more a theory of personal salvation than of writing; in putting this theory into practice, what Wordsworth discovers is that the psychic divisions attending a modern awareness of the world supersede the simple cate' gories of affect versus intellect. That is, the expansive, mystical or quasi-mystical experience of life, which consists in a lack of conscious' ness of self and in complete well-being, conflicts with the heightened insecurity and need for self-protection based in a reinforced knowledge of the *essential* changefulness of human existence.

The capacity to maintain the tension between the two perspectives inherent in Wordsworth's naturalistic monism, between the demands of the self and the recognition that such demands are ultimately insig' nificant, depends to a certain extent on an individual's temperament as well as on the degree to which that individual's personal security is threatened and challenged. The single fact that Wordsworth was ahead of his time in intuiting that our continuity with nature breaks apart the relative facility with which individuals establish their identi' ties against and within institutional belief is explanation enough for his later renunciation of this profound perception; in the nearly two hundred years since Wordsworth wrote *The Prelude*, developments in the natural sciences have led not to a general acceptance of the priority of nature either in the academy or among the general popula' tion but to stridently irrational forms of denial. In the humanities and social sciences today, the discourse of radical constructivism has be' come so pervasive that reference to the natural parameters of our constructions has all but disappeared; certainly, there is scant interest in the difficult question of what actions and decisions may not be subject to choice.[1] Given that our need for survival militates against this sort of self-understanding, it is perhaps a wonder that humankind has ever grasped the priority of nature at all.

For Wordsworth, the pressures against maintaining this vision were far more substantial than the simple fact that his discovery was, given its ruinous nature, eternally premature: both his professional and per' sonal security were subject to a repeated series of tests that were unendurable on any terms. Exposed to outright ridicule at the hands of reviewers, Wordsworth was to retreat into a defensive posture that became increasingly self-righteous in tone. Commenting on *The White Doe of Rylstone*, Kristine Dugas remarks:

Certainly the openly derisive reception accorded the informal reading of *The White Doe,* along with a less than enthusiastic response to other poems Wordsworth thought highly of—such as the 1807 volumes, *Peter Bell,* and *Benjamin the Waggoner*—confirmed his insistence on the increasingly hortatory, often meditative-religious bent to his poetry evidenced in some of these works, in *The Excursion,* and in many of the later revisions of *The Prelude.* It was as if, goaded by the poor reception of poem after poem, Wordsworth had been pushed toward defining, even limiting, his objectives. He insisted on valuing what he found devalued, even to the exclusion of a range of previous concerns.[2]

Often taken as an index of Wordsworth's self-satisfaction, the poet's increasing insistence on the high office of the poet bears the marks of too much protestation, of a fight to maintain the image of his professional integrity amidst growing self-doubt. This seems especially true given Wordsworth's simultaneous, contrary tendency to renounce all that had led to or constituted that ridiculed vision: the self's interaction with the world as the basis of meaning and knowledge; the priority of nature; and the epistemological implications of creativity manifested in language. Paradoxical as it may seem, the poet's hortatory self-presentation is consistent with the attempt to democratize poetry out of existence, for both find their source in a reinvigorated control of individual emotion and response.

Moreover, Wordsworth's lack of confidence in himself and in his vision can only have been exacerbated by the continuous—even relentless—series of deep personal losses that he experienced. If nature was a source of recompense for the child who lost both his parents at an early age, it was less so for the adult poet in the process of completing *The Prelude,* whose sense of achievement was utterly overshadowed by his brother John's recent death. Indeed, it seems hardly an exaggeration to suggest that the deaths of Wordsworth's children Catherine and Thomas in 1812 cynically mirrored the deaths of his parents, cutting the poet off from both the primary source and the outward flow of nurture that was central to his vision. At some point he must surely have felt unjustly mocked by the creative force of the universe to which he had paid such full tribute.

From *The Excursion* onward, Wordsworth was to move progressively away from personal expression and from the flexibilities of blank verse, seeking to contain the self within institutional forms, both social and aesthetic, and to thus realize a norm of Englishness.[3] The sonnet that serves as an epigraph for this chapter appeared in *Poems, in Two Volumes,* published in 1807, and its composition is thus roughly contemporaneous with the writing of *The Prelude.* This small poem encapsulates every aspect of the humility that stood as the perpetual

counterpart to the heroic endeavor to compose a philosophical master-
work, and in so doing defines the tendency away from statement—
perhaps, away from language itself—toward which Wordsworth anx-
iously strives in *The Prelude*. Like the cells, rooms, and citadels of
nuns, hermits, and students, the defined contours of the sonnet enable
productivity and beget contentment. Like these figures, the poet, far
from seeking answers to questions of universal scope, participates in
a modest and circumscribed labor which has, by turns, a devotional,
educational, or economic purpose. Yet the sonnet is at once the safe
and secure haven within which the poet can reflect on a single theme
and an emblem of imprisonment or burial, a scanty plot of ground; in
imposing strict limits, it both enables and deadens. In fact, the light
and contented mood of this particular sonnet derives from Wordsworth's recognition that the solace of the form depends on a prior
experience of greater excursiveness, that the perception of the salutary
effects of aesthetic restriction only arises where the threat of aesthetic
formlessness has occurred. Thus the seemingly idyllic images of the
first few lines are a product of the poet's anxiety over unwonted
freedom, whereas perpetual containment within a delimited physical
space or prescribed aesthetic form is akin to imprisonment or inter-
ment. Given that Wordsworth was to work more and more inten-
sively in the form as the years progressed, this early sonnet anticipates
an artistic death wish in its acknowledgment that persistently narrow
parameters reduce the quantity and quality of human life.[4]

Wordsworth, however, was to complete *The Excursion* before aban-
doning blank verse for experimentation with the sonnet cycle. In completing the poem, Wordsworth avoided studiously the self-exploratory
mode of *The Prelude*, a mode to which he had been unwillingly drawn
in the first place. Instead, he strove for an objective voice and, as a
result, produced what Laura Dabundo calls a piece of "literary jour-
nalism," a poem in which the viewpoint of the first-person poet-
narrator is conspicuously absent.[5] Wordsworth removes both the self
and the radical conception of nature from the poem, thus avoiding
the epistemological dynamic that is the generative principle of *The
Prelude*. The absence, in fact, of an encompassing narrative point of
view is one of the most interesting features of a poem comprised of a
series of narratives, particularly since these tales reflect differently on
the human capacity to survive and generate meaning within existence.

Considered for its religious perspective, *The Excursion* is an odd
poem indeed, and Gill is right to suggest that it is an exploration of
faith rather than a confession thereof.[6] Since the Pastor emerges as
the key authority in the second half of the poem, conceptual logic
suggests that "[t]he parsonage is in effect the institutional renovation

of all *The Recluse*'s ruined cottages and completes a frame around the graveyard stories by presenting an idealized place to match Book V's ideal person, the Pastor," presumably providing recognition and redemption of human sorrow and suffering.[7] Yet this conceptual logic is not borne out in the details of the poem, for what Wordsworth most particularizes are the many scenes of human suffering, a suffering which seems to far outweigh any explanation or justification the Pastor might give. In a hesitant attempt to demonstrate that human suffering and limitation are transcended by Christian faith, Wordsworth reveals, perhaps unwittingly, how the impersonality of organized religion constitutes its fundamental inadequacy. The poem, indeed, seems ethically and philosophically split between, on the one hand, the recognition that there is no justification or compensation for the sufferings of humble people, irrespective of whether the causes are social or natural, and, on the other, an antihumanist need to assert a transcendent order whose magnitude renders such human sorrows insignificant.

Since, therefore, not only individual experience of an extraordinary kind, but the particulars of the most mundane and common individual lives, tend to highlight the inadequacy of and therefore subsequently erode orthodox frameworks, Wordsworth would, in the *Ecclesiastical Sonnets* and other late poems, extend the renunciation of his poetical self to his ideal of the common individual. Through several drastic reductions and alterations—in the space devoted to humble lives, in the restriction of any single tale to the length of a sonnet, and in the creation of an impersonal, institutional voice—Wordsworth ultimately controls the religious doubts arising from personal experience, both extraordinary and ordinary, by effectively canceling individualism.

Book I of *The Excursion* alone exemplifies the contradictory religious values and attitudes that Wordsworth never resolves within the poem and thus attests to a transitional phase between the poet's celebration of the interactive relationship of self and world and his late attempts to define the individual according to institutional norms. If "Tintern Abbey" describes experiences with significant correspondences to traditional mystical experience and if *The Prelude* suggests how this sort of experience leads to a belief in reality as a unified whole, *The Excursion* works, albeit ambivalently and inconsistently, toward aesthetic and institutional containment of such experiences. In this poem, Wordsworth never renders quasi-mystical or visionary experience from the individual perceiver's point of view, consequently eliminating the threat of subjectivism that haunts "Tintern Abbey."

The experiences are thus contained within and subordinated to the narrative purpose.

In Book I, the Poet describes the Wanderer's education in nature, suggesting the sort of mystical communion with outward forms attributed to Wordsworth himself in "Tintern Abbey." This passage, in fact, reads rather like a synopsis of Wordsworth's earlier poem:

> Such was the Boy—but for the growing Youth
> What soul was his, when, from the naked top
> Of some bold headland, he beheld the sun
> Rise up, and bathe the world in light! He looked—
> Ocean and earth, the solid frame of earth
> And ocean's liquid mass, in gladness lay
> Beneath him:—Far and wide the clouds were touched,
> And in their silent faces could he read
> Unutterable love. Sound needed none,
> Nor any voice of joy; his spirit drank
> The spectacle: sensation, soul, and form,
> All melted into him; they swallowed up
> His animal being; in them did he live,
> And by them did he live; they were his life.
> In such access of mind, in such high hour
> Of visitation from the living God,
> Thought was not; in enjoyment it expired.
> No thanks he breathed, he proffered no request;
> Rapt in silent communion that transcends
> The imperfect offices of prayer and praise,
> His mind was a thanksgiving to the power
> That made him; it was blessedness and love!
>
> (I. 197–218)

The scene the young Wanderer observes contains all the key elements of both the second quasi-mystical experience in "Tintern Abbey" and the monistic perception of reality achieved on top of Snowdon in *The Prelude*: the ocean, earth, and clouds are fused into a single entity by a sun that "[bathes] the world in light." And although lines 205–10 report rather than recreate the boy's experience of unity with the outward scene, the experience is clearly identical to the "sense sublime" of "Tintern Abbey"; "the spectacle," the outward scene, becomes indistinguishable from the boy, as he simultaneously takes in the scene and is taken in by it. Wordsworth is insistent on the identification of boy and physical nature, emphasizing the unity of inner spirit and outward forms by specifying that the boy's life was constituted by the natural world in which he lived.[8]

As in *The Prelude*, however, Wordsworth tempers the emotional-

ism of this experience and downplays its extraordinary nature, first
by having the Poet rather than the Wanderer himself relate the experience, and second by giving it neither the dynamic disjunctiveness of
the "Tintern Abbey" passage nor the descriptive specificity of the
Simplon Pass and Snowdon passages from *The Prelude*. Whereas in
"Tintern Abbey" and *The Prelude*, Wordsworth struggles to convey
the full intensity of this kind of experience, here he studiously avoids
techniques that will invite an emotional response that might detract
from the purpose of this description, which is presumably to define
the Wanderer's moral character and thus justify his status as the
object of the Poet's regard, the teller of Margaret's tale, and the guide
through the day's events. Wordsworth implicitly makes a connection
between the Wanderer's capacity for quasi-mystical experience and
his capacity to bring diverse and geographically dispersed people
into communion.

Additionally, while the Poet of *The Excursion* seems anxious to give
this experience an immediate theological explanation, his explanation
is not particularly orthodox. He identifies mystical experience as "visi-
tation for the living God," placing it within a Christian dualist framework; nature is not the infinite force of *The Prelude*, but the medium
through which God makes himself apparent to man. However, in the
final lines of this paragraph and the opening lines of the subsequent
one, the Poet emphasizes the superiority of such communion over both
ritual and sacred text. In the process, the intense emotion characteristic of religious faith is once again identified not with "the living God,"
but with nature. Asserting that the boy's experience "transcends /
The imperfect offices of prayer and praise," the poet suggests that the
traditionally central mediation provided by the church operates in
accord with human need rather than divine dispensation. His insistence on the imperfection of these institutions indicates an awareness
that they are humanly structured forms of mediation, not divinely
ordained entities.

Furthermore, in the following paragraph, the Poet asserts that the
Wanderer repeatedly experienced spiritual communion with nature
and identifies nature itself as the source of faith:

> A herdsman on the lonely mountain-tops,
> Such intercourse was his, and in this sort
> Was his existence oftentimes *possessed*.
> O then how beautiful, how bright, appeared
> The written promise! Early had he learned
> To reverence the volume that displays

> The mystery, the life that cannot die;
> But in the mountain did he *feel* his faith.
>
> (219–26)

Significantly, the Poet makes a distinction here between the boy's knowledge of and reverence for the Bible and his personal experience of faith, which takes place alone in nature. What challenges orthodoxy in this description of mystical communion is not the implication that such experiences can or might occur in the natural world rather than in a church (for as I explained in chapter 2, this is fully a part of orthodox Christianity) but that they *always* occur there. With religious emotion and spiritual communion continually assigned to nature—here as well as in "Tintern Abbey" and *The Prelude*—the mediatory function of the Word and of all those rituals which constitute it as a social practice is undercut, if not fully undermined. Moreover, what is particularly significant in these two passages is that, rather than describing how Christian tradition explains, illuminates, and reinforces the Wanderer's spiritual experience, Wordsworth is intent on differentiating an intellectual knowledge of religion, familiarity with Christianity's offices and central text, from an affective experience of heightened consciousness. In sum, the Poet's interpretation of the Wanderer's religiosity points toward no orthodox system of belief which provides psychic unity; on the contrary, it highlights a seemingly inevitable gulf between private experience and the capacity of institutional religions to explain, reinforce, or effect the psychic integration imperative for stable belief.

Furthermore, Wordsworth reinforces the suggestion that nature, in its capacity to elicit a deep emotional response, is superior to institutional religion:

> The Scottish Church, both on himself and those
> With whom from childhood he grew up, had held
> The strong hand of her purity; and still
> Had watched him with an unrelenting eye.
> This he remembered in his riper age
> With gratitude, and reverential thoughts.
> But by the native vigour of his mind,
> By his habitual wanderings out of doors,
> By loneliness, and goodness, and kind works,
> Whate'er, in docile childhood or in youth,
> He had imbibed of fear or darker thought
> Was melted all away; so true was this,
> That sometimes his religion seemed to me
> Self-taught, as of a dreamer in the woods;

Who to the model of his own pure heart
Shaped his belief, as grace divine inspired,
And human reason dictated by awe.

(397–413)

In fact, this passage implies that the Wanderer's ability to supersede
his Scots Calvinist upbringing with a self-taught naturalism makes
him superior in his sympathy for others, perhaps the quality for
Wordsworth most reflective of divinity. It is nature's ability to assuage
"fear or darker thought"—possibly itself the product of a Calvinist
upbringing, as "the strong hand of purity" and "the unrelenting eye"
seem to indicate—that makes the Wanderer exceptional. But while
the Poet's speculations here indicate that institutional religion offers a
fundamental basis for superior, self-fashioned religion, the Wanderer's
own words at the end of Book I directly contradict the Poet's implication of the insufficiency of religious institutions.

Discouraging the Poet from brooding morbidly on the tale of Margaret, the Wanderer exclaims:

"My friend! enough to sorrow you have given,
The purposes of wisdom ask no more:
Nor more would she have craved as due to One
Who, in her worst distress, had ofttimes felt
The unbounded might of prayer; and learned, with soul
Fixed on the Cross, that consolation springs,
From sources deeper far than deepest pain,
For the meek Sufferer."

(I. 932–39)

One could conceivably argue that these remarks of the Wanderer's
both offer a religious perspective from within which Margaret's suffering is redeemed and correct the Poet's earlier imputation that the
Wanderer's natural religion is purer and superior to institutional religion, but such an explanation would be problematic on both counts.
First, what Margaret's tale most impresses upon the reader is that
absolutely nothing could alleviate the pain caused by separation from
her husband, a sense of loss so deep it destroys both her ability to
care for her child and her desire to live. If prayer has "unbounded
might," then, it is of a decidedly abstract and unpalatable kind. Second, the mere fact that the Poet himself does not comment upon the
Wanderer's Christian interpretation leaves these two perspectives in
tension. The irony, of course, is that while the Poet has specifically
sought the Wanderer and recorded the tale of Margaret because the
Wanderer's wisdom and spirituality surpass those taught by institu-

tions, the Wanderer's final statement about Margaret suggests that the institution of Christianity is the ultimate and profoundest resource.

The ambiguous status of institutional religion and of the medium of its creation and perpetuation, language, is paralleled by the ambiguous status and definition of the poet in *The Excursion*. In describing the Wanderer, the Poet calls him a poet, iterating a distinction Words-worth makes in *The Prelude* between natural poets, men sympatheti-cally responsive to the universe, and actual poets, those who render their responses in verse:

> Oh! many are the Poets that are sown
> By Nature; men endowed with highest gifts,
> The vision and the faculty divine;
> Yet wanting the accomplishment of verse,
> (Which, in the docile season of their youth,
> It was denied them to acquire, through lack
> Of culture and the inspiring aid of books,
> Or haply by a temper too severe,
> Or a nice backwardness afraid of shame)
> Nor having e'er, as life advanced, been led
> By circumstance to take unto the height
> The measure of themselves, these favoured Beings,
> All but a scattered few, live out their time,
> Husbanding that which they possess within,
> And go to the grave unthought of. Strongest minds
> Are often those of whom the noisy world
> Hears least; else surely this Man had not left
> His graces unrevealed and unproclaimed.
>
> (77–94)

This passage simultaneously suggests that it is the duty of visionary folk to write verse and that those prone to vision are least likely to have the training and skill to be poets. In having the Poet address a less than self-evident question—Why doesn't the Wanderer write his own story?—Wordsworth once again implicitly assumes that poetry can operate as a medium through which private vision becomes public experience. Yet the distinction between the man of "inward light," the Wanderer, and the humble scribe, the Poet, dramatizes the diffi-culty of rendering profound experience in literary language. Describ-ing his own task, the Poet says:

> And some small portion of his eloquent speech,
> And something that may serve to set in view
> The feeling pleasures of his loneliness,
> His observations, and the thoughts his mind

Had dealt with—I will record in verse;
Which, if with truth it correspond, and sink
Or rise as venerable Nature leads,
The high and tender Muses shall accept
With gracious smile, deliberately pleased,
And listening Time reward with sacred praise.

(98–106)

The Poet's description of his own task is extremely tentative and his expectation of success not particularly high; at best, he hopes to cap-ture a "small portion" of the Wanderer's wisdom and eloquence. *If* he captures truth, his verse will be acknowledged with the highest possible reward, of course, but what the phraseology here stresses is the conditional and unpredictable nature of poetic achievement. Wordsworth places a double emphasis on the difficulty of poetic ex-pression: not only is the task of rendering experience and thought into literary language itself subject to uncertain results, but the people whose thoughts, in Wordsworth's view, are most suited to poetry are "those of whom the noisy world / Hears least," not being graced with literary accomplishments. Wordsworth's decision to separate the writer from the visionary distinguishes this later doubt regarding the efficacy of poetry from that in Book I of *The Prelude,* where the matter is simply one of finding a subject and getting started, not of the requisite poetical abilities being paradoxically divided between persons. Indeed, the fragmentation of literary ability is emblematic of Wordsworth's divided attitude toward poetry in *The Excursion;* in conferring experiences of vision on the Wanderer and in creating an essentially characterless narrator, the Poet, to write the Wanderer's story, Wordsworth partially renounces both vision and poetry.

Finally, it is the particularity of Margaret's grief, and of *The Excur-sion*'s many sufferers, which makes the poem's elements of Christian doctrine seem like rationalization rather than legitimate explanation. While Wordsworth's renunciation of his own experience as the sub-ject matter for poetry constitutes an attempt to reconcile individual with institutional values, his particularization of the lives and deaths of simple rural folk ultimately undermines any potential reconciliation, proving as threatening to institutional authority and doctrine as was personal experience in *The Prelude.* If *The Prelude* demonstrates how Wordsworth's personal experience conflicts with, indeed leads away from, institutional forms of explanation, *The Excursion* demonstrates, however unintentionally, the pervasiveness of the unresolvable ten-sion between individuals and institutions that is endemic to modern life and in so doing points precisely to the conflict Wordsworth was trying to resolve.

Wordsworth's recognition that stable belief rests not simply on self-renunciation, but on the renunciation of individualism per se, is embodied in *Ecclesiastical Sonnets*. Considered together, the handful of sonnets in the first person constitute a reconsideration and redefinition of individualism, ultimately replacing the visionary prophet of nature with the nunlike female as the new ideal of the individual. Additionally, in contrast to the particularized tales of humble country folk in *The Excursion,* numerous sonnets in this cycle focus on the exemplary status of figures from ecclesiastical history. Operating as exempla rather than individuals, these historical personages have identity only to the extent that it corresponds to their institutional function and aids in the perpetuation and improvement of Anglicanism.

Of those sonnets in the first person, the introductory sonnet is characteristic of Wordsworth in its focus on the teller and his qualifications. Yet in contrast to *The Prelude,* which opens with a self-conscious meditation on the poet's ability to tell the tale, this sonnet identifies the role that Wordsworth intends to adopt:

> I, who accompanied with faithful pace
> Cerulean Duddon from its cloud-fed spring,
> And loved with spirit ruled by his to sing
> Of mountain-quiet and boon nature's grace;
> I, who essayed the nobler Stream to trace
> Of Liberty, and smote the plausive string
> Till the checked torrent, proudly triumphing,
> Won for herself a lasting resting-place;
> Now seek upon the heights of Time the source
> Of a HOLY RIVER, on whose banks are found
> Sweet pastoral flowers, and laurels that have crowned
> Full oft the unworthy brow of lawless force;
> And, for delight of him who tracks its course,
> Immortal amaranth and palms abound.

(1.1)

Although the very first word of the sonnet insists on the person of the writer, it does so only to the extent that it identifies the speaker's faithfulness to his subject and accordingly justifies him as the chronicler of the spiritual history of his people. In fact, the sonnet stresses Wordsworth's fidelity to the subjects of his several sonnet cycles, which are linked by the trope of the river but are increasingly more ambitious in subject matter—having traced the River Duddon and the stream of liberty in previous cycles, he is now ready to chronicle

the holy river of Anglican history. Whereas in *The Prelude* Wordsworth immediately turns to developmental evidence to justify himself
as the poet, in this sonnet he offers faithfulness to his subject as the
primary evidence of his fitness to write an ecclesiastical and spiritual
history of the British people—in following the Duddon with "faithful
pace," he has been ruled by its spirit. And so faithful has he been in
tracing the course of liberty that he has aided the course of this figurative river, helping to unleash the "checked torrent." Likewise, the
highest tributes ("immortal amaranth and palms") are due to the poet
who submerges himself in the course of ecclesiastical history.

In her recent study of *Ecclesiastical Sonnets*, Anne L. Rylestone
says that the series effects a merger of the self with ecclesiastical
history such that "history becomes not only communal memory but
personal experience."[9] While I ultimately question the extent to
which Wordsworth succeeds in this endeavor, Rylestone's statement
describes how fully the poet has reversed his approach since *The
Prelude,* wherein through the memory of personal experience Wordsworth hopes to constitute communal memory and history. But both
the emphasis on and the denial of individual perspective reinforce the
overarching continuity of the difficult relationship of the individual
to social institutions, of which orthodox religions are perhaps the
most salient manifestation. In these sonnets, Wordsworth effectively
minimizes the conflict by describing individual identity as a by-
product of social institutions. The emphatic "I"'s of the first sonnet,
far from identifying the independent authority of the poet, demonstrate that he is virtually brought into existence by his social function.
In striking contrast to the Wordsworth of *The Prelude,* who celebrates
the mind's innate capacity to reconstruct reality, the poet of the *Ecclesiastical Sonnets* is a practiced cartographer, a tradesman who assumes
an objective reality to which he maintains an entirely dependent relation. Defining himself as a writer of sonnet cycles and thus implicitly
creating an identity distinct from the writer of philosophical blank
verse, the suppression rather than the assertion of self acts as a catalyst
for a quasi-historical meditation on public history.[10]

Indeed, considering the *Ecclesiastical Sonnets* in its entirety, the
poet's personal voice and his characteristic sympathy with his subjects
are most conspicuous for their absence. Although Wordsworth pe-
riodically resorts to the first person, this is predominantly a device for
dramatizing the merging or alignment of the self with history. For the
most part, however, Wordsworth's self-reference in these sonnets does
not have the intended dramatic effect and points rather awkwardly
to its own rhetorical function:

REDOUBTED King, of courage leonine,
I mark thee, Richard! urgent to equip
Thy warlike person with the staff and scrip;
I watch thee sailing o'er the midland brine;
In conquered Cyprus see thy Bride decline
Her blushing cheek, love-vows upon her lip,
And see love-emblems streaming from thy ship,
As thence she holds her way to Palestine.
My Song, a fearless homager, would attend
Thy thundering battle-axe as it cleaves the press
Of war, but duty summons her away
To tell—how, finding in the rash distress
Of those Enthusiasts a subservient friend,
To Giddier heights hath clomb the Papal sway.

                                                              (1.35)

As in the introductory sonnet, the poet, rather than merging with the history he relates, as Rylestone contends, is more accurately *constituted* through his reimagination and description of Richard I's journey to the Holy Land. Consistent with the introductory sonnet, this poem defines the poet in terms of his capacity for faithful observation; in his ability to fix his attention on Richard, to imagine accurately the ships "sailing o'er the midland brine," he paradoxically produces his song and establishes personal identity.

In general, the sonnets throughout the series which resort to the first person follow this pattern, suggesting that the poet is essentially created by his immersion in history. This is the case with "Eminent Reformers":

METHINKS that I could trip o'er heaviest soil,
Light as a buoyant bark from wave to wave,
Were mine the trusty staff that JEWEL gave
To youthful HOOKER, in familiar style
The gift exalting, and with playful smile:
For thus equipped, and bearing on his head
The Donor's farewell blessing, can he dread
Tempest, or length of way, or weight of toil?—
More sweet than odours caught by him who sails
Near spicy shores of Araby the blest,
A thousand times more exquisitely sweet,
The freight of holy feeling which we meet,
In thoughtful moments, wafted by the gales
From fields where good men walk, or bowers wherein they rest.

                                                              (2.39)

In imagining himself as Hooker, in fact, Wordsworth attains fuller identity through a more complete immersion in ecclesiastical history. If in the first sonnet he demonstrates his qualifications for tracing ecclesiastical history, and if in the sonnet on Richard I he traces the voyage of a specific figure, here he enhances that identification, no longer simply charting the stream of ecclesiastical history but now figuratively merged with it, envisioning himself "[l]ight as a buoyant bark from wave to wave." And whereas "Tintern Abbey" and *The Prelude* delineate the problematical relationship between extraordinary modes of consciousness and institutional forms of explanation, here reflection on the figures of religious history produces "[t]he freight of holy feeling." Just as, for the Wordsworth speaking in this poem, identity is fundamentally a void without religious history, holy feeling is nonexistent without the religious institution.

To this extent, then, the *Ecclesiastical Sonnets* shares the teleological function of conversion narrative, traditional religious meditation, and seventeenth-century meditative poetry: the series is structured to initiate and ultimately complete the identification of the poet and his readers with aspects of Christianity and finally with Christ. Yet two things differentiate the series from these traditional forms. First, rather than focusing on specific images, symbols, or beliefs, as is the case in meditative practice, Wordsworth focuses on historical personages and events. Second, while the series shares the psychosocial purpose of conversion, it does not, on the whole, dramatize the psychological dynamic of the conventional forms. Traditionally, those forms enact a struggle between doubt and faith, acknowledging the sufferings of the individual as a means of making personal and corporate identity compatible rather than mutually exclusive. Because Wordsworth comes into existence only through the progress of the sonnets, the process is not one of doubt into faith but of nothingness into nearly absolute identification with Anglican history. If the religion of the sonnets seems superficial, it is because, in not acknowledging the tension between individuals and their religious institutions, Wordsworth denies the inevitable difficulty of belief. The focus on history rather than the content of belief furthermore elides the struggle, defining religion as a concrete historical process instead of a set of creeds and dogmas which theoretically embodies transcendent truths.

Although the overriding indication of the series is that the poet essentially comes into being through his meditation on ecclesiastical history, and consequently feels little or no conflict between personal experience and the desire for normative belief, a few sonnets do address the poet's struggle to move from private experience to institutional belief. Yet these sonnets represent a mere handful among the three-hundred-odd *Ecclesiastical Sonnets*. In each of these rare in-stances, furthermore, the private experience is contextualized and im-portantly qualified by the subsequent poem, which most frequently adopts the institutional voice and perspective and disciplines the doubts and desires that arise from personal experience. Since the son-net form lends itself to a concise, pictorial presentation of experiences and images, it discourages the fluid, speculative movement of creative thought characteristic of "Tintern Abbey" and *The Prelude*. Thus, while the qualification of individual experience in *The Prelude* leads to an expansive sense cf individual experience as an aspect of human participation in a shared reality, the cancellation of individual doubts and experiences in the *Ecclesiastical Sonnets* reveals the poet's need for the solace of conformity, for self-abnegation in his commitment to a fixed community. It is history's capacity to serve as proof of the persistence of human society, rather than any specifically Anglican or Christian doctrines, that fulfills this need.

Chief among the sonnets concerned with the relationship between private and institutional experience is a sequence of three poems in Part I which expresses Wordsworth's attraction to meditative with-drawal from the world and corrects the impulse to withdraw. Signifi-cantly, both the desire for withdrawal and the admonition of that desire are effected by the poet's identification with historical figures. In "Seclusion," the first of these sonnets, Wordsworth describes a Saxon king who has renounced his rule to become a monk:

> LANCE, shield, and sword relinquished—at his side
> A bead-roll, in his hand a clasped book,
> Or staff more harmless than a shepherd's crook,
> The war-worn Chieftain quits the world—to hide
> His thin autumnal locks where Monks abide
> In cloistered privacy. But not to dwell
> In soft repose he comes. Within his cell,
> Round the decaying trunk of human pride,
> At morn, and eve, and midnight's silent hour,
> Do penitential cogitations cling;
> Like ivy, round some ancient elm, they twine
> In grisly folds and strictures serpentine;
> Yet, while they strangle, a fair growth they bring,
> For recompense—their own perennial bower.
>
> (1.21)

The king's cloistered life is hardly the fruit of a miraculous conversion; like the withdrawal into nature of Yeats's King Goll, it results in a seemingly inevitable self-destruction that is the outgrowth a life of extremes. Having lived a life inextricably entwined with strife and war, he has been defined according to the evils that threaten to destroy the values of love, charity, and compassion that Wordsworth has come to identify with Christianity, and expedient forms of penitence are simply insufficient. Penitence is, in effect, necessarily relentless, strangling the remnants of the Saxon tyrant just as new vines strangle a dying tree. Thus, the king's withdrawal brings no healing solitude but a necessary self-immolation, one in which the annihilation of self identified with a destructive culture anticipates a "fair growth"—a new culture and a new mode of being.

This quietly unsentimental depiction of guilt and penitence is followed, paradoxically but appropriately, by a personal expression of longing for a secluded place in nature. Basing this next poem on the story of Fursa, who built monasteries but then chose to live as a hermit and gave up all association even with the monasteries themselves, Wordsworth implicitly associates Fursa's behavior with his personal longing for total withdrawal from worldly affairs as well as with the tendency of poetry itself to provide an unmerited fulfillment of this longing.[11] Through self-admonition, Wordsworth dramatizes the irresponsibility of certain modes of withdrawal, which are the product of misinterpretation and engage with an impossible desire to create an enclosure for the self only realizable in abstract form.

Here, the separation of the historical episode from the first-person meditation enacts the poet's failure of identification with the Saxon king, and in so doing represents the sole instance of failed interpretation and identification in the *Ecclesiastical Sonnets*:

> METHINKS that to some vacant hermitage
> My feet would rather turn—to some dry nook
> Scooped out of living rock, and near a brook
> Hurled down a mountain-cove from stage to stage,
> Yet tempering, for my sight, its bustling rage
> In the soft heaven of a translucent pool;
> Thence creeping under sylvan arches cool,
> Fit haunt of shapes whose glorious equipage
> Would elevate my dreams. A beechen bowl,
> A maple dish, my furniture should be;
> Crisp, yellow leaves my bed; the hooting owl
> My night-watch: nor should e'er the crested fowl
> From thorp or vill his matins sound for me,
> Tired of the world and all its industry.
>
> (1.22)

In contrast to the Saxon king's place of ceaseless penitential meditation, this idyllic natural scene is literally designed for (as well as designed by) daydreaming. Whereas nature in the previous sonnet symbolizes the difficult process of moral and spiritual change, here it is emblematic of the desires of the speaking poet, actually altering physically to complement his mood. Somehow, the scene of the poet's retreat, "[s]cooped out of living rock, and near a brook / Hurled down a mountain cove from stage to stage," will have all of the sublime force of *The Prelude*'s Ravine of Gondo, yet will adjust its force to his pastoral mood. And while the Saxon king of the previous sonnet, exhausted in his old age by both the world's unmitigated strife and his part in it, is driven into hiding both psychologically and physically, the poet is simply "[t]ired of the world and all its industry." As for Tennyson's Ulysses, it is the ceaselessness of mundane labor and responsibility in the modern world which makes the poet yearn for a route out of society; however, while Ulysses chooses to forego his social responsibilities for exactly the sort of heroic life that has driven the Saxon king into penitential isolation, the poet desires the other extreme, a carefully styled natural retreat. Despite the poet's apparent solitude, birds keep him company day and night, filling the woods with song and figurative prayer unknown to the Saxon king in his sleepless and guilty isolation. In addition, the nature that provides a warm home for the poet, delivering comfort and utility in the shape of a "beechen bowl" and a couch of leaves, starkly contrasts with the decaying and constricting force that invades human life in "Seclusion."

The contrast between the details of the poet's retreat and that of the Saxon king's ultimately identifies the "vacant hermitage" as an invented place, and in so doing provides a cautionary reminder against the tendency of poetry in general and the sonnet form in particular to invite inappropriate withdrawal. The capacity of this retreat to elevate the poet's dreams is, in fact, a product of imagining such a place rather than being in it, for what Wordsworth describes is neither a remembered nor a reimagined place but a scene only constituted in the poem itself, a representation of a purportedly natural retreat that lures the reader with its perfection.

Nature this seductive is always, in Wordsworth's poetry, a self-evident projection of the human desire for an unthreatening and eternally benign nature, and also, always, a recognition of both the importance and falsity of that desire. Expressive of a subtle but necessarily profound drive toward dominance, this sonnet demonstrates how the recognition of the inseparability of man and nature that Wordsworth depicted in *The Prelude* entails, in the anxiety and insecurity which are its inevitable concomitants, a constant longing to see nature as more human than it is. As David Ferry points out, this dynamic is repeatedly and self-reflexively enacted in *Poems, in Two Volumes*; here, however, the context of the poem insists that such dreaming is not only fantastical but also irresponsible.[12] Following "Seclusion" in the sonnet sequence and therefore demanding to be read against it, "Continued" is clearly not a simple continuation of the previous theme. Hardly based in imagining what isolation, penitence, and life in nature felt like to the Saxon king, it embodies the musing poet's own idea of a "vacant hermitage"; itself followed by "Reproof," the state of mind and the fantasy of retreat are overtly condemned. Wordsworth thus takes a decisively didactic stance toward a desire whose source he nonetheless fully understands.

While both "Seclusion" and "Continued" represent imperfect forms of retreat as well as imperfect attitudes toward the social realm, "Reproof" insists that privacy and social involvement, understood correctly, are interdependent. If the Saxon king's destructive mode of engagement in public life entails final years of crushing isolation, and if the poet's weariness in the face of constant change prompts a longing to withdraw into fantasy, Bede, embodying the figure of the "Sublime Recluse," represents a form of withdrawal that is by its nature social:

> BUT what if One, through grove or flowery mead,
> Indulging thus at will the creeping feet
> Of a voluptuous indolence, should meet
> Thy hovering Shade, O venerable Bede!
> The saint, the scholar, from a circle freed
> Of toil stupendous, in a hallowed seat
> Of learning, where thou heard'st the billows beat
> On a wild coast, rough monitors to feed
> Perpetual industry. Sublime Recluse!
> The recreant soul, that dares to shun the debt
> Imposed on human kind, must first forget
> Thy diligence, thy unrelaxing use
> Of a long life; and, in the hour of death,
> The last dear service of thy passing breath!
>
> (1.23)

Both the Saxon king's and the poet's withdrawal begin and end with the interests of self; notwithstanding the differences between penitential cogitation and dreaming, Wordsworth classifies these modes of retreat as two sides of the same coin. By contrast, Bede's retreat constitutes a higher mode of social engagement.[13] Removed from the "toil stupendous" and "perpetual industry" of the everyday world, Bede becomes the reclusive scholar whose body of work gives back to the world the knowledge he garners from private meditation. If Bede is the "Sublime Recluse," the Saxon king is a lost cause and the poet is a "recreant soul"; neither can envision privacy as a mode of service to the social realm.

This sequence of three sonnets thus dramatically demonstrates the proper form of relationship between the individual and historical figures as well as the proper use of poetry. As such, it implicitly revises Wordsworth's previous theories of poetry, providing a corrective whose self-reflexivity is signaled in the use of the first person, an "I" who simultaneously both is and is not Wordsworth. The Saxon king does not in any sense embody Wordsworth's ideal Christianity, but instead represents progress toward that ideal; moreover, in depicting how the poet-speaker misconstrues what he himself describes—the tangled growth becomes a pastoral enclosure in the poet's subsequent reverie—Wordsworth acknowledges the tendency to project selfish desires onto both nature and history. The personal first-person voice likewise connects the poet himself with the tendency to romanticize available historical lessons and in the process connects the misuse of imagination with solipsism and escapism. To put this in the context of Wordsworth's own metaphors for the sonnet form, the scanty plot of ground that comprises the poet's pastoral enclosure is in fact a prison or gravesite rather than the modest and fitting enclosure of the nun or hermit because it is based in a willful misreading of the Saxon king's story. Unlike Bede, the Saxon king is not a figure to emulate, and the attempt to find an exemplary life in his leads further into isolation rather than toward communion. While the poet can produce a fuller understanding of history through creating, both for himself and his readers, imaginative participation in it, he also runs the risk of improper construction, of shedding a redeeming light on an individual life that cannot, in fact, be fully redeemed. By contrast, identification with an exemplary person like Bede leads toward a correct understanding of the relationship between solitude and communion as well as between the individual and religious history.

The self-reflexiveness of these three sonnets is reinforced by the fact that Bede's *Ecclesiastical History* served as an important source for the *Ecclesiastical Sonnets,* as Wordsworth acknowledges in the title of the sonnet series. The poet who writes with an honest eye on history here replaces the meditative poet of nature, and the authority of history and of its exemplary figures replaces that of the poet. Poetry does not supersede but rather supplements factual knowledge, and the ecclesiast replaces the poet as the exemplary Wordsworthian personage. Properly shaped and understood, then, the sonnet's modest and contained form is a poetic embodiment, on a lesser scale, of Bede's cell, an emblem of the containment and withdrawal tied to self-renunciation and necessary for social devotion of a higher order.

Significantly, while the poet's identification with the figure of Bede, and with other major figures of religious history, seems largely rhetorical, suggesting total self-abnegation in the face of incontrovertible authority, identification on a more personal level occurs with humble figures who are most frequently female. As the nunlike female becomes the emblem of the ideal poet, poetry joins the hierarchy of religious forms of discourse, and the poet replicates Bede's cloistered existence on a more modest scale.

Among the handful of first-person sonnets in the entire series is one that describes an actual vision that Wordsworth had of his daughter Dora. It is important within the series as a whole because it represents the sole instance of anything resembling religious vision, and in this describes a markedly different experience than those of "Tintern Abbey," *The Prelude,* and *The Excursion:*

> I SAW the figure of a lovely Maid
> Seated alone beneath a darksome tree,
> Whose fondly-overhanging canopy
> Set off her brightness with a pleasing shade.
> No Spirit was she; *that* my heart betrayed,
> For she was one I loved exceedingly;
> But while I gazed in tender reverie
> (Or was it sleep that with my Fancy played?)
> The bright corporeal presence—form and face—
> Remaining still distinct grew thin and rare,
> Like sunny mist;—at length the golden hair,
> Shape, limbs, and heavenly features, keeping pace
> Each with the other in a lingering race
> Of dissolution, melted into air.
>
> (3.1)

In contrast to the mystical or quasi-mystical experiences described in "Tintern Abbey," *The Prelude,* and *The Excursion,* this experience resembles, to some extent, the lower-order religious experience of visions and voices. Whereas the genesis of Wordsworth's poetic conception of the episodes is more difficult to establish with regard to those earlier texts, this one is evidently the product of both autobiographical and literary influence. Wordsworth himself had this to say about the composition of the sonnet:

When I came to this part of the series, I had the dream described in this sonnet. The figure was that of my daughter, and the whole passed exactly as here represented. The sonnet was composed on the middle road leading from Grasmere to Ambleside: it was begun as I left the last house of the vale, and finished, word for word as it now stands, before I came in view of Rydal. I wish I could say the same of the five or six hundred I have written: most of them were frequently retouched in course of composition, and not a few, laboriously.[14]

Moreover, as Potts notes, Walton's *Book of Lives*, another source for Wordsworth in the composition of the sonnets, recounts similar types of experiences. What is in fact most notable about this experience of vision is its extreme ordinariness; if "Tintern Abbey" shows the discrepancy between other modes of consciousness and workaday reflection while striving to establish a relationship between the two, and if *The Prelude* and *The Excursion* point to the functional significance of extraordinary consciousness, this sonnet shows vision and common perception to be *fundamentally* the same thing. The sonnet describes an experience that is neither distinctly religious nor unusual, but one that is more or less an integral part of human love. Unlike traditional religious visions, this one involves not unknown beings and dramatic actions, but an entirely familiar personage; here, instead of seeing the potentially illusory as real, Wordsworth imagines his living and beloved daughter as a dissolving illusion. While traditional visions frequently foreshadow the apocalypse and the second coming, this one anticipates the most inevitable of events, a human death. Far from reminding Wordsworth of a universe that extends beyond the self, this vision embodies the impermanence of human existence, and in so doing reinforces the dependent relationship of love and mutability.

Whereas both the language and the effects of extraordinary experiences in the other texts I have discussed associate them with religious forms of experience, this sonnet contains very little specifically religious language, and its ultimate effect, in the sonnet that follows, is to connect the poet not with God or nature, but with his nation. It is therefore more accurately a moment of insight rather than a religious experience. Wordsworth imagines Dora as he must have seen her many times, sitting beneath a tree whose shade sets off her beauty. Moreover, Wordsworth specifically asserts her human rather than spiritual reality, a fact of which he was fully conscious at the time of the dream itself. And whereas the "presence" of "Tintern Abbey" is a ubiquitous power, a motion and a spirit, in which matter and spirit coinhere, in this sonnet it is simply the living Dora. Thus one of Wordsworth's most reverential words is invoked to speak of what is manifestly this-worldly, the "bright *corporeal* presence" of another human being (my italics). Similarly, it is the poet's vivid imagining of Dora's face that makes her features "heavenly."

Like the sonnet that describes the poet's desire for withdrawal from the industrious world, this sonnet is followed by another that places it in a larger context and thus establishes its significance. But unlike the contemplation of idyllic withdrawal in "Continued," the move-ment in this sonnet from private perception to public reflection sug-gests the continuity and consistency of the two, as the personal image of mutability expands into a meditation on the mutability of nations:

> LAST night, without a voice, that Vision spake
> Fear to my Soul, and sadness which might seem
> Wholly dissevered from our present theme;
> Yet, my beloved Country! I partake
> Of kindred agitations for thy sake;
> Thou, too, dost visit oft my midnight dream;
> Thy glory meets me with the earliest beam
> Of light, which tells that Morning is awake.
> If aught impare thy beauty or destroy,
> Or but forebode destruction, I deplore
> With filial love the sad vicissitude;
> If thou has fallen, and righteous Heaven restore
> The prostrate, then my spring-time is renewed,
> And sorrow bartered for exceeding joy.
>
> (3.2)

The relationship between this sonnet and the vision of Dora indicates the extent to which this series of ecclesiastical poems is less religious in every sense—in both the personal and spiritual and the institutional and doctrinal—than "Tintern Abbey" and *The Prelude,* notwith-standing the knowledge and celebration of nature which emerge from these verses. For if the vision of Dora is both secular and ordinary, reinforcing the poet's awareness of mutability, the "kindred agitations" he experiences in the subsequent sonnet are for England itself, not Anglican Christianity. As Galperin points out, the sonnets celebrate the ameliorative nature of the English character rather than religious orthodoxy[15]; "Patriotic Sympathies" clarifies why that ameliorative character and the distinct form of Christianity compatible with it are subjects worthy of poetry. Since only the restoration of England will renew the poet's "spring-time," individual existence and identity are utterly dependent upon the state of the nation. Should England, dur-ing the upheavals of the Restoration which this section of the series relates, be destroyed, the premonition of the poet's vision is realized as the simultaneous dissolution of nation, poet, and daughter.

As the first poem in the third and final section of the series, the vision of Dora also invites comparison to the opening, hortatory son-

net of the entire series, and as a poem acknowledging personal experience, it invites comparison to the sonnet containing the pastoral
reverie. To a certain extent, this sonnet reinforces the poet's initial,
impersonal announcement of the accuracy of his observations by demonstrating how private reflection not only corresponds to but also
illuminates historical reflection. If the sonnet "Continued" indicates
a moment of delinquency, as the poet envisions a pastoral retreat and
desires to withdraw into it, the vision of Dora demonstrates, by contrast, the proper place of personal vision or reflection within public
history. Significantly, this appropriate form of vision involves not solitude but imagined human contact with one whom Wordsworth loves
perhaps better than himself; the counterpoint of the voice that merges
with history is a voice so aware of mutation and individual vulnerability that it dissolves in the image of the "lovely Maid," who embodies
both human frailty and the drive toward extreme renunciation that
is one result of an intense consciousness of mutability.

As in *The Prelude,* the capacity to imagine things larger than the
self—by turns nature, God, history, poetry—depends, to a degree,
upon either an insight into or an idea of the particular characteristics
of female existence. But while in *The Prelude* the identification of
various women with a maternal and nurturing function emphasizes
that woman is both source of and paradigm for human love and creativity, the modest "lovely Maid" of *Ecclesiastical Sonnets* connects
women with purity, self-renunciation, and mutability. Although on
superficial analysis this might seem to suggest the diminished significance of the female in Wordsworth's view, such an analysis would
overlook the fundamental continuity that Wordsworth describes between male and female existence, and the correspondingly intense
identification between himself and the female figures in his poetry.
Arguably, the figures in Wordsworth's poetry that stand as morally
and emotionally compelling role models for the poet himself are nearly
always female. Just as the nurturing sister of *The Prelude* both reflects
and is responsible for Wordsworth's own ability to produce that poem
and, in turn, thus nurture Coleridge, the daughter of the sonnet embodies an ideal of modesty and self-renunciation to which Wordsworth himself aspires. This later emphasis on female humility does
not contradict the poet's earlier conception of female nature but is in
fact its logical reduction, a reduction fully consistent with Wordsworth's diminished notion of poetry and the self and by no means
indicative of a pejorative view of actual woman. The constitutional
desire to nurture which Wordsworth recognizes in women and celebrates in *The Prelude* represents, at the time of writing that poem,
the perfect embodiment of personal fulfillment combined with self-

renunciation whose source is entirely natural. Consistent with the poet's general curtailment of nature in the late poetry, then, his identification of women with self-renunciation alone mirrors his personal attempt to reduce his own intense perception of the insecurity contingent upon mutability by constructing the paradoxical ideal of the self-denying individual.

My association of the "lovely Maid" with the consciousness of mutability and with a self-renunciation that Wordsworth tended to identify with women rests not only on the recurrence of this theme within the *Ecclesiastical Sonnets* but also on similar images that recur in various sonnets over the years.[16] Indeed, the sonnet stands out in this long series by virtue of its fidelity to a personal experience; as an unexpected confession of the depth of the poet's love, the fleeting image that he has no power to retain embodies his own vulnerability. The still picture of Dora recalls the initial image of "Nuns fret not," in which the nun's narrow room provides a protective enclosure, just as the "fondly-overhanging canopy" both shelters Dora and offsets her beauty. But this sonnet bears an even more distinct resemblance to one from the series *Memorials of a Tour of the Continent, 1820,* where the poet describes female forms in the waning light of Bruges:

> Bruges I saw attired with golden light
> (Streamed from the west) as with a robe of power:
> The splendour fled; and now the sunless hour,
> That, slowly making way for peaceful night,
> Best suits with fallen grandeur, to my sight
> Offers the beauty, the magnificence,
> And sober graces, left her for defence
> Against the injuries of time, the spite
> Of fortune, and the desolating storms
> Of future war. Advance not—spare to hide,
> O gentle Power of darkness! these mild hues;
> Obscure not these silent avenues
> Of stateliest architecture, where the Forms
> Of nun-like females, with soft motion, glide!
>
> (III. 165)

In contrast to the vision of Dora, which leads toward a deeper concerned expression for the mutability of human social orders, the Bruges sonnet progresses in the opposite direction, down the scale of mutable forms. Paradoxically, Bruges is most beautiful and magnificent in the waning light of day, for it is just this dying light that arouses the poet's fears about the future desolation of the city. Like the city itself, the beauty of the "nun-like females" inheres in their mutability, for notwithstanding the poet's plea, both architectural and human forms will be obliterated in the literal, if not the figurative, darkness of "future war." But it is the self-renunciatory aspect of the women, conveyed through their nunlike appearance and impalpable gliding, that counterbalances and finally cancels the apprehensions contingent upon the poet's knowledge of impermanence. If the vision of Dora seems, in its accuracy, so close to her real appearance that it is hardly a vision at all, the women in this sonnet, gliding silently through the streets of Bruges, seem more imagined than real. This recourse to the controlling dynamic of *The Prelude,* whereby the poet seeks to align ordinary and extraordinary experience in pursuit of an overarching vision, occurs here with a significant difference. No longer is the aim an all-encompassing perspective. As usual and unusual perception appear indistinguishable once again, Wordsworth depicts the shadowy and fleeting nature of human existence, finding in this evanescence its own transcendence.

This aspect of Wordsworth's late poetry, in which "vision" involves an intensified focus on a particular image or scene and no longer includes the drive to interpret the experience and fit it in a religious or philosophical context, is more characteristically a Keatsian rather than Wordsworthian mode of perception. As in "To Autumn," the perception of a warm and expansive beauty depends upon both the physical fact and the psychological acceptance of mutability. John Rudy comments that the Bruges sonnet, unlike other poems that relate extraordinary experience, embodies the extreme selflessness of Zen Buddhism, as the poet's individual consciousness is entirely merged with the scene.[17] To a certain extent, this quietistic contentment, which can be conveyed so perfectly through the sonnet form, is less in keeping with orthodox Christianity than Wordsworth's earlier depictions of mysticism and anticipates the aesthetics of symbolism and imagism. The vision of Dora, despite its inclusion in a series of ecclesiastical poems, also has something of this quality, in which the acceptance and even appreciation of mutability entails the poet's extreme self-renunciation, as his excessive love seemingly succumbs, like the vision itself, to the "lingering race / Of dissolution [melting] into air." In both poems, the poet renounces the claims of self in his ability to supersede fears of impermanence with a simple acceptance of its beauty and in so doing mirrors his own image of self-renunciation, the nunlike female.

In the *Ecclesiastical Sonnets,* then, heightened consciousness is transformed into an aesthetically and psychologically more manageable entity than the quasi-mystical experiences of "Tintern Abbey," *The Prelude,* and *The Excursion;* additionally, it plays a far less important part in the overall function of the work. As beautiful as the vision of Dora is, and as much of a welcome relief as the personal voice is from the more typical hortatory voice of the sonnets—an intentionally impersonal voice echoed and produced by history—the vision itself is relatively incidental to the series as a whole.

Predictably, the self-renunciation evident in Wordsworth's contracted presentation of vision as well as his decision to adopt a predominantly impersonal voice also entails a far more traditional view of nature than that of The Prelude. The initial sonnet of the series introduces, somewhat blatantly, the trope of the holy river, and in his not entirely consistent or skillful use of the river symbol throughout the series Wordsworth reestablishes the division between nature and humanity that he had shown to be a humanly constructed binary opposition in The Prelude. Although nature is not simply reduced to symbolic uses in the Ecclesiastical Sonnets, its other function as a force cooperative with the course of religious history places it nonetheless in a role subordinate to that history itself. Moreover, unlike The Prelude, where human development and creativity are themselves both testimony to and an actual expansion of nature, the Ecclesiastical Sonnets trace a positivistic course of history which entails a reduction in the significance of nature; as Rylestone points out, there is a shift in the third part of the series away from nature as a context for the church to "the church appropriating nature and some of nature's roles."[18]

Perhaps the most telling example of Wordsworth's attempt to contain nature within the purposes of the series is that discussed by Johnson in Wordsworth and the Sonnet, the revision of "Author's Voyage Down the Rhine (Thirty Years Ago)" from the Memorials.[19] In its description of the journey down the river, the original sonnet reveals how the configuration of the Rhine guides the experience of the travelers:

> The confidence of Youth our only Art,
> And Hope gay Pilot of the bold design,
> We saw the living Landscapes of the Rhine,
> Reach after reach, salute us and depart;
> Slow sink the Spires,—and up again they start!
> But who shall count the Towers as they recline
> O'er the dark steeps, or on the horizon line
> Striding, with shattered crests, the eye athwart?
> More touching still, more perfect was the pleasure,
> When hurrying forward till the slack'ning stream
> Spread like a spacious Mere, we could measure

> A smooth free course along the watery gleam,
> Think calmly on the past, and mark at leisure
> Features which else had vanished like a dream.

It is the qualities of leisure and unpredictability that lend the original experience, expressed in this early version of the poem, its distinct pleasure; in appropriating his own past experience and poetry to the quite different aims of the *Ecclesiastical Sonnets*, Wordsworth reduces the Rhine to an emblem of direction and purpose:

> DOWN a swift Stream, thus far, a bold design
> Have we pursued, with livelier stir of heart
> Than his who sees, borne forward by the Rhine,
> The living landscapes greet him, and depart;
> See spires fast sinking—up again they start!
> And strives the towers to number, that recline
> O'er the dark steeps, or on the horizon line
> Striding with shattered crests his eye athwart.
> So have we hurried on with troubled pleasure:
> Henceforth, as on the bosom of a stream
> That slackens, and spreads wide a watery gleam,
> We, nothing loth a lingering course to measure,
> May gather up our thoughts, and mark at leisure
> How widely spread the interests of our theme.
>
> (3.12)

Whereas the lack of human control over the river's movement becomes the chief source of pleasure in the initial sonnet, the stream of the second sonnet, as a metaphor for the poet's recreation of ecclesiastical history, and the new shape of the stream, "[t]hat slackens, and spreads wide a watery gleam," is entirely the creation of the poet. As Johnson points out, Wordsworth knew he needed a sonnet that would prepare the reader for the digressiveness of the later sonnets on liturgy and ecclesiastical architecture, but as he also suggests, the revised sonnet attests "in miniature [to] the failure of the ecclesiastical emblem and narrative to elicit statements which are comparable to the strength of sonnets written out of personal observation."[20] What this sonnet usefully demonstrates, however awkward its aesthetics, is that a dual tendency toward depersonalizing the personal and denaturalizing nature was required for the poet's goal of relating religious history.[21]

In those sonnets in which nature is not reduced to emblems and metaphors that embellish Wordsworth's historical account, it serves a cooperative but ultimately subservient function. For instance, in

"Dissolution of the Monasteries," nature is depicted as a force that engages with the course of ecclesiastical history:

> THREATS come which no submission may assuage,
> No sacrifice avert, no power dispute;
> The tapers shall be quenched, the belfries mute,
> And, 'mid their choirs unroofed by selfish rage
> The warbling wren shall find a leafy cage;
> The gadding bramble hang her purple fruit;
> And the green lizard and the gilded newt
> Lead unmolested lives, and die of age.
> The owl of evening and the woodland fox
> For their abode the shrines of Waltham choose:
> Proud Glastonbury can no more refuse
> To stoop her head before these desperate shocks—
> She whose high pomp displaced, as story tells,
> Arimathean Joseph's wattled cells.

(2.21)

This poem follows one entitled "Monastic Voluptuousness," which describes the bacchanalian festivities within the monasteries during the thirteenth and fourteenth centuries. As Rylestone notes, the image of the ruins overrun by nature is part of a "tendency toward healing," in which nature participates in the correction and amelioration of the clerical and monastic abuses related in the three preceding sonnets.[22] Far from representing a permanent decay of Christian values and institutions, then, the naturalized ruin symbolizes the end of a corrupt order and anticipates the birth of a new one. And just as the image of the Saxon king as a tree trunk entangled in vines foreshadows both natural and cultural renewal, nature's invasion of the monastery betokens the impermanence of human excess. Autocratic rule, abuse of power, violence, and immorality, all manifestations of the "deeper nature" Wordsworth speaks of in *The Prelude,* are ultimately susceptible to the unassuming force of regenerative nature, which reinhabits the abandoned monastery. The small woodland creatures— wren, lizard, newt, owl, fox—remind the reader of the peaceful contentment the monks have foregone in their pursuit of pleasure; like true recluses or hermits, these animals find a haven in a humble spot, and "[l]ead unmolested lives, and die of age." In this transitional phase, their minimal existences provide crucial evidence for the perpetuity of life amidst seeming desolation.

Hence, while nature cooperates with the onward course of Christianity, providing a vital continuity when culture and religion are in a state of decay and decline, it never threatens the positivist epistemology of the sonnets by asserting its priority over human culture or by replacing Anglican history as the series' praiseworthy subject. Its function, rather, is to ameliorate the transition from one phase of culture to the next. Wordsworth delineates the course of ecclesiastical history as a natural process whose progress and productions, in the shape of religious rites and architecture, constitute an improvement on nature. In this, Wordsworth reverts to the binaristic distinction between nature and culture characteristic of Enlightenment thought. It is the separation of human culture from the inevitable forces of nature, and not a particularly strong belief in Anglican dogma, that motivates even the later sonnets on liturgy and ecclesiastical architec' ture. The focus on history itself, in fact, which attests to the trans' formative nature of belief, militates against orthodoxy to some extent. Outside of values such as love, charity, and humility, certainly never exclusively Christian values, it is not so much the content or theologi' cal significance of beliefs that concerns Wordsworth but the perpetu' ity of human institutions and their related rites per se. For if an intense consciousness of mutability compels the poet to self-renunciation as a paradoxical mode of self-protection, institutions, as embodiments of human solidarity and as emblems of the perpetuity of human culture, guard against utter insignificance.

It is therefore hardly surprising that the sonnets on liturgy are as much concerned with mutability as with specific religious rites. Not added to the series until 1845, over twenty years after the composition of the original pieces, the sonnets on liturgy are generally interpreted as evidence of Wordsworth's increasing adherence to high church orthodoxy. While they no doubt attest to this tendency, they also demonstrate the extent to which Wordsworth's embrace of orthodoxy derived from his relentless awareness of mutability rather than any particular belief in Anglican creeds. Even on the evidence of these particular sonnets, then, the religion of the *Ecclesiastical Sonnets* is no less problematical than that of "Tintern Abbey" and *The Prelude,* although the poet's desire to submit to the institutional perspective is unequivocally stronger. But ultimately the sonnets on liturgy illustrate the same disjunction between the knowledge of relentless and unre' deemed loss taught by personal experience and the institutional rites that presumably allow the individual to place such losses in a larger context.

Several of the sonnets, in particularizing the loss of parents by chil' dren or vice versa—those very subjects that undermine Christian be' lief in *The Excursion*—threaten to undo the meaning of the liturgical rituals they purportedly endorse. In one of these poems, "Catechis' ing," Wordsworth describes one of his few memories of his mother:

From Little down to Least, in due degree,
Around the Pastor, each in new-wrought vest,
Each with a vernal posy at his breast,
We stood, a trembling, earnest Company!
With low soft murmur, like a distant bee,
Some spake, by thought-perplexing fears betrayed;
And some a bold unerring answer made:
How fluttered then thy anxious heart for me,
Beloved Mother! Thou whose happy hand
Had bound the flowers I wore, with faithful tie:
Sweet flowers! at whose inaudible command
Her countenance, phantom-like, doth re-appear:
O lost too early for the frequent tear,
And ill requited by this heartfelt sigh!

(3.22)

If nature in *The Prelude* offers evidence that human nurture is abun-
dant enough to alleviate the destitution of the young Wordsworth
after his mother's death, here the memory of catechism ameliorates,
however imperfectly, the poet's loss. It is his own anxious participation in the "trembling, earnest Company," his desire to perform satis-
factorily within a small community, that enshrines both the moment
and the image of his mother in his memory. Yet in its very demonstra-
tion of the significance of human community, this sonnet embodies
the fragility of human institutions; the children, novice members of
the religious community, answer tentatively and not always correctly,
and the last line of the sonnet is an overt statement that the loss the
incident evokes is permanently unredeemed.

This dynamic, in which there is a fragile balance between the continuity provided by the institutional occasion and a specific memory of
loss related to it, also occurs in "Confirmation Continued":

I SAW a Mother's eye intensely bent
Upon a Maiden trembling as she knelt;
In and for whom the pious Mother felt
Things that we judge of by a light too faint:
Tell, if ye may, some star-crowned Muse, or Saint!
Tell what rushed in, from what she was relieved—
Then, when her Child the hallowing touch received,
And such vibration through the Mother went
That tears burst forth amain. Did gleams appear?
Opened a vision of that blissful place
Where dwells a Sister-child? And was power given
Part of her lost One's glory back to trace

Even to this Rite? For thus *She* knelt, and, ere
The summer-leaf had faded, passed to heaven.

(3.24)

In spite of the assertion of the last line, this poem is hardly a triumphant declaration of the older daughter's ascent into heaven. Focusing
sympathetically on the mother, for whom the loss of the older child
can only have been keenly felt, and adopting the interrogative mode,
Wordsworth celebrates confirmation in a quintessentially ambivalent
fashion. The questions Wordsworth asks—"Did gleams appear? /
Opened a vision of that blissful place / Where dwells a Sister-
child?"—hopefully imagine that the mother's suffering is redeemed by
a glorious vision of her child's heavenly afterlife. But the questions
are not merely rhetorical, as the poet leaves it to "some star-crowned
Muse, or Saint" to reveal what the mother has seen. Given the hortatory tone of so many sonnets in the series, it is perhaps surprising that
Wordsworth questions rather than asserts the dead child's transcendence. Indeed, the tentative insistence of the poet's questions, like the
questions of "Tintern Abbey" and the speculative tone of large sections of *The Prelude,* constitutes a delicate plea that the poet's intuition be correct. For the repetition of the ceremony with another
daughter must also inevitably be a reminder of the loss of the first
child and, in keeping with this, would be likely to arouse the fear of
a repetition of that loss. Whatever continuity the ceremony involves,
and whatever joyous vision attends it, ultimately, it is the hard fact
of the girl's death that Wordsworth reserves for the last lines of the
sonnet, just as he catechizes his reader with his own "ill requited"
loss in the final line of "Catechising."

With few other exceptions, however, the other sonnets on liturgy
adopt the impersonal, hortatory voice that predominates throughout
the *Ecclesiastical Sonnets.* For example, "Sacrament," which directly
follows "Confirmation Continued," is perhaps intended to cancel the
painful ambivalences of the previous sonnet:

> BY chain yet stronger must the Soul be tied:
> One duty more, last stage of this ascent,
> Brings to thy food, mysterious Sacrament!
> The Offspring, haply at the Parent's side;
> But not till they, with all that do abide
> In Heaven, have lifted up their hearts to laud
> And magnify the glorious name of God,
> Fountain of Grace, whose Son for sinners died.
> Ye, who have duly weighed the summons, pause
> No longer; ye, whom to the saving rite

The Altar calls; come early under laws
That can secure for you a path of light
Through gloomiest shade; put on (nor dread its weight)
Armour divine, and conquer in your cause!

(3.25)

If the sonnet on Bede in section 1 effectively corrects the desire for a
pastoral retreat, this sonnet virtually shouts down the apprehensions
and pain of the preceding one. The commanding voice cannot cancel
mutability and human suffering, but it can strive to render them
irrelevant in the face of institutional imperatives. In contrast to the
pathetic tale of mother and daughters, this poem relates a generalized
and impersonal situation, in which the proximity of "offspring" to
parent accords with the ritual of communion. And whereas "Confirmation Continued" reflects upon the tenuous ability of ceremonial
ritual to ameliorate personal pain, this poem speaks out of righteous
indignation against those who delay their commitment to the church.

To a certain extent, the manifest inhumanity of "Sacrament" is
precisely its point; only in returning to the impersonal voice of authority can Wordsworth supersede sympathy and memory and with them
the fear of loss and religious doubt they necessarily entail. The replacement of human love with institutional commitment necessitates, finally, imaginative self-annihilation.

In "Mutability," the one acknowledged great poem of the entire
series and the final sonnet in the short series on liturgy, Wordsworth
speaks in neither the modest, self-renunciatory voice of the few sonnets reflective of personal emotions and events, nor in the predominant
self-annihilating hortatory voice of the series. Instead, the authority
of the voice in "Mutability" derives from its subject, the impersonality
of mutability itself:

FROM low to high doth dissolution climb,
And sink from high to low, along a scale
Of awful notes, whose concord shall not fail;
A musical but melancholy chime,
Which they can hear who meddle not with crime,
Nor avarice, nor over-anxious care.
Truth fails not; but her outward forms that bear
The longest date do melt like frosty rime,
That in the morning whitened hill and plain
And is no more; drop like the tower sublime
Of yesterday, which royally did wear
His crown of weeds, but could not even sustain

Some casual shout that broke the silent air,
Or the unimaginable touch of Time.

(3.34)

In this poem, Wordsworth transcends both the painful insecurity of
the individual perspective and the stridency of the institutional perspective in a moment of dignified poetic observation. In contrast to
that of the institutional perspective, the voice here is authoritative
rather than authoritarian, arising not from a desire to embrace normative values but from repeated confrontations with the fact of mutability itself. The depth of Wordsworth's recognition is reflected in what
is this time a sympathetically impersonal voice, for, in recognizing
mutability's ubiquitous reign, Wordsworth transcends personal pain
in an overarching awareness of death and dissolution as the quintes-
sential common experience. Far from being a burden to the reflective
individual, then, this consciousness of mutability is a gift to the good,
to those "who meddle not with crime / Nor avarice, nor over-anxious
care." It is precisely in our inability to sustain "the unimaginable touch
of Time" that we witness our very existence.

It is an odd conclusion to the sonnets on liturgy, notwithstanding
the concern with mutability that permeates the series, for "Mutability" suggests the irrelevance of the institutional voice. In calmly asserting that both natural and man-made forms—the snow on the hill
and the tower—are subject to decay, the sonnet apparently mocks the
pettiness of the bracing call to Anglicanism. Indeed, nowhere in the
sonnet does Wordsworth indicate that this saving insight results from
the forms of ritual awareness he has just been recommending to the
reader, nor does he imply that mortality is redeemed by a heavenly
afterlife.

If this poem stood as the final piece in the *Ecclesiastical Sonnets,* it
might effectively cancel the generative force of the entire series, the
desire to embrace religious history. But in fact, the last sonnet, "Conclusion," returns predictably to the river emblem introduced in the
beginning of the series, construing it as a sign of the eschatological
direction of Anglican history:

WHY sleeps the future, as a snake enrolled,
Coil within coil, at noon-tide? For the WORD
Yields, if with unpresumptuous faith explored,
Power at whose touch the sluggard shall unfold
His drowsy rings. Look forth!—that Stream behold,
THAT STREAM upon whose bosom we have passed
Floating at ease while nations have effaced
Nations, and Death has gathered to his fold

Long lines of mighty Kings—look forth, my Soul!
(Nor in this vision be thou slow to trust)
The living Waters, less and less by guilt
Stained and polluted, brightened as they roll,
Till they have reached the eternal City—built
For the perfected Spirits of the just!

(3.47)

If "Mutability" intimates that the appreciative awareness of life and
the feeling of belonging with the things of this world are constituted
in a knowledge of our mutual transience, this sonnet instructs us that
the stream of religious history transcends the knowledge of mutability.
Although death touches even the mightiest of monarchs and nations,
"[t]he living Waters" of the river, embodying our common and perpetual participation in history, represent a part of the ultimate immortality to which they lead, "the eternal City." In envisioning along with
the poet the ongoing course of ecclesiastical history, we travel toward
and anticipate the immortality beyond death.

The commanding, institutional voice of this sonnet, fraught with
imperatives and exclamation points, is finally irreconcilable with the
personal voice that only occasionally arises throughout the series.
Wordsworth's tentative expressions of personal feeling and experience
throughout the *Ecclesiastical Sonnets,* including the desire to withdraw into a pastoral retreat, the vision of Dora, the memory of his
mother, all signify the insufficiency of conformity and institutional
explanations, and are manifestations of the problematical nature of
Wordsworth's willed belief in the efficacy of ecclesiastical history.
The overriding impersonal voice attests to the extent that Wordsworth's faith is a product of psychic necessity and self-discipline rather
than of felt belief.

Wordsworth's desire to reform the self in accord with institutional
imperatives constitutes, like so much Victorian poetry to follow, a
denial of his awareness that belief is shaped in a dynamic relationship
between the individual and other realities, religious institutions and
nature perhaps the most salient among them. The drive to bury this
knowledge, which leads in romanticism to a strong awareness of the
human mind's creative role in institutional beliefs and structures, is
not without its own wisdom, because the capacity for absolute acceptance of institutional values lessens individual insecurity and so militates, in this respect at least, in favor of human survival. But it is also
a drive destined to failure for, as someone has said, once something is
known, it cannot be unknown, it can only be forgotten. Wordsworth's
profound insight into the priority of nature and the corresponding

insignificance of human beings and their institutions, so profoundly and thoroughly put forth in "Tintern Abbey" and *The Prelude,* is not an insight that can be easily unknown or forgotten, notwithstanding the fact that his own effort to do so included strenuous self-denial and a severely contracted notion of creativity. Having once intuited that, as a part of nature, our own culture represents not a transcen- dence of nature but our unique form of participation in it, Words- worth cannot claim the absolute truth of religious institutions without his assertions appearing rather suspect.

Played out in his poetry over the course of his career, Wordsworth's conflicted beliefs illustrate the profoundly human problem of adopting a naturalistic epistemology, and in so doing illuminate a psychological dilemma still central to our culture. Huizinga has this to say about modern ambivalence toward cultural forms:

> The nearer we come to our own times the more difficult it is to assess objectively the value of our cultural impulses. More and more doubts arise as to whether our occupations are pursued in play or in earnest, and with the doubt comes the uneasy feeling of hypocrisy, as though the only thing we can be certain of is make-believe. But we should remember that this precarious balance between seriousness and pretence is an unmistakable and integral part of culture as such, and that the play factor lies at the heart of all ritual and religion. So that we must always fall back on this lasting ambiguity, which only becomes really troublesome in cultural phe- nomena of a non-ritualistic kind ... insofar as Romanticism and kindred movements are divorced from ritual we shall inevitably, in our assessment of them, be assailed by the most vexing ambiguities.[23]

Latent in Wordsworth's knowledge of the priority of nature is a suspi- cion that religion, like poetry, derives not from God-given truths but from what Huizinga calls the "play-factor." And to apprehend that religion is created rather than given places it in competition with poetry: both represent strivings toward truth in the face of an underly- ing awareness that ultimate truths are not available to man.

Why not simply abandon the effort? Ironically, consciousness of truth's limited availability reinforces the insecurity that motivates man to discover truth in the first place. In its increasing agnosticism and atheism, literary culture continues to address art with a need whose depth art cannot supply. As one of the first to demonstrate that the vexing ambiguities we discover in our pragmatic approach to reality constitute a truth we are constitutionally unable to accept, Wordsworth is, as Bloom so preciently tells us, more modern than Pynchon, Beckett, Freud. If art seems to fail us, it is only because we ask too much of it, wanting simultaneously a reflection of reality and some transcendent consolation, in spite of our awareness that the two represent incompatible epistemologies.

Notes

Chapter 1. Transcendent Experience, Religious Orthodoxy, and the Mediations of Poetry

1. See Frederick Crews, "The Unknown Freud," *New York Review of Books* 40, no. 19 (1 November 1993), and the subsequent responses to Crews's attack: Crews et al., "The Unknown Freud: An Exchange," *New York Review of Books* 41, no. 3 (3 February 1994), and Thomas Nagel, "Freud's Permanent Revolution," *New York Review of Books* 41, no. 9 (12 May 1994). Also see Frederick Crews, *Skeptical Engagements* (Oxford: Oxford University Press, 1986).

2. See Nagel's defense of Freud, above. Though claiming that Freudian hypotheses are untestable because they rely on commonsense insight, Nagel misses the point that within the domain of psychology it is exactly those purportedly commonsensical perceptions—that is, perceptions signifying the commonality of human mental organization—which ought to be verifiable. See William James, *Pragmatism* (c. 1910; reprint, Cambridge and London: Harvard University Press, 1975), 75–76.

3. Crews, "The Unknown Freud: An Exchange," 43.

4. Daniel N. Stern, *The Interpersonal World of the Infant: A View from Psychoanalysis and Developmental Psychology* (New York: Basic Books, 1985).

5. Stern, *The Interpersonal World*, 26–28.

6. Barbara A. Schapiro, *The Romantic Mother: Narcissistic Patterns in Romantic Poetry* (Baltimore: Johns Hopkins University Press, 1983), 95.

7. Thus Schapiro's tendency, in *The Romantic Mother*, to read nature symbolically as the lost mother.

8. Joseph F. Byrnes, *The Psychology of Religion* (New York: Free Press, 1984).

9. Sigmund Freud, *Totem and Taboo*, trans. A. A. Brill (1912–13; reprint, New York: Moffat, Yard, and Company, 1920), 206.

10. See Donald E. Brown, *Human Universals* (Philadelphia: Temple University Press, 1991), 32–37 and 118–29. While competition between males is widespread, it appears manifestly not the case, in light of the studies of incest avoidance that Brown summarizes, that sons are competing for the sexual attentions *of their mothers*, as Freud imagined.

11. E. E. Evans-Pritchard, *Theories of Primitive Religion* (Oxford: Clarendon Press, 1965), 42.

12. Sigmund Freud, *Civilization and Its Discontents*, trans. and ed. James Strachey (1930; reprint, New York: W. W. Norton and Company, 1961), 19.

13. For a typical Freudian analysis of romanticism which identifies throughout romantic poetry a pattern of return to an undifferentiated, pre-Oedipal state, see Gerald B. Kauver, "The Psychological Structures of English Romantic Poetry," *The Psychoanalytic Review* 64, no. 1 (1977).

14. Sigmund Freud, *Moses and Monotheism*, trans. Katherine Jones (1939; reprint,

New York: Vintage, 1955); and Sigmund Freud, *The Future of an Illusion,* trans. W. D. Robson-Scott (1927; reprint, New York: Liveright, 1949).

15. Evans-Pritchard, *Theories of Primitive Religion,* 15.

16. Wayne Proudfoot offers a restrained defense of the Freudian hypothesis of religion in *Religious Experience* (Berkeley: University of California Press, 1985), addressing the claim of religion's defenders that Freud's view is reductive. Proudfoot suggests that this accusation is a protective strategy that rests on a failure to discriminate between descriptive reduction and explanatory reduction. In Proudfoot's words, "The analyst must cite, but need not endorse, the concepts, beliefs and judgments that enter into the subject's identification of his experience" (196). This seems a legitimate scientific discrimination, and yet in the particular case of Freud there was never even an attempt to satisfy the first phase of this analytic process, an accurate description of a subject's religious experience (or better yet, those of several subjects drawn from diverse populations and across the spectrum of mental health).

17. Here is a sample overview of some of the criticism of psychoanalysis across the disciplines:

William W. Meissner takes on the subject of Freud's views of religion at length in *Psychoanalysis and Religious Experience* (New Haven: Yale University Press, 1984). Meissner (in what seems to be standard form among psychoanalysts) first offers a psychoanalytic interpretation of Freud's personal reasons for a bias against religion, including Freud's ambivalence about his Jewishness. Meissner then criticizes Freud's tendency to see all behavior as a mode of repetition and, drawing on such practitioners as D. W. Winnicott and Erik Erikson, provides an overview of a developmental orientation within psychoanalysis that modifies Freud's assumptions about the dynamics of behavior and of religious experience. In support of this newer model, Meissner cites Robert Holt's criticism of the scientific premises of Freud's theories and George Klein's elaboration of the distinction between Freud's mechanistic metapsychology and his hermeneutic clinical theory.

Like Meissner, the folklorist David Hufford also looks specifically at the shortcomings of Freud's views of religion in "Ambiguity and the Rhetoric of Belief," *Keystone Folklore Quarterly* 21 (1976) and in his commentary to Genevieve Foster's *The World Was Flooded with Light* (Pittsburgh: University of Pittsburgh Press, 1985). Describing some of his own research on mystical experiences and demonic assaults, Hufford asserts that such experiences are not only far more common than is generally held, but also by no means less common among the mentally healthy than the disordered.

For a more general condemnation of Freud's theories, see Crews's *Skeptical Engagements* and "The Unknown Freud." Crews's work also provides an informed account of the challenges to Freudianism and responses from the psychoanalytic establishment.

18. Crews, *Skeptical Engagements,* 34.

19. See especially Richard Rorty, *Contingency, Irony, Solidarity* (New York: Cambridge University Press, 1989). While Rorty is a primary spokesperson for this view of knowledge, similar assumptions and attitudes underwrite the extreme constructivism of other poststructuralist positions. For a thorough critique of the notion that knowledge consists solely of culturally generated constructions, see the discussion of framework relativism in Paisley Livingston, *Literary Knowledge: Humanistic Inquiry and the Philosophy of Science* (Ithaca: Cornell University Press, 1988), 55–65.

20. Though evolutionary explanations are still erroneously equated with biological determinism and social Darwinism, the primary contemporary researchers in evolutionary psychology point out that choice or plasticity in behavior is possible *because of* domain-specific competences. That is, without a "panhuman psychological architecture," the overwhelming number of possible behaviors in a given situation would

prove incapacitating. See John Tooby and Leda Cosmides, "The Psychological Foundations of Culture," in Jerome H. Barkow, Leda Cosmides, and John Tooby, *The Adapted Mind: Evolutionary Psychology and the Generation of Culture* (Oxford: Oxford University Press, 1992), 54–62.

21. A word needs to be said here about the history of the field. Initially a subdiscipline of psychology, the psychology of religion actually began before James with Edwin Starbuck's *Psychology of Religion* and continued as such through the 1920s. Its decline and ultimate demise as a unified discipline in the thirties is accounted for by numerous factors, including the following: the advent of psychoanalysis; the apologetic and protective strategies of theologians, which eroded the empiricist approach; the growth of behaviorism and its focus on simple behaviors; the lack of a comprehensive theory; the difficulty of data collection; and the lack of interest in the field due to declining religious commitments within society at large. But since the sixties, a resurgent interest in the study of religion has coincided with an upswing in religious attendance, and the scholarship that has appeared since then attests to the revitalized interest in a scientific approach to religion.

22. Jack T. Hanford, "A Synoptic Approach: Resolving Problems in Empirical and Phenomenological Approaches to the Psychology of Religion," *Journal for the Scientific Study of Religion* 14, no. 2 (1976), 225.

23. For a discussion of the modified scientific realism that characterizes the conception of knowledge operative in the sciences today, see Livingston's *Literary Knowledge,* chapter 3.

24. See the discussion of the Integrated Causal Model in Barkow, Cosmides, and Tooby, *The Adapted Mind.* One literary scholar has recently written a history of methodological dualism and called for its replacement with a holistic or integrated model of knowledge; see Betty Jean Craige, *Reconnection: Dualism to Holism in Literary Study* (Athens: University of Georgia Press, 1988).

25. James, *Pragmatism,* 18, 28.

26. William James, *The Principles of Psychology* (New York: H. Holt and Company, 1899).

27. James, *Pragmatism,* 83.

28. Leon Festinger, *A Theory of Cognitive Dissonance* (Evanston, Ill.: Row, Peterson, 1957).

29. See Michael Ruse, "The View from Somewhere: A Critical Defense of Evolutionary Epistemology," in Kai Hahlweg and C. A. Hooker, eds., *Issues in Evolutionary Epistemology* (Albany: State University of New York Press, 1989); Roger D. Masters, "Evolutionary Biology, Human Nature, and Knowledge," and Michael Ruse, "Evolutionary Epistemology: Can Sociobiology Help?" in *Sociobiology and Epistemology,* ed. James H. Fetzer (Dordrecht, Holland: Reidel, 1985).

30. Rorty, *Contingency, Irony, Solidarity,* 9.

31. Erving Goffman, *Frame Analysis: An Essay on the Organization of Experience* (Cambridge: Harvard University Press, 1974), 2; Michael Morton, "Strict Constructionism: Davidsonian Realism and the World of Belief," in *Literary Theory after Davidson,* ed. Reed Way Dasenbrock (University Park: Penn State University Press, 1993).

32. Jacques Barzun, *Romanticism and the Modern Ego* (Boston: Little, Brown, and Company, 1943), 211.

33. Robert Langbaum, *The Poetry of Experience: The Dramatic Monologue in Modern Literary Tradition* (New York: W. W. Norton and Company, 1957), 22.

34. Langbaum, *The Poetry of Experience,* 28.

35. Sydney E. Ahlstrom, "Romantic Religious Revolution and the Dilemmas of Church History," *Church History* 46, no. 2 (1977), 155.

36. Hoxie Neale Fairchild, *Religious Trends in English Poetry*, vol. 3 (New York and London: Columbia University Press, 1949), 11; M. H. Abrams, *Natural Supernaturalism* (New York: W. W. Norton and Company, 1971), 13.

37. Perhaps the most notorious definition of romanticism as a religious phenomenon is T. E. Hulme's "Romanticism and Classicism" in *Speculations* (New York: Harcourt, Brace, and World, 1936). This essay is as astute in its perception of the underlying religious contradictions as it is both unsympathetic to the era's pervasive spiritual malaise and assuredly subversive of psychoanalytic discourse. Hulme posits belief in a deity as part of man's fixed instinctual nature which, repressed because of the rationalist tide of the eighteenth century, results in the symptomatic and illogical formulation of heaven-on-earth purportedly central to romanticism. Hulme thus reaches the conclusion that romanticism is "spilt religion" through his own unique version of Freudian one-upmanship: the psychological analyst can as easily call orthodox religious belief an instinct as a neurosis as long as he feels no compunction to demonstrate either point.

38. All references to Wordsworth's poetry throughout this volume are to the following editions: *The Ecclesiastical Sonnets of William Wordsworth: A Critical Edition*, ed. Abbie Findlay Potts (New Haven: Yale University Press, 1922); *The Excursion*, in *The Poetical Works of William Wordsworth*, ed. E. de Selincourt and Helen Darbishire, 2d ed., vol. 5 (Oxford: Clarendon Press, 1959); *Lyrical Ballads, and Other Poems, 1797–1800*, ed. James Butler and Karen Green (Ithaca: Cornell University Press, 1992); *Memorials of a Tour of the Continent, 1820*, in *The Poetical Works of William Wordsworth*, ed. E. de Selincourt and Helen Darbishire, 2d ed., vol. 3 (Oxford: Clarendon Press, 1952); *Poems, in Two Volumes, and Other Poems, 1800–1807*, ed. Jared Curtis (Ithaca: Cornell University Press, 1983); *The Thirteen-Book Prelude*, ed. Mark L. Reed, vol. 1 (Ithaca: Cornell University Press, 1991); *The White Doe of Rylstone; or The Fate of the Nortons*, ed. Kristine Dugas (Ithaca: Cornell University Press, 1988).

39. See M. H. Abrams, *The Mirror and the Lamp: Romantic Theory and the Critical Tradition* (New York: Oxford University Press, 1953), for a discussion of the nineteenth-century theologian John Keble as an important figure who traced a functional similarity between poetry and religion. Noting the proto-Freudianism of Keble's view that art is a cathartic form of veiled self-expression, Abrams points to the parallels between poetry and prayer and confession. But there is also an extraordinary formal difference between writing or reading a poem and partaking of orthodox confession, which suggests that the functional similarity is not exact. The religion of art, such as it is, arises in the nineteenth century and survives today on the elision of these crucial distinctions.

40. See John Herman Randall, "Romantic Reinterpretations of Religion," *Studies in Romanticism* 22, no. 4 (1963). According to Randall, Hegelianism, which stressed rational understanding of the supernatural, continued to represent God as an absolute and insisted that religion was a form of knowledge; ironically, this was the permutation of romantic philosophy most readily secularized in the nineteenth century. The other two directions taken by theology redefined religion as a subjective, aesthetic experience (Schleiermacher and Herder) and as action and moral striving (Kant, Fichte, Ritschl, and Arnold). Both contemporary fundamentalism and liberal religion, in Randall's view, are indebted to these later reinterpretations; however, from another perspective, they serve an apologetic function, defending religious doctrine and experience from scientific inquiry.

41. For a discussion of imaginative experience as an adaptive behavior derived from play and primitive ritual, see my essay "Play, Mutation, and Reality Acceptance: Toward a Theory of Literary Experience" in *After Poststructuralism: Interdisciplinarity and Literary Theory*, ed. Nancy Easterlin and Barbara Riebling (Evanston, Ill.: Northwestern University Press, 1993).

42. Freud, *The Future of an Illusion*, 8.

43. Henry James, *The Art of the Novel*, rev. ed. (1907; reprint, New York: Charles Scribners and Sons, 1934), 32.

44. James, *Pragmatism*, 56.

45. William James, *The Varieties of Religious Experience: A Study in Human Nature* (c. 1902; reprint, New York: New American Library, 1958).

46. In his rebuttal to Fairchild's *Religious Trends in English Poetry*, Benziger writes: "Professor Fairchild never actually says that the Romantics could have avoided their anguish and melancholy simply by consulting the nearest clergyman, that the Church had the answer which would have given them assurance. But some such judgment seems to be implied. If so, it is questionable. The poets under consideration did not wilfully involve themselves in uncertainty. Their adult intellectual lives may be said to have started in division and uncertainty. They could not simply accept the clergyman's answer, because the validity of this answer was one of the great points at issue." Benziger's implicit understanding that poetic ability does not constitute a superior capacity to control or solve personal anguish and metaphysical crisis renders his study of romanticism and religion one of the most balanced and psychologically perceptive of the earlier studies in this area. Where my study differs from Benziger's— and, in like fashion, from David Perkins's *Quest for Permanence: The Symbolism of Wordsworth, Shelley and Keats* (Cambridge: Harvard University Press, 1965)—is first in its correlation of psychological and social data with the religious aspects of the poems, and second in its interpretive focus on the process of language rather than on the recurrence of specific images or symbols within the poems. James Benziger, *Images of Eternity* (Carbondale and Edwardsville: Southern Illinois University Press, 1962), 9, 23.

47. Laurence Lockridge, *The Ethics of Romanticism* (Cambridge: Cambridge University Press, 1989), 3.

48. James, *Pragmatism*, 61.

49. Lionel Trilling, "The Immortality Ode," in *English Romantic Poets: Modern Essays in Criticism*, ed. M. H. Abrams (New York: Oxford University Press, 1960), 138.

50. Morse Peckham, *The Triumph of Romanticism* (Columbia: University of South Carolina Press, 1970), 208.

51. Although Peckham takes pains to disassociate himself from the strict behaviorists, his tendency to emphasize the socializing nature of norms, behaviors, and institutions (i.e., the policing function of art) reflects an overall orientation toward humans as preeminently conditioned animals.

52. G. K. Nelson, "Cults and Religion: Toward a Sociology of Religious Creativity," *Sociology and Social Research* 68, no. 3 (1984).

53. Proudfoot traces an entire tradition of religious apologetics, based in this affective tradition, back to Schleiermacher. Both theological writings and psychological studies that focus solely on individual experience and therefore do not address the issue of the origins of religious belief can indeed serve as a protective strategies for existing institutions; this is not to say, however, that experience-centered approaches to religion *inevitably* serve such a purpose.

54. James, *The Varieties of Religious Experience*, 42.

55. James, *The Varieties of Religious Experience,* 47.

56. Gerald Graff, *Literature against Itself: Literary Ideas in Modern Society* (Chicago: University of Chicago Press, 1979), 35.

57. James, *The Varieties of Religious Experience,* 42, italics mine.

58. See Rudolph Otto, *Mysticim East and West: A Comparative Analysis of the Nature of Mysticism* (New York: Macmillan Company, 1932). In this comparative, selective study of two mystics, Otto makes this discrimination between the function of mystical experience within Eastern and Western religious traditions.

59. Ellen Dissanayake, *What Is Art For?* (Seattle: University of Washington Press, 1988), 143–44.

60. See Lockridge, *The Ethics of Romanticism,* 20.

61. James B. Twitchell, "Romanticism and Cosmic Consciousness," *Centennial Review* 14, no. 4 (1975), 289.

62. James, *The Varieties of Religious Experience,* 141.

63. More recently, Ashton Nichols has directed attention to the difference between the modern literary epiphany and its religious antecedents in *The Poetics of Epiphany* (Tuscaloosa: University of Alabama Press, 1987). Unlike the traditional religious epiphany, which fuses experience and interpretation, the modern epiphany beginning with Wordsworth leaves ultimate meaning unstated and depends on the emotions associated with perceptual transformation rather than the interpretation of the event. My reading is consistent with Nichols's on this central point about the relationship of emotion to interpretation, although it differs in emphasizing the psychologically destabilizing effect of insufficient interpretation or explanation.

64. See Larry C. Ingram, "Testimony and Religious Cohesion," *Religious Education* 81, no. 2 (1986).

65. James, *The Varieties of Religious Experience,* 322.

66. Hufford, "Ambiguity and the Rhetoric of Belief."

67. Robert D. Margolis and Kirk W. Elifson, "A Typology of Religious Experience," *Journal for the Scientific Study of Religion* 18, no. 1 (1978).

68. In Foster, *The World Was Flooded with Light,* 169.

69. David Hufford, *The Terror That Comes in the Night* (Philadelphia: University of Pennsylvania Press, 1982), xviii.

70. Proudfoot, *Religious Experience,* 123. Proudfoot is adopting this argument from Ninian Smart.

71. Paul W. Pruyser, "Lessons from Art Theory for the Psychology of Religion," *Journal for the Scientific Study of Religion* 15, no. 1 (1976).

72. Proudfoot, *Religious Experience,* 215.

73. Johan Huizinga, *Homo Ludens,* trans. anon. (c. 1920; reprint, New York: Roy Publishers, 1950), 120.

74. Langbaum, *The Poetry of Experience,* 79.

Chapter 2. Intellectual Vision and Self-Qualifying Structure in "Tintern Abbey"

1. I use the word *objective* here not to suggest that the beliefs of the individual's religious community represent acknowledged facts, but to indicate their importance in establishing continuity in the individual's faith. As a social institution representing an ongoing consensus of belief, an orthodox religion appears *to the believer* to substantiate his or her religious experiences. In keeping with my frame of inquiry, then, orthodoxies are crucially important in a psychological sense.

2. The perennial misconception that romantic poetry embodies a titanic rejection

of form, celebrating raw emotion in opposition to conceptual thought and its attendant orders, persists despite much recent thoughtful criticism to the contrary. It is not so much M. H. Abrams's identification, in *The Mirror and the Lamp*, of an expressivist aesthetic within romanticism that is to blame for the now habitual slighting of artistic self-awareness among these poets, but instead the pervasive tendency in literary culture to conflate Wordsworth's rhetoric of feeling with later cultural developments. As Lockridge points out, Wordsworth follows the associationists in his belief that feeling is the base of conduct (207–10); while we may dislike this insistence that our actions are not rationally motivated, such a point of view is hardly naive from the perspective of contemporary neurophysiology.

As Stuart Curran makes amply clear in *Poetic Form and British Romanticism* (New York and Oxford: Oxford University Press, 1986), the romantic poets worked self-consciously from an extensive knowledge of classical literature, purposely extending, inverting, or combining traditional aesthetic forms.

Wordsworth studies specifically have also benefitted from a renewed recognition that poetic creation takes place only within the arena of formal considerations. Paul Sheats's study of Wordsworth's early development, *The Making of Wordsworth's Poetry, 1785–1798* (Cambridge: Harvard University Press, 1973), explicates, in sensitive detail, the tension between personal expression and aesthetic discipline in Wordsworth's career. Sheats points out that although the lyric mode came most naturally to Wordsworth, he avoided writing in all lyric forms for the ten years prior to 1798 and only returned to these forms when he felt capable of controlling their potential subjectivism. In *Wordsworth's Metaphysical Verse: Geometry, Nature, and Form* (Toronto: University of Toronto Press, 1982), Lee M. Johnson suggests that Wordsworth's most important philosophical passages exhibit the rule of continuous geometric proportion. Johnson's analysis provides an important starting point for criticism capable of dealing with the romantic perception that linear forms represent a simplified version of reality, that form, far from being a straightforward matter, mutates and regenerates in a dynamic universe of order and disorder.

3. John Stuart Mill, "Thoughts on Poetry and Its Varieties," in *Collected Works of John Stuart Mill*, ed. John M. Robson and Jack Stillinger, vol. 1, *Autobiography and Literary Essays* (Toronto: University of Toronto Press, 1981), 349.

4. David Hartley, "Observations on Man, His Frame, His Duty, and His Expectations," in *Backgrounds of Romanticism: English Philosophical Prose of the Eighteenth Century*, ed. Leonard M. Trawick (Bloomington: University of Indiana Press, 1967), 53.

5. For instance, Jerome Bruner discusses the recent effects of mechanical metaphors on cognitive psychology in the preface to *Acts of Meaning* (Cambridge: Harvard University Press, 1990). Arguing that psychology needs more than the positivist ideal of reduction, causal explanation, and prediction, Bruner asserts that the cognitive revolution in the 1950s was initially an attempt to move away from objectivism and place meaning at the center of psychology. However, early on there was a shift away from meaning construction toward an adoption of the computational metaphor derived from information processing and a corresponding reabsorption of stimulus-response theory.

6. Sheats, *The Making of Wordsworth's Poetry*, 227.

7. In Earl Wasserman's memorable words, "Within itself the modern poem must both formulate its own cosmic syntax and shape the autonomous poetic reality that the cosmic syntax permits: 'nature,' which once was prior to the poem and available for imitation, now shares with the poem a common origin in the poet's creativity" (*The Subtler Language: Critical Readings of Neoclassical and Romantic Poems* [Balti-

more: Johns Hopkins University Press, 1959], 11). Thus, the twin romantic aware-
nesses of nature as a dynamic force and the mind as an interpreting organ
simultaneously frame our reconstructions and knowledge of the physical world.

8. Pruyser, "Lessons from Art for the Psychology of Religion"; F. C. Happold,
Mysticism: A Study and an Anthology (1963; reprint, Harmondsworth: Penguin
Books, 1970).

9. Although literary criticism has witnessed profound changes in recent years,
approaches in romanticism have remained consistent, from New Criticism through
poststructuralism, in their rationalist and Germanic interpretations of extraordinary
mental events. This is most evident in the persistence of Freudian terminology within
purportedly distinct, even opposed, schools of criticism. In 1965 David Perkins carefully corrected R. D. Havens for applying the word *mystic* to Wordsworth in *The
Mind of the Poet* (Baltimore: Johns Hopkins University Press, 1941), explaining that
the so-called mystical experiences are different only in intensity from other imaginative experiences recorded in Wordsworth's poetry. Thus, in Perkins's analysis, "the
life of the mind was wholly *projected* upon external nature" (Perkins, *The Quest for
Permanence*, 59, my italics). While the explanation of these states as imaginative
projection is reasonable and plausible, it is not self-evidently true; moreover, it is not
an explanation that takes account of the poet's perpetual equivocation about the locus
of spiritual force, nor of his conception of the fundamental interrelatedness of mind
and nature.

Albert O. Wlecke, who provides a phenomenological reading that explicitly aims
at and in many ways achieves a sympathetic description of the poet's consciousness,
also borrows psychoanalysis's rhetoric of self-trickery in his discussion of "Tintern
Abbey," finding in the poem's transcendent moments a "displacement" of imaginative
activity into "a 'something' dwelling throughout the universe" (*Wordsworth and the
Sublime* [Berkeley: University of California Press, 1979], 22). While much is valuable
in Wlecke's book, the suggestion that Wordsworth's experience can only be understood as imaginative—and therefore self-delusive—activity slights the poet's own
sense of the problematic nature of these experiences.

Some recent deconstructive-materialist critics combine Marxist and Freudian perspectives to create a revised concept of displacement. In McGann's interpretation of
the poem, "Everything [except the initial scene] has been erased—the abbey, the
beggars and displaced vagrants, all that civilized culture creates and destroys, gets
and spends. We are not permitted to remember 1793 and the turmoil of the French
Revolution . . . Wordsworth displaces all that into a spiritual economy where disaster
is self-consciously transformed into the threat of disaster . . . and where that threat,
fading into a further range of self-conscious anticipation, suddenly becomes a focus
not of fear but of hope. For the mind has triumphed over its times" (Jerome McGann,
The Romantic Ideology [Chicago: University of Chicago Press, 1983], 88). No longer
infusing nature with imagined spirit, the creative imagination shields the self from
social reality. McGann's reading, like Perkins's and Wlecke's, emphasizes the will-to-
power of the creative imagination characteristic of the German romantic tradition.
In my view, the interactive, pragmatic mode of "Tintern Abbey" more accurately
suggests that spirituality and creativity are valuable for Wordsworth because they
are potential avenues back into the human community. David Simpson, a historicist
whose views have not been heavily influenced by German models and are therefore
more in keeping with my own, asserts a general dependency of private moments on
social circumstance in Wordsworth's poetry, criticizing other Marxist and historicist
scholars for thinking in too exclusively theoretical terms. Simpson modifies the notion
of *displacement* by essentially redefining it in non-Freudian terms (David Simpson,

Wordsworth's Historical Imagination: The Poetry of Displacement [New York and London: Methuen and Company, 1987]).

Several other recent books, informed by religious traditions, seek to correct the dominant tendency to read private, spiritual experience as an escape from or displacement of social reality. In *Wordsworth and the Hermeneutics of Incarnation* (University Park: Pennsylvania State University Press, 1993), David Haney points out that deconstructive and ideological critics, in ignoring the theological, historical, and ethical aspect of Wordsworth, have binarized and simplified Christian history. Informing his discussion with Augustine's conception of the inner word, Haney contrasts Wordsworth's incarnational language, which is both productive and substantial, with representational language.

Likewise, by emphasizing the *process* by which epiphanies come to have meaning in Wordsworth as well as the crucial role of the ordinary in Wordsworthian self-transcendence, Nichols demonstrates, in *The Poetics of Epiphany,* that neither such experiences nor the attempt to interpret them is inherently escapist. And finally, in a discussion of sublime aesthetics, Jack Voller maintains that Wordsworth is fundamentally uninterested in literary supernaturalism, in large part because rendered visions are potentially atypical and subjective and thus oppose the poet's preference for the normatively human and social (Jack G. Voller, *The Supernatural Sublime: The Metaphysics of Terror in Anglo-American Romanticism* [DeKalb: Northern Illinois University Press, 1994]).

10. Solomon F. Gingerich, *Wordsworth: A Study in Memory and Mysticism* (Elkhart, Ind.: Mennonite Publishing Company, 1908), 121.

11. Gingerich offers the first and probably best existing discussion of mystical experience in Wordsworth, finding in the "serene and blessed mood" of "Tintern Abbey" the ineffability and noetic quality James identifies as characteristic of mystical experience. Havens's correlations of Wordsworth's work with mystical experience rest not so much on James (whom he mentions in a footnote) as on other prominent scholars of religion, including J. H. Leuba, Evelyn Underhill, Dean Inge, and Rufus M. Jones. In keeping with early studies in religious psychology, Gingerich and Havens tend not to differentiate kinds of religious experience, using the term *mysticism* as a general rubric (see my discussion of differing states in chapter 1).

Both Perkins and Frances Ferguson complain, with much justice, of the vagueness of the term *mysticism* and of its application to Wordsworth. In commenting on the Lucy poems, Ferguson writes, "While one might say that Wordsworth's poetry thus creates a mystical realm beyond experience, it seems to me mistaken to characterize Wordsworth as a mystic in any meaningful sense of the word. Rather, he virtually parodies mysticism by demonstrating the futility of the hope that experience will ever enter the mystical realm" (*Wordsworth: Language as Counter-Spirit* [New Haven and London: Yale University Press, 1977], 193). First, I hope to avoid the potential amorphousness of the word by relying on a psychological definition; given this considered use, it seems to me that *mysticism* nowhere courts the treacheries of insignificance as ardently as *sublime,* a hopelessly skating signifier if there ever was one. In keeping with this, *mysticism* refers not to a hypothesized realm beyond the material world, but to an evanescent state of consciousness that may attest to contact with a transcendent reality. Second, I draw a sharp distinction between what in the poetry corresponds to mystical experience and any claim that Wordsworth himself was a mystic. Third, I distinguish between individual poems: Wordsworth both idealizes mystical experience ("Tintern Abbey") and parodies or declaims quasi-mystical or imaginative withdrawal from the world (the yew tree lines and "The Blind Boy"). The diverse experiences related in these poems and the values attributed to them cannot be contained within a single generalization about the nature or function of mystical and/or visionary experience in Wordsworth's poetry.

12. As Havens points out, Wordsworth himself never called these experiences mystical: "Indeed, there is no evidence that he had heard of the term or the thing it designates, which is more surprising in view of Coleridge's familiarity with Plotinus, Boehme, and similar writers" (167). In view of the fact that mystical practices are more common within Catholicism and radical Protestantism than in Anglicanism, it is likely that Wordsworth either was unaware of mysticism's traditional religious associations or avoided the term precisely because of them. For Wordsworth, the term might have prompted demands to clarify his doctrinal position, demands he clearly avoided.

Since contemporary use of the term tends to emphasize its psychological aspects rather than its religious connotations, we can assume (as Wordsworth perhaps could not) that mysticism refers to a state of mind not necessarily engaged with orthodox religious practices. Happold divides these experiences into the categories of nature, soul, and God mysticism, and within these distinguishes between practicing mystics who follow a "way" of three or more stages, depending on their denomination (e.g., Christianity's threefold way, Buddhism's eightfold path) and nonpracticing mystics, whose experiences appear spontaneous, unprovoked by religious traditions, and often occur out of doors.

13. In James, *The Varieties of Religious Experience*, 313–14.

14. My research does not indicate that Wordsworth read St. Teresa, although the rhetoric of common prayer shares some of the tropes of her description. But establishing influence would have little impact on my particular reading of the poem, which is guided by the poet's representation of such an experience as an authentic reality, not a hypothesis about the source of transcendent experience.

15. Andrew Greeley, *The Sociology of the Paranormal: A Reconnaissance* (Beverly Hills, Calif. and London: Sage Publications, 1975). For additional descriptions of experiences of nature mysticism, see Happold, Greeley, and Hufford in Foster, *The World Was Flooded with Light*.

16. Richard E. Brantley, *Wordsworth's Natural Methodism* (New Haven: Yale University Press, 1975).

17. Hufford, in Foster, *The World Was Flooded with Light*; Greeley, *The Sociology of the Paranormal*, n. 87.

18. Stephen Gill, *William Wordsworth: A Life* (Oxford: Clarendon Press, 1989), 154. Frank McConnell stresses Wordsworth's yearning for community: "*The Prelude*, in its assured and complex use of audience, represents a personal assurance and technical skill even greater than that of the lyrics of the major period. For these lyrics, too, especially 'Tintern Abbey,' 'Stepping Westward,' and 'The Solitary Reaper,' depend upon a named or implied personal audience for much of their distinctive power. But often their invocation of audience seems to be a *plea* for the ratification of human company rather than the triumphant assertion of community which is *The Prelude*" (*The Confessional Imagination: A Reading of Wordsworth's Prelude* [Baltimore and London: Johns Hopkins University Press, 1974], 47).

19. See "Some Historical Patterns in Criticism" in Karl Kroeber's Wordsworth essay in Frank Jordan's *The English Romantic Poets: A Review of Research and Criticism*, 4th ed. (New York: Modern Language Association of America Publications, 1985). Using Jonathan Arac's "Bounding Lines: The Prelude and Critical Revision" (*Boundary 2*, 1979) as a starting point, Kroeber traces the two Wordsworths within criticism: (1) the poet of joy, extending from Arnold through Abrams, and (2) the brooding poet on the verge of crisis, stemming from A. C. Bradley and continuing

through Hartman. Arac himself here serves as an example of the recent trend to accommodate the extremes of tradition and countertradition, associated in Arac's model with Pater and Lindenberger. Critics endeavoring to depict this third Words-worth of the middle way stress the vitality of writing in Wordsworth but avoid the simplifications of redemption and conflict models.

20. James, *The Varieties of Religious Experience*, 293.

21. Greeley, *The Sociology of the Paranormal*, 50.

22. Starbuck's study reports a 6 percent lapse in faith in a survey of a hundred evangelical church members, according to James, *Varieties*, 206.

23. Happold, *Mysticism*, 130.

24. This theological point is central to Wordsworth's *"Natural Methodism,"* in which Brantley insists on the poet's fidelity to Christian orthodoxy. The validity of Brantley's theological point notwithstanding, it is indeed curious that Wordsworth's most vivid depictions of spiritual experience make scant connection between these experiences and Christian belief.

Happold makes the crucial point that belief in the coinherence of matter and spirit—that God is living in the things of the world as well as transcendent above them—is central to the development of humanism and belief in progress. It leads to the mysticism of action, or the "lesser" mystical way, characteristic of the Bhagavad Gita and Christianity.

In contemporary theology, emphasis on coinherence is associated with Alfred North Whitehead and Charles Hartshorne. The development out of Whitehead's process philosophy is called process theology or panentheism, a word meaning "all in God." As Daniel Dombrowski explains it, "God [in panentheism] is neither completely removed from the world, or unmoved by it, as in classical theism, nor completely identified with the world, as in pantheism" ("Wordsworth's Panentheism," *The Wordsworth Circle* 16, no. 3 [1985], 137). While this concept seems to explain or justify Wordsworth's religious sensibility, it also tends to suggest that Wordsworth had intellectually accommodated his feelings for nature to Christian belief. This is a misleading suggestion, since all indications are that Wordsworth consciously avoided logical or systematic articulation of his religious position. See also W. Widick Schroeder, "Evolution, Human Values and Religious Experience: A Process Perspec-tive," *Zygon: Journal of Religion and Science* 7, no. 3 (1982), for an overview of process theology, which attempts to reconcile Christianity and evolutionary theory.

25. My interpretation relies on the connections Abrams and McConnell have made between poetry and the forms of crisis autobiography and Protestant confession and by no means constitutes a rejection of these interpretations. I question Abrams's larger implication that religion can be secularized, but I do not dispute the tropological and dynamical similarities between some of Wordsworth's poetry and religious dis-course. At issue here is how such religious tropes, patterns, and discourse are to be interpreted. Likewise, McConnell's emphasis on the pattern of mediation in the *The Prelude* and thus on the significance of audience is enormously important in correcting the longstanding charge that Wordsworth's is an indulgent and subjectivist poetry. But I will distinguish between the mediation Wordsworth accomplishes through poetry and testimony as part of a mediating system in the church.

Pointing out that the manifestations of spiritual crises in romantic poems are akin to those in metaphysical verse, Abrams himself cautions against interpretations stress-ing the similarity of the two in "Structure and Style in the Greater Romantic Lyric," in *Romanticism and Consciousness: Essays in Criticism*, ed. Harold Bloom (New York: W. W. Norton and Company, 1970). In particular, Abrams notes that the meaning derived from the scene is the product of individual mind rather than communal symbolism.

26. Augustine, *Confessions,* trans. and intro. R. S. Pine-Coffin (1961; reprint, Harmondsworth: Penguin Books, 1983), 21.

27. Ingram, "Testimony and Religious Cohesion," 308.

28. Ingram, "Testimony and Religious Cohesion," 303.

29. Louis L. Martz, *The Poetry of Meditation* (1954; reprint, New Haven and London: Yale University Press, 1962), 127.

30. Commenting upon the evidence in his research which suggests that adult mystical experience is linked with closeness to parents in childhood and particularly with the religious joy of the father, Greeley hypothesizes that the belief system mediates between the two. But he is quick to point out that the causality could be reversed, acknowledging that the pattern probably depends upon the individual. What is important for my analysis is the sheer significance of a belief system as part of this dynamic, not that the belief system is consistently the mediating (and therefore schematically central) factor. (Obviously, the religious joy of the father is not of much relevance to Wordsworth's case, the parent's separation from his son and early death rendering him of little influence, religious or otherwise, on the poet's life.)

31. Robley Edward Whitson, *Mysticism and Ecumenism* (New York: Sheed and Ward, 1966), 27.

32. Abrams, *The Mirror and the Lamp,* 296.

33. Geoffrey Hartman, *Wordsworth's Poetry* (New Haven: Yale University Press, 1964), 26.

34. John Hollander makes a comment about the syntactic ambiguity of Milton's blank verse that applies as well to Wordsworth: "Milton was to see that the *simultaneous* variousness of the drawing-out of sense from one verse to another could produce such hovering effects, which would vanish in the paraphrase of prose as totally as those of their Latin counterparts would do in translation" *Vision and Resonance: Two Senses of Poetic Form* (New York and Oxford: Oxford University Press, 1975), 116.

35. These comments on Wordsworth's style draw on many valuable and relatively recent critical observations. See Robert Rehder, "Wordsworth's Long Sentences," in *Wordsworth and the Beginnings of Modern Poetry* (Totowa, N.J.: Barnes and Noble Books, 1981) for a discussion of the syntactic freedom Wordsworth gains by eliminating rhyme, which cooperates with radical enjambment to delay meaning, thus enabling the poet to merge disparate experiences. For an analysis of Wordsworth's movement away from a nominal view of language, which leads toward an emphasis on communication and rhetorical modes of address and results in the outward tendency of Wordsworth's common nouns (nominals) to move outward toward metonomy, see J. P. Ward, *Wordsworth's Language of Men* (New York: Barnes and Noble Books, 1984). Ward's insight is related to Hartman's comment, in the introduction to *Wordsworth's Poetry,* that metaphor in Wordsworth's poetry apparently operates as a generalized structure rather than a specific verbal figure. Both Hugh Sykes Davies in *Wordsworth and the Worth of Words,* ed. John Kerrigan and Jonathan Wordsworth (Cambridge: Cambridge University Press, 1986) and Ferguson point to the effects of repeated words or word groups both within particular poems and throughout the body of Wordsworth's poetry which, in Ferguson's terms, create an echo effect between poems.

36. Ninian Smart, *The Concept of Worship* (London: Macmillan and Company, 1972), 27.

37. While Abrams asserts that the form of the poem is a new lyric species that replaces English versions of the Pindaric ode, Johnson and Curran prefer to emphasize

its traditional associations: Johnson identifies it with the Pindaric ode, Curran with the Horatian. But as Curran makes clear in his thorough overview of eighteenth-century manifestations of the ode forms in English, the forms tended to be misinterpreted and hybridized in their translation from their classical origins. The insight that the form of "Tintern Abbey" rests on unresolved dialectical progression is Curran's.

38. Martz, *The Poetry of Meditation,* 28.

39. The image in meditation, then, centers activity as does the phenomenological focus in worship. Smart asserts the centrality of such a focus in worship.

40. Curran, *Poetic Form and British Romanticism,* 76.

41. In Bloom, *Romanticism and Consciousness,* 227.

Chapter 3. Self-Qualification and Naturalistic Monism in *The Prelude*

1. See Roy Rappaport, "The Sacred in Human Evolution," *Annual Review of Ecology and Systematics,* vol. 2 (Palo Alto, Calif.: Annual Reviews, 1971). Rappaport argues that institutional religion, through its capacity to reduce ambiguity, served a crucial adaptive function in human evolution. A religion—a set of sacred beliefs and its standard actions (rituals)—acts as an information system, one in a series of interlocking, hierarchically arranged information systems that comprise human society. The adaptive function of all ritual lies in its ability to binarize ambiguous information; male puberty rites, for instance, redefine the adolescent initiate as a man, while his physiological transition from boyhood to manhood is in fact less clear.

2. I used the word *object* advisedly here and throughout the rest of the chapter because the object of emotion in Wordsworth's poetry is never as conceptually discrete as that word implies. Part of the problem of belief in Wordsworth's poetry is that nature, because it is indeterminately expansive and inclusive of humanity (and hence of the poet himself), cannot have the apparently objective status of a deity within a belief system.

3. Abrams, Hartman, and Bloom are the most prominent among these critics.

4. In this chapter, I deal only with the correspondences between a selection of passages from *The Prelude* and mystical and vertigo experience. However, lower-order visionary experience also has an aesthetic counterpart in the poem. The dream of the Arab in Book V, for instance, has the prophetic and apocalyptic qualities associated with visionary experience, but Wordsworth uses the dream not to suggest access to a supernatural reality but to dramatize how fantasy and excess extend the imagination and consequently allow for the renewal of meditation. The episode is framed in terms of its fictiveness: drowsing on the beach, Wordsworth's friend has been reading, of all things, "The famous History of the Errant Knight / Recorded by Cervantes" (V. 59–60). While reading of the Don who cannot distinguish illusion from reality, and subsequently entering a state in which illusion and reality are indistinguishable, the friend apprehends the enormous force of the human imagination and of books. The dream, like fairytale, fantasy, and romance, allows a temporary reprieve from reality, a momentary self-forgetfulness (V. 364–69). Thus, in *The Prelude,* experiences of this kind signify and celebrate the power of imagination, not of metaphysical vision.

5. Gingerich, *Wordsworth: A Study in Memory and Mysticism,* 143.

6. For an explanation of this dynamic, see chapter 2 for my discussion of Happold's interpretation of his own mystical experience.

7. See J. T. Ogden, "The Structure of Imaginative Experience in *The Prelude,*" *The Wordsworth Circle* 6, no. 4 (1975); Kenneth R. Johnston, *Wordsworth and "The*

Recluse" (New Haven: Yale University Press, 1984), and Nichol's *The Poetics of Epiphany.* These critics supply important revisions to the traditional emphasis on apocaplytic moments in Wordsworth criticism. Applying DeQuincy's conversations with Wordsworth to a reading of *The Prelude*, Ogden identifies a four-stage structure of imaginative experience which includes expectation, interruption and/or disappointment, interpenetration of mind and object, and poetic explanation. Ogden's assertion that imaginative experience always contains these dimensions is somewhat problematic, begging the question of how one marks off discrete experiences. But as Ogden implies, temporal variations qualify this nonetheless identifiable structure: experiences are superimposed upon and interpenetrate one another in infinitely subtle ways not susceptible to logical formulation, but suggested through subtle effects like rhetorical and figural repetition. More emphatic than Ogden in moving Wordsworth criticism away from its emphasis on isolated, apocalytic moments, Nichols claims that Wordsworth's means of organizing experience by recourse to the commonplace is his most significant contribution to modern poetry.

8. James indicates that, among mystics with "natively strong minds and characters," the extraordinary state in general contributes to energy and action rather than encourages withdrawal and overabstraction (*The Varieties of Religious Experience*, 317–19).

9. See Herbert Lindenberger, *On Wordsworth's "Prelude"* (Princeton: Princeton University Press, 1963). Especially in chapter 2, "The Rhetoric of Interaction," Lindenberger elaborates the significance of process and refinement, which supersedes discrete moments and images by projecting a unified vision of reality. One of Lindenberger's important insights is that the interchange of characteristics between animate and inanimate objects becomes an aesthetic means of demonstrating the unity of all existence. Thus, Wordsworth guides his reader toward a perspective that emphasizes the similarity and relatedness of various episodes and downplays the objective integrity of particular phenomena and events.

10. Key critical works here include Perkins's *Quest for Permanence*, Benziger's *Images of Eternity*, and M. H. Abrams's "The Correspondent Breeze: A Romantic Metaphor," rev. version, reprinted in *English Romantic Poetry: Modern Essays in Criticism*, ed. M. H. Abrams (New York: Oxford University Press, 1960).

11. Hartman, for instance, identifies these two episodes as rival high points in the poem (*Wordsworth's Poetry*, 63).

12. Lindenberger, *On Wordsworth's "Prelude,"* 59.

13. Susan Wolfson, *The Questioning Presence: Wordsworth, Keats, and the Interrogative Mode in Romantic Poetry* (Ithaca: Cornell University Press, 1986), 31.

14. See, for example, Bruner's *Acts of Meaning* and Mihaly Csikszentmihalyi and Eugene Rochberg-Halton, *Domestic Symbols and the Self* (Cambridge: Cambridge University Press, 1981).

15. Lindenberger, *On Wordsworth's "Prelude"*; Ogden, "The Structure of Imaginative Experience in *The Prelude.*"

16. Ironically, Wordsworth's use of self-qualification and association seems to cry out for a metaphor to contain it, for this progressive technique reveals the poet's dissatisfaction with static figures and representations. In relating Wordsworth's poetry to the geometric golden section and to David Bohm's theory of the implicate order respectively, Johnson in *Wordsworth's Metaphysical Verse* and Barbara Schapiro in "Wordsworth Visionary Imagination: A New Critical Context," *The Wordsworth Circle* 18, no. 3 (1987) come closest to finding appropriate critical metaphors for Wordsworth's conception of reality and its attendant aesthetic. Both metaphors, borrowed from the sciences, stress complexity, dynamism, dimension, and interrelat-

edness, and thus both are appropriate to a modern view of reality which seeks to understand the links between the known and the unknown. Johnson, for instance, maintaining that the poet perceives objects geometrically, along intersecting planes, suggests that this mode of perception links permanence and mutability within the open and restless system of reality. The appropriateness of these abstract, contemporary metaphors indicates the modernity of Wordsworth's view of nature and of his monism; like the modern scientist, the poet has variable and limited access to the whole of reality.

17. See chapter 1 for Margolis's and Elifson's definition of vertigo experience.

18. According to Lindenberger, Wordsworth's interest is in the dichotomy between inertia and movement rather than that between the abstract and the concrete. In fact, I would go further to say that Wordsworth is interested in the relationship between this *apparent* dichotomy and a higher vision of relatedness (or interaction, to use Lindenberger's term).

19. See John Hodgson, *Wordsworth's Philosophical Poetry, 1797–1814* (Lincoln: University of Nebraska Press, 1980), 39. Hodgson notes that such shifts to the third person are characteristic of Wordsworth's visionary moments. Just as images and incidents in *The Prelude* merge with one another, then, the self merges with a larger conception of humanity. Moreover, the sense of oneness resulting from this shift has a general correspondence to the mystical experience of wholeness and unity.

20. In his recent reading of this passage, Alan Liu is also concerned with how it is to be integrated with the rest of *The Prelude*. Liu claims that "Wordsworth inserted background reminders of historicity in the Imagination passage as avenues toward a realization that 'the mind' must finally enroll . . . in a collective system authorized from some source 'elsewhere' than the self: in the grounded or demystified Nile that is history." While I agree with Liu that Wordsworth questions the very self-sufficiency the passage on imagination seems to posit, I locate the poet's awareness of dependency, contingency, and community not, as Liu does, in the "collective system" of public history but in the collective reality of human nature (*Wordsworth: The Sense of History* [Stanford, Calif.: Stanford University Press, 1989], 23).

21. Lindenberger observes that the "spots of time" passages follow the pattern I describe here: in his words, the passages, beginning with impersonal, prosaic openings, move from casual reminiscence to vision, enabling the poet to put emotion at a distance and to release long-forgotten feelings. Hence, the pattern both exemplifies the concept of feeling Wordsworth outlines in the Preface and corresponds to the psychodynamics of conversion: "feeling" embodies the integration of affect and intellect, as the reconsideration and control of past spontaneous emotions enables a higher level of feeling which attests to psychic integration.

22. This sense of shared or reciprocal revelation is itself an instance of repetition and refinement. In Book IV, when the poet feels his first excitement in returning from Cambridge to his native countryside, it is "a rough terrier of the hills" whose loyalty and companionship encourages and inspires the youthful poet (IV. 96–109). The appearance of the brother of this humble creature in the final vision on Snowdon thus joins the seemingly mundane experience of the rough young poet with the sublime experience of the slightly older poet in the Alps, qualifying and uniting the two earlier experiences by integrating mundane and magnificent—the dog's companionship with the grandeur of the mountains and the recognition of imagination—into the seamless perception that mature vision affords.

23. For discussions of the indefinite relationship between the literal and the figurative in Wordsworth's language, see, for example, Paul de Man, "Intentional Structure of the Romantic Image," reprinted in *Romanticism and Consciousness: Essays in Criti-*

cism, ed. Harold Bloom (New York and London: W. W. Norton and Company, 1970), 65–77; W. K. Wimsatt, Jr., "The Structure of Romantic Nature Imagery," in *Romanticism and Consciousness,* 77–88; Perkins's *Quest for Permanence;* Hartman's *Wordsworth's Poetry;* Ward's *Wordsworth's Language of Men;* and McConnell's *Wordsworth's Confessional Imagination.* Since de Man is concerned specifically with the philosophical implications of this technique, he is particularly relevant to my argument. Wimsatt observes that Wordsworth's superimpositions of images amount to a "sleight of words" (35). Perkins discusses, within romanticism in general, the dual tendency toward literal statement and suggestion through symbolism, and points out that this dual procedure allows latitude for truth. Noting that metaphor operates on the level of overall structure in Wordsworth's poetry, Hartman touches on the relationship between Wordsworth's aesthetic practice and his philosophical outlook, tentative in its conceptualization of reality and therefore of language. Ward connects Wordsworth's linguistic practices with a movement away from a nominal view of language; thus, nouns remain stable as *passing* references, but also tend toward metonomy. Whereas de Man, in the essay I discuss below, notes the tendency of the romantics to take the figurative as literal, McConnell points toward the reverse of this—the tendency of the literal to become figurative.

24. De Man, "Intentional Structure of the Romantic Image," 70, 76–77. De Man's interpretation is marred by a totalizing definition of romanticism, which homogenizes the concerns of poets of diverse nationality, sensibility, and historical periods. Certainly any allegations of a willed denial of reality carries more weight in an analysis of the works of the symbolists Baudelaire and Rimbaud than it does in an analysis of Wordsworth's poems.

25. Lockridge, *The Ethics of Romanticism,* 213.

26. Sheats, *The Making of Wordsworth's Poetry,* 208.

27. *The Letters of William and Dorothy Wordsworth,* ed. E. de Selincourt, *The Early Years, 1787–1805,* vol. 1, rev. Chester L. Shaver (Oxford: Oxford University Press, 1967), 594.

28. James, *Pragmatism,* 95–96.

29. In these passages about the church, then, and in some of what follows above about Wordsworth's use of the word *God,* I agree with Abrams that Wordsworth has secularized aspects of traditional religion. But this is neither a conscious nor consistent practice on Wordsworth's part, since those very terms that accede to a secular interpretation in one part of the poem have a distinctly orthodox meaning in others.

30. D. H. Lawrence, *Apocalypse* (1931; reprint, Harmondsworth: Penguin Books, 1960).

31. Typology is the hermenuetical practice of finding analogues for persons, animals, and objects (the types) in the Old Testament with those of the New Testament (the antitypes). Thus, in contrast to Wordsworth's abstract reference to "types and symbols," typological practice focuses on distinct Biblical phenomena as the source of spiritual meaning. After the Reformation, the mystical and allegorical tendencies of the medieval period, which allowed for more speculative scriptural interpretation, were generally abandoned, and the church returned to the practice of true typology: the types of the Old Testament are completed and corrected by the New Testament antitypes, creating a spiritual bond between the two books and reinforcing an eschatological vision. The practice stresses literal interpretation of the Bible, which is taken for an accurate historical record. Typology therefore rests in notions about language and truth that are diametrically opposed to the assumptions underlying Wordsworth's philosophical poetry. For a discussion of the history of typological practices, see

Thomas M. Davis, "The Traditions of Puritan Typology," in *Typology and Early American Literature*, ed. Sacvan Bercovitch (Amherst: University of Massachusetts Press, 1972), 11–45.

32. For the sake of simplicity, I ascribe masculine gender to God and feminine gender to nature, following Wordsworth's own practice.

33. Meissner, *Psychology and Religious Experience*, 157. Meissner's assumption that primitive religion is literalistic while modern religion is metaphoric seems logical, but Prickett in *Romanticism and Religion* argues persuasively that Enlightenment rationalism is responsible for the literal attitude toward religion.

34. Hartman, *Wordsworth's Poetry*, 31.

35. See Alan Richardson, "Romanticism and the Colonization of the Feminine," and Marlon Ross, "Troping Masculine Power in the Crisis of Poetic Identity," in Anne K. Mellor, ed., *Romanticism and Feminism* (Bloomington: Indiana University Press, 1988); and Barbara Schapiro, *The Romantic Mother: Narcissistic Patterns in Romantic Poetry* (Baltimore: Johns Hopkins University Press, 1983), 113, and Judith W. Page, *Wordsworth and the Cultivation of Women* (Berkeley: University of California Press, 1994), 24–25. Children (male and female) do not absorb their mother's sympathetic faculties, as Richardson, drawing on Nancy Chodorow, asserts; they either develop or fail to develop their own affective and social natures depending on the success of primary bonding. See John Bowlby, *Attachment and Loss*, 3 vols. (New York: Basic Books, 1969). Likewise, Wordsworth's focus on growth and development does not so much suggest the unmasking of an authentic or aboriginal self, as Ross claims, but instead reflects a fairly accurate intuition that self-making is a process; for this, see Stern's *Interpersonal World of the Infant*.

Page's recent book modifies the image (here encouraged by Richardson and Ross) of a poet driven sheerly by a masculine desire for dominance over the feminine. Placing feminist Wordsworth criticism in a biographical context, Page, in a reading consistent with Schapiro's and my own, notes that the nurture and support of the women in his life enabled sublime vision.

36. Discussing the sources of this passage in Wordsworth's domestic life and early poetry, Kurt Heinzelman points to the poet's persistent identification of himself and the Grasmere household with the mountaintop of Stone Arthur. For this fascinating reading of these lines, see "The Cult of Domesticity: Dorothy and William Wordsworth at Grasmere," in *Romanticism and Feminism*, 65–68.

37. While not offering the naturalistic interpretation I provide here, Haney in *The Hermeneutics of Incarnation* nevertheless stresses the exemplary and expansive function of the final part of the poem. Haney points out that the poem, as a gift to Coleridge, is not contained by economies of exchange some recent critics invoke and instead includes an overflow of meaning.

38. As Lockridge says, "The poem narrates the eclipse of its own ethical imperatives and prophesies the exhaustion of its author beyond its own ending. The poet, who is preparing to write a philosophical poem largely ethical in character, has in effect disqualified himself by the poem's end for those large pronouncements on man and society, and has already treated of the only ethical dynamic he could convert into a strong poetry: the confrontation of his personal imagination with ethical pressure from without and within" (*The Ethics of Romanticism*, 226).

Chapter 4. Too Much Liberty: The Sonnet and the Recompense of Institutions

1. There is, however, some indication that the wisdom of radical constructivism and cultural relativism in the humanities and social sciences is being put into question.

For a critical assessment of the cultural relativism traditionally dominant in anthropology, see Donald E. Brown, *Human Universals* (Philadelphia: Temple University Press,
1991). For discussions of bioepistemology (an evolutionary theory of knowledge), see
Kai Hahlweg and C. A. Hooker, eds., *Issues in Evolutionary Epistemology* (Albany:
State University of New York Press, 1989).

2. Preface in Wordsworth, *The White Doe of Rylstone*, 11.

3. Willard L. Sperry, *Wordsworth's Anti-Climax* (Cambridge: Harvard University Press, 1935). Sperry offers the standard account of Wordsworth's "anti-climax,"
hypothesizing, first, that Wordsworth's late arrival as a poet prophesied his early
decline, and second, that the poet accepted Hartley's and Addison's system, according
to which the imagination is superseded by moral principles in the course of human
development. With regard to the first point, there is no logical reason why a late
artistic development need necessarily entail less permanent ability; the assertion
hardly seems supported by literary history. With regard to the second, it is not
clear that Wordsworth's subject matter or aesthetics was the product of the poet's
investment in a given system of ideas rather than arrived at intuitively.

See Ferguson, Johnston in *Wordsworth and "The Recluse,"* and William H. Galperin, *Revison and Authority in Wordsworth: The Interpretation of a Career* (Philadelphia: University of Pennsylvania Press, 1989) for recent revisions to Sperry's
interpretation. These critics explain the puzzling aspects of the poet's late work in
light of his troubled and tenuous belief in poetic authority. Ferguson and Galperin
see in Wordsworth's poetry a renunciatory drive; for Ferguson, this drive is fundamentally beyond language and consciousness, whereas for Galperin it is more specifically a quarrel with authority. Johnston, by contrast, suggests that the idea of *The
Recluse* as an ongoing project was necessary to the sense of self required for Wordsworth's best poetry, and that, once Wordsworth gave up the project in 1815, his
poetry was never the same.

4. Lee M. Johnson comments on this tendency toward containment and personal
constriction in Wordsworth's late poetry. As Johnson points out, "A major critical
problem about Wordsworth's later poems is to discern whether 'blest tranquillity' is
attained chiefly by encompassing or by excluding the sublime and humble aspects of
his poetical character . . . 'Musings near Aquapendente' suggests that tranquil perceptions are exclusive, which might argue that the range of his poetical character has
contracted severely." Since so many of Wordsworth's late poems are sonnets (as
Johnson notes, the poet was the most prolific sonneteer in English, producing a total
of 535), it seems reasonable to speculate that the decision to write predominantly in
that form was in part motivated by a desire to limit the range of emotion and experience (*Wordsworth and the Sonnet* [Copenhagen: Rosenhilde and Bagger, 1973], 32).

5. Laura Dabundo, "The Extrospective Vision: *The Excursion* as Transitional in
Wordsworth's Poetry and Age," *The Wordsworth Circle* 19, no. 1 (1988).

6. Gill, *William Wordsworth*, 295.

7. Johnston, *Wordsworth and "The Recluse,"* 319. Johnston's thorough study of
The Recluse establishes how abundantly conceptualized *The Excursion* is, in spite of
how mediocre much of it is as verse.

8. In spite of this praise of nature as a beneficent formative influence on the young
Wanderer, nature also has a sinister aspect in *The Excursion* which has not gone
unnoticed by the critics. Galperin points to the discord between man and nature
evident from the beginning of the poem, and Johnston says that "nature is interposed
as a covert or shade between the characters and their respective horizons" (*Wordsworth and "The Recluse,"* 274).

9. Anne L. Rylestone, *Prophetic Memory in Wordsworth's "Ecclesiastical Sonnets"*

(Carbondale: Southern Illinois University Press, 1991), 11. Rylestone's central thesis is that the *Ecclesiastical Sonnets* constitutes a powerful poetic realization of "the individual's struggle . . . with faith and service in the fallen world," and she submits that the series has been unjustly neglected. I am in partial agreement with this statement. As a substantial piece of work by a major English-language poet, the *Ecclesiastical Sonnets* should be subject to greater critical attention than it has met with in the past for the way it can illuminate our understanding of the entire Words-worth canon; on the whole, however, I believe the series has received exactly the aesthetic evaluation it deserves, and I would positively hide it from students who had not yet achieved an appreciation of Wordsworth's major poetry.

10. Here my analysis parts ways with Galperin's. Observing that the sonnets tend to reincorporate the church into the world rather than promote Christian doctrine, Galperin asserts that Wordsworth's late poetry is not simply a capitulation to author-ity but the continuation of a quarrel with it. Instead, I see a drive toward conformity in the sonnets in which Wordsworth seeks identification with a survivalist course of history rather than specific doctrines connected with it. Wordsworth's limited presentation of Christian myth and ritual indicates not so much a desire to control or redefine these entities, but their relative unconvincingness in the face of mutability. Wordsworth quarrels with specific authorities but not authority per se; in the *Eccle-siastical Sonnets,* his particular quarrel is with the Catholic church's abuse of power.

11. See Potts's commentary in Wordsworth, *Ecclesiastical Sonnets,* 229.

12. David Ferry, *The Limits of Mortality: An Essay on Wordsworth's Major Poems* (Middletown, Conn.: Wesleyan University Press, 1977). As Ferry so ably demon-strates, *Poems, in Two Volumes* turns on an ironic perspective in which the poet's persistent questionings of natural phenomenon reveal the discrepancy between human consciousness and nature's unconsciousness. In Ferry's analysis, because nature, un-like man, is not conscious of itself, it is virtually eternal, and it is this perception of its practical eternity which constitutes the poet's interest in it.

13. Johnston points out that reclusiveness for Wordsworth is distinct from isola-tion and withdrawal, and that, for the poet, the term *recluse* represents an ideal that merges solitude with socially meaningful activity (*Wordsworth and "The Recluse,"* 13).

14. In Wordsworth, *Ecclesiastical Sonnets,* 280, n.3.1.1–14.

15. Galperin, *Revision and Authority,* 225.

16. In *Wordsworth and the Sonnet,* Johnson notes that the sonnets closest to the great sonnet "Mutability" in themes and images all concern female figures; it seems that Wordsworth had a general tendency to connect women with the theme of mutability.

17. Rudy, "Wordsworth's 1820 Memorials." In his analysis of this sonnet, Rudy questions the necessity of conflict in art, maintaining that the aesthetic pleasure the sonnet elicits is the product of Wordsworth's accepting and selfless consciousness of the scene itself.

18. Rylestone, *Prophetic Memory,* 91. A major aspect of Rylestone's interpretation, her assertion that Wordsworth effects a synthesis of nature and the church through the series, suggests that the poet was, as in *The Prelude,* once again working toward continuity of perspective.

19. See Johnson's discussion of these two sonnets in *Wordsworth and the Sonnet,* 159–61.

20. Johnson, *Wordsworth and the Sonnet,* 161.

21. Rylestone maintains that the river image successfully merges the church and nature, but I share Johnson's opinion that it is simply an obvious expedient: "The

stream in the *Ecclesiastical Sonnets* has no physical basis. Wordsworth proclaims its use as an emblem of church history at the beginning, and such it remains throughout the series" (*Wordsworth and the Sonnet*, 146).

22. Rylestone, *Prophetic Memory*, 85.
23. Huizinga, *Homo Ludens*, 191.

Bibliography

Primary Works

Wordsworth, William. *Ecclesiastical Sonnets.* 1845. Reprinted in *The Ecclesiastical Sonnets of William Wordsworth: A Critical Edition.* Edited by Abbie Findlay Potts. New Haven: Yale University Press, 1922.

———. *The Excursion.* 1815. Reprinted in *The Poetical Works of William Wordsworth.* Edited by E. de Selincourt and Helen Darbishire. 2d ed. Vol. 5. Oxford: Clarendon Press (1949), 1959.

———. *The Letters of William and Dorothy Wordsworth.* Edited by E. de Selincourt. *The Early Years, 1787–1805.* Vol. 1. Revised by Chester L. Shaver. Oxford: Oxford University Press, 1967.

———. *Lyrical Ballads, and Other Poems, 1797–1800.* 1800. Edited by James Butler and Karen Green. Ithaca: Cornell University Press, 1992.

———. *Memorials of a Tour of the Continent, 1820.* 1822. Reprinted in *The Poetical Works of William Wordsworth.* Edited by E. de Selincourt and Helen Darbishire. 2d ed. Vol. 3. Oxford: Clarendon Press (1949), 1952.

———. *Poems, in Two Volumes, and Other Poems, 1800–1807.* 1807. Edited by Jared Curtis. Ithaca and London: Cornell University Press, 1983.

———. *The Prose Works of William Wordsworth.* Edited by W. J. B. Owen and Jane Worthington Smyser. Vol. 1. Oxford: Clarendon Press, 1974.

———. *The Thirteen-Book Prelude.* 1850. Edited by Mark L. Reed. 2 vols. Ithaca: Cornell University Press, 1991.

———. *The White Doe of Rylstone; or The Fate of the Nortons.* 1814. Edited by Kristine Dugas. Ithaca and London: Cornell University Press, 1988.

Literary Criticism and Literary History

Abrams, M. H. "The Correspondent Breeze: A Romantic Metaphor." In *English Romantic Poets,* edited by M. H. Abrams, 37–57.

———. *The Mirror and the Lamp: Romantic Theory and the Critical Tradition.* New York: Oxford University Press, 1953.

———. *Natural Supernaturalism.* New York: W. W. Norton and Company, 1971.

———. "Structure and Style in the Greater Romantic Lyric." In *Romanticism and Consciousness,* edited by Harold Bloom, 201–29.

———, ed. *English Romantic Poets: Modern Essays in Criticism.* New York: Oxford University Press, 1960.

Ahlstrom, Sydney E. "Romantic Religious Revolution and the Dilemmas of Religious History." *Church History* 46, no. 2 (1977): 149–70.

Armstrong, Isobel. "Wordsworth's Complexity: Repetition and Doubled Syntax in *The Prelude*." *Oxford Literary Review* 4, no. 3 (1981): 20–42.

Barzun, Jacques. *Romanticism and the Modern Ego*. Boston: Little, Brown and Company, 1943.

Benziger, James. *Images of Eternity*. Carbondale and Edwardsville: Southern Illinois University Press, 1962.

Bercovitch, Sacvan. *Typology and Early American Literature*. Amherst: University of Massachusetts Press, 1972.

Bloom, Harold. "The Internalization of the Quest Romance." *Yale Review* 58, no. 4 (1969): 526–36.

———. *Ruin the Sacred Truths: Poetry and Belief from the Bible to the Present*. Cambridge: Harvard University Press, 1987.

———, ed. *Romanticism and Consciousness: Essays in Criticism*. New York: W. W. Norton and Company, 1970.

Bradley, A. C. "Wordsworth." In *Wordsworth: A Collection of Critical Essays*, edited by M. H. Abrams, 13–21. Englewood Cliffs, N.J.: Prentice-Hall, 1972.

Brantley, Richard E. *Wordsworth's "Natural Methodism."* New Haven: Yale University Press, 1975.

Craige, Betty Jean. *Reconnection: Dualism to Holism in Literary Study*. Athens: University of Georgia Press, 1988.

Chandler, James K. *Wordsworth's Second Nature: A Study of the Poetry and Politics*. Chicago: University of Chicago Press, 1984.

Curran, Stuart. *Poetic Form and British Romanticism*. New York and Oxford: Oxford University Press, 1986.

Dabundo, Laura. "The Extrospective Vision: The Excursion as Transitional in Wordsworth's Poetry and Age." *The Wordsworth Circle* 19, no. 1 (1988): 8–14.

Davies, Hugh Sykes. *Wordsworth and the Worth of Words*. Edited by John Kerrigan and Jonathan Wordsworth. Cambridge: Cambridge University Press, 1986.

Davis, Thomas M. "The Traditions of Puritan Typology." In *Typology and Early American Literature*, edited by Sacvan Bercovitch, 11–45.

De Man, Paul. "Intentional Structure of the Romantic Image." In *Romanticism and Consciousness*, edited by Harold Bloom, 65–77.

Dombrowski, Daniel. "Wordsworth's Panentheism." *The Wordsworth Circle* 16, no. 3 (1985): 136–42.

Easterlin, Nancy. "Play, Mutation, and Reality Acceptance: Toward a Theory of Literary Experience." In *After Poststructuralism: Interdisciplinarity and Literary Theory*, edited by Nancy Easterlin and Barbara Riebling, 105–25. Evanston, Ill.: Northwestern University Press, 1993.

Eldridge, Richard. "Self-Understanding and Community in Wordsworth's Poetry." *Philosophy and Literature* 10, no. 2 (1986): 273–94.

Fairchild, Hoxie Neale. *Religious Trends in English Poetry*. Vol. 3. New York and London: Columbia University Press, 1949.

Ferguson, Frances. *Wordsworth: Language as Counter-Spirit*. New Haven and London: Yale University Press, 1977.

Ferry, David. *The Limits of Mortality: An Essay on Wordsworth's Major Poems*. Middletown, Conn.: Wesleyan University Press, 1977.

Galperin, William H. *Revision and Authority in Wordsworth: The Interpretation of a Career*. Philadelphia: University of Pennsylvania Press, 1989.

Gates, Barbara T. "Wordsworth's Mirror of Morality: Distortions of Church History." *The Wordsworth Circle* 12, no. 2 (1981): 129–32.

Gill, Stephen. *William Wordsworth: A Life*. Oxford: Clarendon Press, 1989.

Gingerich, Solomon F. *Wordsworth: A Study in Memory and Mysticism*. Elkhart, Ind.: Mennonite Publishing Company, 1908.

Graff, Gerald. *Literature against Itself: Literary Ideas in Modern Society*. Chicago: University of Chicago Press, 1979.

Haney, David. *Wordsworth and the Hermeneutics of Incarnation*. University Park: Pennsylvania State University Press, 1993.

Havens, Raymond Dexter. *The Mind of the Poet*. Baltimore: Johns Hopkins University Press, 1941.

Hartman, Geoffrey H. "Romanticism and 'Anti-Self-Consciousness.'" In *Romanticism and Consciousness: Essays in Criticism*, edited by Harold Bloom, 46–56.

———. *Wordsworth's Poetry*. New Haven: Yale University Press, 1964.

Hearn, Ronald B. *The Road to Rydal Mount: A Survey of William Wordsworth's Reading*. Austria: Institut für Englische Sprache und Literatur, 1973.

Heinzelman, Kurt. "The Cult of Domesticity: Dorothy and William at Grasmere." In *Romanticism and Feminism*, edited by Anne K. Mellor, 25–78.

Hodgson, John A. *Wordsworth's Philosophical Poetry, 1797–1814*. Lincoln: University of Nebraska Press, 1980.

Hollander, John. *Vision and Resonance: Two Senses of Poetic Form*. New York and Oxford: Oxford University Press, 1975.

Hulme, T. E. "Romanticism and Classicism." In *Speculations*, 113–40. New York: Harcourt, Brace and World, 1936.

James, Henry. *The Art of the Novel*. Rev. ed. New York: Charles Scribner's Sons (1907), 1934.

Jasper, David. *The Interpretation of Belief: Coleridge, Schleiermacher, and Romanticism*. Hampshire and London: Macmillan and Company, 1986.

Johnson, Lee M. *Wordsworth and the Sonnet*. Copenhagen: Rosenhilde and Bagger, 1973.

———. *Wordsworth's Metaphysical Verse: Geometry, Nature, and Form*. Toronto: University of Toronto Press, 1982.

Johnston, Kenneth R. "The Politics of *Tintern Abbey*." *The Wordsworth Circle* 14, no. 1 (1983): 6–14.

———. *Wordsworth and "The Recluse."* New Haven: Yale University Press, 1984.

Jordan, Frank, ed. *The English Romantic Poets: A Review of Research and Criticism*. 4th ed. New York: Modern Language Association of America Publications, 1985.

Kauver, Gerald B. "The Psychological Structure of English Romantic Poetry." *The Psychoanalytic Review* 64, no. 1 (1977): 21–40.

Kelley, Theresa M. *Wordsworth's Revisionary Aesthetics*. Cambridge: Cambridge University Press, 1988.

Langbaum, Robert. *The Poetry of Experience: The Dramatic Monologue in Modern Literary Tradition*. New York: W. W. Norton and Company, 1957.

Lawrence, D. H. *Apocalypse*. 1931. Reprint. Harmondsworth: Penguin Books, 1960.

Levinson, Marjorie. *Wordsworth's Great Period Poems*. Cambridge: Cambridge University Press, 1986.

Lindenberger, Herbert. *On Wordsworth's "Prelude."* Princeton: Princeton University Press, 1963.

Liu, Alan. *Wordsworth: The Sense of History.* Stanford, Calif.: Stanford University Press, 1989.

Livingston, Paisley. *Literary Knowledge: Humanistic Inquiry and the Philosophy of Science.* Ithaca: Cornell University Press, 1988.

Lockridge, Laurence. *The Ethics of Romanticism.* Cambridge: Cambridge University Press, 1989.

Lovejoy, Arthur O. *The Great Chain of Being: A Study of the History of an Idea.* Cambridge: Harvard University Press, 1936.

Martz, Louis L. *The Poetry of Meditation.* 1954. Reprint. New Haven and London: Yale University Press, 1962.

McConnell, Frank D. *The Confessional Imagination: A Reading of Wordsworth's "Prelude."* Baltimore and London: Johns Hopkins University Press, 1974.

McFarland, Thomas. "Wordsworth's Best Philosopher." *The Wordsworth Circle* 13, no. 2 (1982): 59–68.

McGann, Jerome. *The Romantic Ideology.* Chicago: University of Chicago Press, 1983.

McGhee, Richard D. "Resistance and Revision in Wordsworth's *Prelude.*" *Literature and Psychology* 32, no. 1 (1986): 37–52.

Mellor, Anne K., ed. *Romanticism and Feminism.* Bloomington: University of Indiana Press, 1988.

Mill, John Stuart. "Thoughts on Poetry and Its Varieties." *Collected Works of John Stuart Mill.* Edited by John M. Robson and Jack Stillinger. Vol 1. *Autobiography and Literary Essays.* Toronto: University of Toronto Press, 1981.

Morton, Michael. "Strict Constructionism: Davidsonian Realism and the World of Belief." In *Literary Theory after Davidson,* edited by Reed Way Dasenbrock. University Park: Penn State University Press, 1993.

Nichols, Ashton. *The Poetics of Epiphany: Nineteenth Century Origins of the Modern Literary Movement.* Tuscaloosa and London: University of Alabama Press, 1987.

Ogden, J. T. "The Structure of Imaginative Experience in *The Prelude.*" *The Wordsworth Circle* 6, no. 4 (1975): 290–98.

Onorato, Richard J. *The Character of the Poet: Wordsworth in "The Prelude."* Princeton: Princeton University Press, 1971.

Page, Judith W. "Style and Rhetorical Intention in Wordsworth's *Lyrical Ballads.*" *Philological Quarterly* 62, no. 3 (1983): 293–313.

———. *Wordsworth and the Cultivation of Women.* Berkeley: University of California Press, 1994.

———. "Wordsworth and the Psychology of Meter." *Papers on Language and Literature: A Journal for Scholars and Critics of Language and Literature* 21, no. 3 (1985): 275–94.

Patterson, Annabel. "Hard Pastoral: Frost, Wordsworth, and Modernist Poetics." *Criticism: A Quarterly for Literature and the Arts* 29, no. 1 (1987): 67–87.

Peckham, Morse. *Romanticism and Behavior.* Columbia: University of South Carolina Press, 1976.

———. *Romanticism and Ideology.* Greenwood, Fla.: Penkvill Publishing Company, 1985.

———. *The Triumph of Romanticism.* Columbia: University of South Carolina Press, 1970.

Prickett, Stephen. *Romanticism and Religion: The Tradition of Coleridge and Wordsworth in the Victorian Church.* Cambridge: Cambridge University Press, 1976.

Randall, John Herman. "Romantic Reinterpretations of Religion." *Studies in Romanticism* 2, no. 4 (1963): 189–212.

Rehder, Robert. "Wordsworth's Long Sentences." In *Wordsworth and the Beginnings of Modern Poetry.* Totowa, N.J.: Barnes and Noble Books, 1981.

Richardson, Alan. "Romanticism and the Colonization of the Feminine." In *Romanticism and Feminism,* edited by Anne K. Mellor, 13–25.

———. "'The Two-Part Prelude' and Spots of Time." *The Wordsworth Circle* 19, no. 1 (1988): 15–20.

Ross, Marlon. "Romantic Quest and Conquest: Troping Masculine Power in the Crisis of Poetic Identity." In *Romanticism and Feminism,* edited by Anne K. Mellor, 26–51.

Roston, Murray. *Prophet and Poet: The Bible and the Growth of Romanticism.* London: Faber and Faber, 1965.

Rudy, John G. "Wordsworth's 1820 Memorials: Emergent Unities in the Selfless Way." *Massachusetts Studies in English* 10, no. 4 (1986): 237–53.

Rylestone, Anne L. *Prophetic Memory in Wordsworth's "Ecclesiastical Sonnets."* Carbondale: Southern Illinois University Press, 1991.

Schapiro, Barbara. *The Romantic Mother: Narcissistic Patterns in Romantic Poetry.* Baltimore: Johns Hopkins University Press, 1983.

———. "Wordsworth's Visionary Imagination: A New Critical Context." *The Wordsworth Circle* 18, no. 3 (1987): 137–43.

Shea, F. X. "Religion and the Romantic Movement." *Studies in Romanticism* 9, no. 4 (1970): 285–96.

Sheats, Paul D. *The Making of Wordsworth's Poetry, 1785–1798.* Cambridge: Harvard University Press, 1973.

Simpson, David. *Wordsworth's Historical Imagination: The Poetry of Displacement.* New York and London: Methuen and Company, 1987.

Sperry, Willard L. *Wordsworth's Anti-Climax.* Cambridge: Harvard University Press, 1935.

Thomas, Keith G. *Wordsworth and Philosophy: Empiricism and Transcendentalism in the Poetry.* Ann Arbor, Mich.: University Microfilms International, 1989.

Trilling, Lionel. "The Immortality Ode." In *English Romantic Poets,* edited M. H. Abrams, 123–43.

Twitchell, James B. "Romanticism and Cosmic Consciousness." *Centennial Review* 14, no. 4 (1975): 287–307.

Vogler, Thomas A. *Preludes to Vision: The Epic Venture in Blake, Wordsworth, Keats, and Hart Crane.* Berkeley: University of California Press, 1971.

Voller, Jack G. *The Supernatural Sublime: The Metaphysics of Terror in Anglo-American Romanticism.* DeKalb: Northern Illinois University Press, 1994.

Ward, J. P. *Wordsworth's Language of Men.* New York: Barnes and Noble Books, 1984.

Wasserman, Earl R. *The Subtler Language: Critical Readings of Neoclassical and Romantic Poems.* Baltimore: Johns Hopkins University Press, 1959.

Wimsatt, W. K., Jr. "The Structure of Romantic Nature Imagery." In *Romanticism and Consciousness,* edited by Harold Bloom, 77–88.

Wlecke, Albert O. *Wordsworth and the Sublime.* Berkeley: University of California Press, 1973.

Wolfson, Susan. *The Questioning Presence: Wordsworth, Keats, and the Interrogative Mode in Romantic Poetry.* Ithaca: Cornell University Press, 1986.

Woodhouse, A. S. P. *The Poet and His Faith: Religion and Poetry in England from Spenser to Eliot and Auden.* Chicago and London: University of Chicago Press, 1965.

Psychology, Philosophy, Anthropology, and Sociology

Augustine. *Confessions.* 1961. Reprint. Translated and introduced by R. S. Pine-Coffin. Harmondsworth: Penguin Books, 1983.

Austin, M. R. "Aesthetic Experience and the Nature of Religious Perception." *Journal of Aesthetic Education* 14, no. 3 (1980): 19–35.

Beit-Hallahmi, Benjamin. "Psychology of Religion 1880–1930: The Rise and Fall of a Psychological Movement." *Journal of the History of the Behavioral Sciences* 10, no. 1 (1974): 84–90.

Bowlby, John. *Attachment and Loss.* 3 vols. New York: Basic Books, 1969.

Brown, Donald E. *Human Universals.* Philadelphia: Temple University Press, 1991.

Bruner, Jerome. *Acts of Meaning.* Cambridge: Harvard University Press, 1990.

Byrnes, Joseph F. *The Psychology of Religion.* New York: Free Press, 1984.

Crews, Frederick C. *Skeptical Engagements.* New York: Oxford University Press, 1986.

———. "The Unknown Freud." *New York Review of Books* 40, no. 19 (18 November 1993): 55–66.

——— et al. "The Unknown Freud. An Exchange." *New York Review of Books* 41, no. 3 (3 February 1994): 34–43.

Csikszentmihalyi, Mihaly, and Eugene Rochberg-Halton. *Domestic Symbols and the Self.* Cambridge: Cambridge University Press, 1981.

Dissanayake, Ellen. *What Is Art For?* Seattle: University of Washington Press, 1988.

Evans-Pritchard, E. E. *Theories of Primitive Religion.* Oxford: Clarendon Press, 1965.

Festinger, Leon. *A Theory of Cognitive Dissonance.* Evanston, Ill.: Row, Peterson and Company, 1957.

Fetzer, James H., ed. *Sociobiology and Epistemology.* Dordrecht, Holland: Reidel Publishing Company, 1985.

Foster, Genevieve W. *The World Was Flooded with Light: A Mystical Experience Remembered.* Pittsburgh: Pittsburgh University Press, 1985.

Freud, Sigmund. *Civilization and Its Discontents.* 1930. Reprint. Translated and edited by James Strachey. New York: W. W. Norton and Company, 1961.

———. *The Future of an Illusion.* 1927. Reprint. Translated by W. D. Robson-Scott. New York: Liveright Publishing Corporation, 1949.

———. *Moses and Monotheism.* 1939. Reprint. Translated by Katherine Jones. New York: Vintage Books, 1955.

———. *Totem and Taboo.* 1912–1913. Reprint. Translated by A. A. Brill. New York: Moffat, Yard, & Company, 1920.

Greeley, Andrew M. *The Sociology of the Paranormal: A Reconnaissance*. Beverly Hills, Calif. and London: Sage Publications, 1975.

Goffman, Erving. *Frame Analysis: An Essay on the Organization of Experience*. Cambridge: Harvard University Press, 1974.

Hahlweg, Kai, and C. A. Hooker, eds. *Issues in Evolutionary Epistemology*. Albany: State University of New York Press, 1989.

Hanford, Jack T. "A Synoptic Approach: Resolving Problems in Empirical and Phenomenological Approaches to the Psychology of Religion." *Journal for the Scientific Study of Religion* 14, no. 2 (1976): 219–27.

Happold, F. C. *Mysticism: A Study and an Anthology*. 1963. Reprint. Harmondsworth: Penguin Books, 1970.

Hartley, David. "Observations on Man, His Frame, His Duty, and His Expectations." In *Backgrounds of Romanticism: English Philosophical Prose of the Eighteenth Century*, edited by Leonard M. Trawick.

Hufford, David. "Ambiguity and the Rhetoric of Belief." *Keystone Folklore Quarterly* 21 (1976): 11–24.

———. "Psychology, Psychoanalysis, and Folklore." *Southern Folklore Quarterly* 38 (1974): 187–97.

———. *The Terror That Comes in the Night*. Philadelphia: University of Pennsylvania Press, 1982.

Huizinga, Johan. *Homo Ludens: A Study of the Play Element in Culture*. 1944. Translated by anonymous. New York: Roy Publishers, 1950.

Ingram, Larry C. "Testimony and Religious Cohesion." *Religious Education* 81, no. 2 (1986): 295–309.

James, William. *Pragmatism*. C. 1910. Reprint. Cambridge and London: Harvard University Press, 1975.

———. *The Varieties of Religious Experience: A Study in Human Nature*. C. 1902. Reprint. New York: New American Library, 1958.

———. *The Will to Believe*. 1897. Reprint. New York: Dover Publications, 1956.

Margolis, Robert D., and Kirk W. Elifson. "A Typology of Religious Experience." *Journal for the Scientific Study of Religion* 18, no. 1 (1978): 61–67.

Masters, Roger D. "Evolutionary Biology, Human Nature, and Knowledge." In *Sociobiology and Epistemology*, edited by James H. Fetzer, 97–113.

Meissner, William W. *Psychology and Religious Experience*. New Haven: Yale University Press, 1984.

Nagel, Thomas. "Freud's Permanent Revolution." *The New York Review of Books* 41, no. 9 (12 May 1994): 34–38.

Nelson, G. K. "Cults and Religion: Towards a Sociology of Religious Creativity." *Sociology and Social Research* 68, no. 3 (1984): 301–25.

Otto, Rudolph. *Mysticism East and West: A Comparative Analysis of the Nature of Mysticism*. New York: Macmillan Company, 1932.

Proudfoot, Wayne. *Religious Experience*. Berkeley: University of California Press, 1985.

Pruyser, Paul W. "Lessons from Art Theory for the Psychology of Religion." *Journal for the Scientific Study of Religion* 15, no. 1 (1976): 1–14.

Rappaport, Roy. "The Sacred in Human Evolution." *Annual Review of Ecology and Systematics*. Vol. 2. Palo Alto, Calif.: Annual Reviews, 1971.

Rorty, Richard. *Contingency, Irony, Solidarity*. Cambridge: Cambridge University Press, 1989.

Ruse, Michael. "Evolutionary Epistemology: Can Sociobiology Help?" In *Sociobiology and Epistemology*, edited by James H. Fetzer, 250–65.

———. "The View from Somewhere: A Critical Defense of Evolutionary Epistemology." In *Issues in Evolutionary Epistemology*, edited by Kai Hahlweg and C. A. Hooker, 185–225.

Saffady, William. "New Developments in the Psychoanalytic Study of Religion: A Bibliographical Review of the Literature since 1960." *Psychoanalytic Review* 63, no. 2 (1976): 291–99.

Schroeder, W. Widick. "Evolution, Human Values and Religious Experience: A Process Perspective." *Zygon: Journal of Religion and Science* 17, no. 3 (1982): 267–91.

Smart, Ninian. *The Concept of Worship*. London: Macmillan and Company, 1972.

Stern, Daniel N. *The Interpersonal World of the Infant: A View from Psychoanalysis and Developmental Psychology*. New York: Basic Books, 1985.

Tooby, John, and Leda Cosmides. "The Psychological Foundations of Culture." In *The Adapted Mind: Evolutionary Psychology and the Generation of Culture*, edited by Jerome H. Barkow, Leda Cosmides, and John Tooby, 19–136. Oxford: Oxford University Press, 1992.

Trawick, Leonard M., ed. *Backgrounds of Romanticism: English Philosophical Prose of the Eighteenth Century*. Bloomington: Indiana University Press, 1967.

Underhill, Evelyn. *Mysticism: A Study in the Nature and Development of Man's Spiritual Consciousness*. 1911. Reprint. London: Methuen and Company, 1957.

Whitson, Robley Edward. *Mysticism and Ecumenism*. New York: Sheed and Ward, 1966.

Winnicott, D. W. *Playing and Reality*. New York: Basic Books, 1971.

Wood, Barry S. "The Religion of Psychoanalysis." *American Journal of Psychoanalysis* 40, no. 1 (1980): 13–22.

Index